AF607854

Empirical Translation Studies

Empirical Translation Studies

Interdisciplinary Methodologies Explored

Edited by Meng Ji

SHEFFIELD UK BRISTOL CT

Published by Equinox Publishing Ltd.

UK: Office 415, The Workstation, 15 Paternoster Row, Sheffield, South Yorkshire S1 2BX
USA: ISD, 70 Enterprise Drive, Bristol, CT 06010

www.equinoxpub.com

First published 2016

© Meng Ji and contributors 2016

All rights reserved. No part of this publication may be reproduced or transmitted in any form or by any means, electronic or mechanical, including photocopying, recording or any information storage or retrieval system, without prior permission in writing from the publishers.

British Library Cataloguing-in-Publication Data

A catalogue record for this book is available from the British Library.
ISBN 978 1 78179 049 6 (hardback)

Library of Congress Cataloging-in-Publication Data
Empirical translation studies: interdisciplinary methodologies explored /
Edited by Meng Ji.
pages cm
Includes bibliographical references and index.
ISBN 978-1-78179-049-6 (hb)
1. Translating and interpreting–Research–Methodology. 2. Metaphor–Research–Methodology. 3. Interdisciplinary research–Methodology. 4. Phraseology. 5. Lexicology. 6. Psycholinguistics. I. Ji, Meng, 1982- editor.
P306.5.E47 2014
418'.02072–dc23
2014038658

Typeset by S.J.I. Services, New Delhi
Printed and bound in Great Britain by Lightning Source UK Ltd., Milton Keynes and Lightning Source Inc., La Vergne, TN

Contents

Contributors

Anna Baczkowska is Associate Professor in the Department of English Studies, Kazimierz Wielki University, Bydgoszcz, Poland.

Veronica Bonsignori is Research Fellow in the Language Centre at the University of Pisa.

Silvia Bruti is Associate Professor of Language and Translation at the University of Pisa.

Mikołaj Deckert works as assistant professor in the Department of Translation Studies, Institute of English Studies, University of Łódź, Poland.

Gert De Sutter is Associate Professor in Translation Studies and Dutch Linguistics in the Department of Translation, Interpreting and Communication at Ghent University, Belgium.

Giacomo Figueredo is Lecturer of Applied Linguistics at the Federal University of Ouro Preto (UFOP), Brazil, where he teaches English as a foreign language and translation theory for undergraduate students.

Meng Ji is Associate Professor/Reader at the University of Sydney, Australia. She is specialised in Corpus Linguistics, Translation Studies and Contrastive Linguistics (Chinese/Spanish/Japanese/English).

Hannu Kemppanen is Professor of Russian Language and Translation at the University of Eastern Finland, Joensuu, Finland.

Defeng Li is Reader in Translation Studies at the School of Oriental and African Studies, University of London.

Annabelle Lukin is Senior Lecturer in Linguistics at Macquarie University, Australia.

Jukka Mäkisalo is Acting Professor in Translation Studies at the University of Eastern Finland, Joensuu, Finland.

Adriana Pagano is Professor in the Graduate Program in Linguistics and Applied Linguistics at the Faculty of Arts, Universidade Federal de Minas Gerais, Brazil.

Iraklis Pantopoulos holds a PhD in translation studies from the University of Edinburgh. He organizes and conducts courses at the Ionian University and the Technological Educational Institute of Epirus, in Greece.

Koen Plevoets lectures in the Department of Linguistics at the University of Leuven, Belgium.

Qing Wang was an Associate Professor at Shandong Jiaotong University, who passed away prematurely in 2012 after a most courageous battle with a brain tumour. She had a strong interest in translation and literary studies and was actively publishing in both areas.

Mark Shuttleworth is Senior Lecturer in Translation Studies in the School of European Languages, Culture & Society, University College London

Lore Vandevoorde is Researcher in Translation Studies at Ghent University, Belgium.

Professor Yuanjian He is a full time professor at Macau University.

Introduction: Advancing Empirical Translation Studies

Meng Ji

This volume focuses on the development of advanced research methodologies for empirical translation studies which include both corpus-based and corpus-driven approaches to translation products and related social and cultural phenomena. Since the introduction of language corpora to translation studies in the 1990s, the descriptive branch of translation studies has seen rapid development mainly due to the experimentation with a variety of corpus materials and corpus methodologies. A distinct feature of current empirical translation studies is the integration of corpus methods with established research techniques used in applied linguistics and literary studies, such as contrastive linguistics, quantitative linguistics and stylistics. Chapters in this book make useful attempts to explore the potential of corpus research methods to advance emerging cutting-edge research areas such as multimedia and multimodal translation.

The combined use of language corpora and research methods borrowed from cognate fields has given rise to new research areas such as corpus translation stylistics, quantitative translation studies, and empirical multimodal translation studies. An important feature shared by these rapidly growing areas of empirical translation studies is that they are highly interdisciplinary, exploratory and experimental, with a strong focus on the development of robust and empirically verifiable research methodologies. In this way, new analytical models proposed and developed for translation studies will be technically modifiable and theoretical extensible, as language processing technologies continue to push back the frontier of the development of multilingual and translational corpus resources.

From a theoretical perspective, the significance of the exploration and establishment of advanced research methodologies is that they can assist translation scholars effectively in the identification and retrieval of useful linguistic units and textual patterns in large-scale translational and multilingual corpora to advance our understanding of translation as a highly purposeful cross-cultural activity and profession which drives the evolving process of globalisation. The study of textual and linguistic patterns in translation lies at the heart of influential contemporary translation theories such as translation norms, laws and universal features since the 1970s. The insight is shared by contributors to this book that many important translation phenomena or recurring corpus patterns that reveal important relations between different sets of contextual and textual factors in translation remain unexplored or have been investigated only to a limited extent due to a lack of robust corpus analytical techniques in empirical translation studies.

Ever since the 1990s, the identification and verification of revealing and widely existing corpus patterns has prepared the ground for the theoretical development of translation studies as an academic discipline. This book builds upon the momentum of existing corpus translation studies by offering a set of original research papers by world-leading translation scholars. Their work illustrates the application of advanced corpus analytical techniques in the study of the translation of a variety of textual genres involving a wide range of language combinations: Finnish-Russian, Chinese-English, Polish-English, Greek-English, Italian-English and Brazilian Portuguese-English.

The four main sets of corpus methodologies explored in this book include: (1) the keyword analysis of translation (Shuttleworth; Kemppanen and Mäkisalo) which applies computer-assisted keyword analysis in the exploration of comparable and parallel corpora; (2) the corpus-based study of stylistic variations in translation (Li and Wang; Pantopoulos); (3) the corpus-driven quantitative study of translation (Pagano et al.; Vandevoorde et al.); and (4) the systematic processing of multimedia translation corpora that cover a range of genres such as learners' corpora, TV series and documentaries (Baczkowska; Bonsignori and Bruti; Deckert). These four areas represent some of the most dynamic fields of corpus translation research which prioritise the exploration and experimentation with advanced research methodologies in empirical translation studies.

As empirical translation studies evolves with advances made in research methodologies, there are a number of issues that seem to divide scholarly efforts in this growing area. One of them is the so-called dichotomy between corpus-based and corpus-driven approaches to translation. It is argued in this book that the two sets of research methods which are both valid in dealing with specific research problems can be integrated effectively to advance empirical translation studies. While the corpus-based approach works well in verifying and revising existing theoretical hypotheses, the corpus-driven approach is particularly useful in the development and testing of new analytical constructs and models as new evidence and textual patterns continue to emerge from computer-aided corpus processing and modelling. It is truly hoped that this latest addition to corpus translation research will contribute to the ongoing debates on developing advanced research methodologies for empirical translation studies. .

Editor
Meng Ji
October 2015

Part I

Mixed Approach to Translation

A Corpus-based Study of Metaphor in Translation

Mark Shuttleworth

1. Introduction

It is now generally accepted that metaphor in language is like the lettering in a stick of Brighton rock: whatever genre or area of language use you examine, metaphor will be found to be present. Given this fact, the importance of metaphor in translation should be quite apparent. Furthermore, the notions of metaphor, transfer and translation are closely related, both etymologically – at least, in many Indo-European languages – and conceptually. When writing on metaphor in translation you therefore have to think simultaneously in terms of two separate types of semantic transfer: not only that of texts moving between languages but also of concepts being borrowed (or 'mapped') from one domain of experience to provide a new way of encapsulating a concept within another domain of experience. This potentially makes the study of metaphor in translation one of the more complex types of translation studies research.

Given this level complexity, why should we devote our energy to studying the topic? For what reason is it of interest and importance? It is my hope that this article will provide detailed answers to these questions, but in brief, I believe there are at least two reasons why this should be the case. First, metaphor is a fundamental part of language. As such it plays a vital role in communication, and one that cannot be ignored by the translator. Second, given the conceptual link between metaphor and translation that was mentioned at the beginning of the article it stands to reason that we can learn about translation from metaphor (and vice versa). Furthermore, as a topic within translation studies it is of potential interest to researchers approaching it from a wide range of different angles: linguistic, cultural, cognitive, processual and, of course, interdisciplinary.

It is of course the interdisciplinary aspect that provides the starting point for this article. Interdisciplinarity implies a two-way interaction between disciplines: it involves not only consulting metaphor studies sources but also being in a position to offer something back to this discipline, from which important theoretical ideas may have been borrowed (see Shuttleworth 2014b). In the case of research into metaphor in translation, the 'loaning' discipline is generally cognitive linguistics, even if some of its concepts need to be adapted to the different context of translation studies, and many researchers in the area recognize that their work will be of interest to cognitive linguists researching metaphor as well as to translation scholars (see Al-Harrasi 2001 and Ding, Noël and Wolf 2010, for example).

2. Planning the project

In his seminal article dating from the early 1970s, which has played a very significant role in forming the discipline as we know it today, Holmes describes translation studies as consisting of three branches: the theoretical, the descriptive and the applied (2004:184–191). Holmes' overall vision of the discipline is often presented visually as a map (see for example Toury 1995:110). Purely theoretical work is certainly being carried out, either on a highly abstract, 'general', all-encompassing theory or on more specific 'partial' ones (2004:186). However, most of the research that is not of an applied nature (or in other words, that deals with practical matters of translation assessment, translator training or the use of translation technology, for example) takes place within the descriptive branch. The non-prescriptive approach adopted here is to investigate translation as both a product and a process, and also to study the functions of translation within a given cultural, social or political context (2004:184–185), the aim being to observe and report on the data examined in as neutral a way as possible, without imposing any preconceived ideas regarding how translation should be performed or what a completed translation ought to look like. The term 'descriptive translation studies' (along with the name of the discipline itself, selected in preference to alternatives such as 'translation theory' or the 'science of translation': 2004:182–183), when applied to the study of translated texts, also generally implies the use of an approach that is committed to the analysis of real instances of translation and firmly oriented towards the target rather than the source (Toury 1995:23–39), or in other words involved with analysing translations as texts existing in the target culture quite independently of their source texts that belong to a different language and culture and maybe serve a different communicative purpose.

For descriptive research into metaphor in translation, as with any kind of research, it helps very much to have a 'hook': an aspect of the subject that will hold the interest of the researcher – and, indeed, that of the reader – throughout all the stages of the project. The reason for my personal fascination with this area is connected to a translation of a musicological monograph that I undertook in the late 1990s. A major feature of this text was the unusual metaphors that it contained, many of which presented serious problems to me as the translator, and as a result of which I became curious as to what precisely the framework was within which translators would make decisions regarding how to translate metaphorical expressions from one language into another.

It was in this context that my own research project got underway. This was – and is – an investigation into how metaphorical expressions in popular science articles are translated into a number of different languages – originally French, Italian, German, Polish and Russian, although more recently a number of Spanish and Chinese examples have also been included in the project. The emphasis in the research is on discovering generalities about the methods used for translating metaphor that are valid across all the target languages studied rather than focusing on the specifics of each individual one. This may in some ways be similar to research into translation universals (see for example Ilisei 2012; Mauranen 2004, 2008), but here the focus is different in that no wide-ranging claims are made regarding the ubiquity of the tendencies that are observed. The research is based on a corpus of *Scientific American* articles and involves a detailed analysis of the types of translation procedure that are given rise to by various kinds of scientific metaphor. The research started life as a PhD project although it is currently being extended.

Whether your research project being planned is for a PhD thesis, a Master's dissertation or a research project leading to publication in article form, the advice remains the same: research is always difficult, challenging and time-consuming so it is important to do everything possible to ensure that it is as simple as the aims permit. This means, for example, ensuring that your data is unproblematic, selecting realistic, achievable aims and using an uncomplicated research methodology (and preferably only one rather than a whole battery of different methods) in order to achieve them. This is of particular importance when researching a relatively complex area such as metaphor in translation.

Right at the start it will be necessary to make a number of initial decisions. The most fundamental of these is probably the selection of aims, although realistically these may only start to crystallise as you begin to examine your data and come to an understanding of its potential. In text-based research into metaphor in translation some of the most usual aims may focus on the procedures used by translators, the difficulty that this textual feature appears to give rise to and the application of the cognitive theory of metaphor to the study of metaphor in translation.[1] Aims more relevant to descriptive translation studies in general rather than to the study of metaphor in translation could, for example, include studying metaphor as a feature of translated texts or investigating what the norms of metaphor in translation can show us about translation norms in general.

Once the aims have been established it will be possible to turn to the methodology. Most fundamental, arguably, is the need to plan everything out in detail in advance and not just allow things to happen. If this is done carefully then the analysis stage, when you finally come to it, will be considerably simpler than if everything is thrown together in a haphazard manner. The most important decision it is usually necessary to take is whether the research is to be qualitative or quantitative in nature. (In point of fact, however, most projects combine the two approaches to some extent – see Olohan 2004:86 – although if you intend to emphasize the purely numerical then you will probably need to have a background – or to receive some training – in statistical analysis.) In other words, are you planning to conduct a detailed investigation of a relatively limited number of metaphorical expressions and their translation into another language, focusing on their contextual meaning and analysing (for example) the procedures used by the translators, or will you employ statistical and other tools to examine the contours of large quantities of data that you have annotated with respect to the features that are of interest to you? As well as determining the kind of insight that your research is likely to result in, this decision may well have a significant bearing on the question of corpus size: generally speaking, a quantitative study requires more data than a qualitative one. Furthermore, if the intention is to conduct an intensive study of a small number of examples then this will also have clear implications for the corpus size – although it has to be said that the trend now is probably in favour of more extensive modes of analysis. However, since there are no hard and fast rules concerning corpus size it is usually a good idea to carry out a pilot study (see Section 5) to help determine the amount of data that is likely to be needed in order to be able to conduct a meaningful investigation of the phenomena being researched.

Stated theoretically, the purpose of this kind of research is to investigate how a limited number of 'variables' – normally no more than two – interact with each other (see Williams and Chesterman 2002:83–89). A variable is a parameter along the lines of which it is possible to observe variation within your data. So for example, if you have classified each metaphorical expression according to how original it is and also in terms of the purpose it is intended to serve you will be able to determine, for example, whether there is a tendency for metaphorical expressions used for explanatory purposes to be innovative in nature or for conventional metaphors to be utilized for reasons of ornamentation. Similarly, by comparing one or other such parameter against the translation procedures that are used it should potentially be feasible to identify any possible correlations there may be between metaphor type and the preferred translation procedure adopted. As stated above, it is important that you only attempt to contrast two variables at a time as otherwise it will be well-nigh impossible – without the aid of specialist statistical software – to make any sense of the complicated interactions that would occur between multiple independent variables. The fact that my project involved an analysis of the data along the lines of seven different parameters does not go against this principle as each variable was analysed in turn against the procedures adopted by the translators.[2] Finally, it should also be noted that it is not important if you are unable to identify any significant correlations between variables: even if this is the case it is just as valid a result as a more positive outcome would be and should certainly be reported as part of your findings.

As stated above, a large proportion of translation studies research is descriptive in nature. However, if the focus of your work is on translation quality or on establishing guidelines or recommendations for how translators should tackle metaphorical expressions then it is research that will be situated within the applied branch of the discipline. This distinction is important as descriptive research needs to avoid any kind of evaluation and simply report on what is discovered about the particular area of translation being researched. Once again, you quite clearly need to establish in advance whether your work is going to be descriptive or applied, as a mixed approach can make for a piece of research that lacks proper focus.

Most, or possibly all, research into translation entails at least an element of interdisciplinarity, and metaphor in translation is no exception. In the case of this topic it is disciplines such as cognitive linguistics that potentially provide the greatest theoretical input, with authors such as Gibbs (1994), Kövecses (2002/10, 2005, 2006), Lakoff (1987; 1993), Lakoff and Johnson (1980, 1999), and Lakoff and Turner (1989) providing a conceptual framework that is potentially highly fruitful for descriptive translation studies research. If there was a weakness in much of the earlier work on metaphor in translation then it was that this important theoretical work was not always taken properly into account. Although there has been something of a greater tendency in recent years to look to this other discipline for a firm theoretical framework, the situation is still not ideal in this respect. This can be seen by looking at the number of articles that use particular keywords. As of February 2013 there were 60 articles listed in the St. Jerome Publishing Translation Studies Abstracts Online (Harding, Saldanha and Zanettin 2013) that were published between 1981 and 2012 and that contain the word *metaphor* in their title; however, only about a quarter use any keywords that would obviously indicate that a serious amount of theoretical input from metaphor scholars had been absorbed. At the very least, researchers working on metaphor in translation would be well advised to follow some of the basic conventions of metaphor research. This will of course vary from one theoretical framework to another, but within the cognitive metaphor theory these would, for example, include distinguishing between conceptual metaphors (or in other words the 'mappings' from one domain of experience to another that make metaphorical language understandable) and individual metaphorical expressions as they occur in texts. However, I would argue that the value of such research is greatly enhanced if it takes full account of the findings of metaphor research: not only will it be using insights and methodologies that have been developed by experts in metaphor, but the readership of your work may in that way be increased.

3. Text selection, data collection and data preparation

> Find all the metaphors in a text: This computer is only a piece of plastic and this software can't do that. It'd be nice if it could, though.
> (WordSmith Tools 3.0 Help topic)

The corpus used in the project comprises 62 *Scientific American* articles that appeared between January 2003 and July 2004 along with their translations into the five target languages included in the project. Altogether it totals 281,305 words of English text, with corresponding or smaller totals in each of the other languages. The reason why the word count in some target languages is lower is that not all articles are translated into all languages. More recently the corpus has been supplemented with some examples for Spanish and Chinese too.

Because of the copious bi- and even multilingual data that they provide *Scientific American* articles have already been used by a number of translation scholars (see for example Rey 2000; Bowker and Pearson 2002; Hoorickx-Raucq 2005; Liao 2007, 2010, 2011; Sharkas 2009; Chan 2011; Liu 2011) and offer a rich resource in terms of the quantity of material and the number of target languages covered. The periodical is in fact translated into 13 different languages on a monthly basis.[3]

What is immediately striking about many (but not all) *Scientific American* articles is the high level of metaphoricity that they possess, which appears to be broadly in line with Knudsen's observation that metaphorical language is far more prominent in the language of popular science than in more specialist scientific genres. However, when I was planning the composition of my corpus not only did it seem highly unlikely that every article would contain similar numbers of metaphorical expressions, but I was even doubtful as to whether each subject area would be characterized by the same levels of metaphor use. Relying on my own possibly faulty intuition, in my selection of texts for inclusion in the corpus I considered subject areas such as neurobiology, biotechnology, cosmology, artificial intelligence and information technology to be potentially of interest, but fields such as pharmaceuticals, therapeutics, gadgets and armaments less so. Whether or not I was right to exclude these topics, those that were included yielded a high proportion of articles that contained large numbers of metaphorical expressions.

Later in the process, articles were informally ranked on the basis of their metaphoricity and some of the more metaphor-rich were analysed in detail. My eventual selection of texts reflects my earlier intuition, and, whether or not they are in fact the most metaphor-rich, my general observation is that it was possible to extract an impressive collection of metaphorical expressions from a relatively small number of texts.

The texts did not make for an easy corpus to work with in their initial form. Specific problems included the fact that the different language editions were available in different formats (usually either PDF or hard copy) and also the extreme complexity of the documents themselves, consisting as they did of columns, captions and text boxes, all of which contained text that needed to be included. By the time all 259 texts had been assembled in electronic form (which in many cases entailed scanning and optical character recognition as well as conversion to text-only format), this internal structure had in many cases been lost. This, along with the fragmentary nature of the corpus that working with so many short texts produced and the fact that each English article had up to five translations, made the possibility of producing a set of aligned corpora totally impracticable – or at least, it was considered that the time needed to do so would not be justified in terms of the time it would save later on. For the same reasons, conducting an exhaustive study of all source texts and up to five target texts in each case was likewise unfeasible. However, because of time constraints and my own developing understanding of how best to access and exploit the considerable volume of data contained within the corpus, no consistent policy was pursued at first in terms of entering examples into the spreadsheet. In the end, the metaphorical expressions from six articles and their translations were identified and entered exhaustively by means of close reading of the source texts and cross-referencing with each target text in turn, but this methodology was not pursued beyond these six first because of the painstaking nature of the work required but also as by that time it was considered that enough data had been collected in that manner.[4] Indeed, with most research into metaphor in translation the consensus seems to be that a preparatory close reading of a sample of texts will give the researcher a clear idea of lexical items likely to be of interest (see for example Charteris-Black 2004:35) but that this needs to be followed up by an examination of concordance lines based on well-chosen search terms. Thus in order to compensate for the limitations of the exclusive use of visual searching and thus ensure that the entire corpus was exploited to at least some extent an additional approach to accessing relevant data had to be employed.

It should of course be pointed out that the use of a corpus-based approach is possibly more problematic in the case of metaphor in translation than elsewhere, as Mike Scott wryly points out in the WordSmith Tools 3.0 help topic quoted above. This is because metaphorical expressions cannot be searched for directly in the same way, for example, as words ending in *-ing*, or be identified on purely statistical principles, as can words that occur only once in a corpus, for example.

In this instance the WordSmith Tools concordancing software was used to search the entire corpus for instances of important keywords taken from examples that had already been manually identified. This approach was experimental and was not implemented on any large scale, which means that the number of expressions that it retrieved only accounted for around 10% of the entire data set. Importantly, it was also at this stage that metaphorical expressions added in the translation process were located, using the same method.

The figure of 10% reflects the fact that I only started to use the concordancing approach to data collection relatively late on in the process. My recommendation now would be to start this wider search for examples when only around 30–40% of the total estimated number of examples needed have been collected. In this way you will help ensure that the entire corpus is properly utilized.

Keywords can either be lexical items that occur frequently in the manually collected data or other items that are semantically related to them. Figure 1 shows a sample of concordance lines drawn from the entire corpus and based on the search term *nature*, which was identified as an important metaphorical keyword in the course of manual data collection.

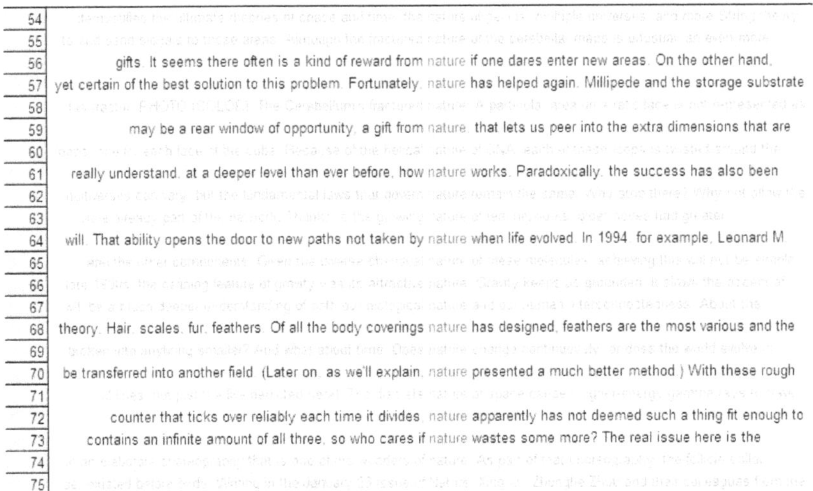

N	Concordance
54	
55	
56	gifts. It seems there often is a kind of reward from nature if one dares enter new areas. On the other hand,
57	yet certain of the best solution to this problem. Fortunately, nature has helped again. Millipede and the storage substrate
58	
59	may be a rear window of opportunity, a gift from nature, that lets us peer into the extra dimensions that are
60	
61	really understand, at a deeper level than ever before, how nature works. Paradoxically, the success has also been
62	
63	
64	will. That ability opens the door to new paths not taken by nature when life evolved. In 1994, for example, Leonard M
65	
66	
67	
68	theory. Hair, scales, fur, feathers. Of all the body coverings nature has designed, feathers are the most various and the
69	
70	be transferred into another field. (Later on, as we'll explain, nature presented a much better method.) With these rough
71	
72	counter that ticks over reliably each time it divides, nature apparently has not deemed such a thing fit enough to
73	contains an infinite amount of all three, so who cares if nature wastes some more? The real issue here is the
74	
75	

Figure 1: Listing of instances of the word *nature* from the English data with all non-metaphorical examples greyed out (WordSmith Tools 4.0).

Examples that are deemed to be non-metaphorical have been greyed out. Nonetheless, the few remaining examples indicate the great diversity of metaphorical mappings that can be found in this corpus of scientific discourse, nature being presented in the guise of a traveller, a designer, a giver of gifts and other anthropomorphic roles besides.

Since for the reasons stated above the source texts were not aligned with their various target texts it then became necessary to conduct similar searches for each target language based on the nearest functional equivalent for the keyword 'nature'; the listing for German is presented in Figure 2.

1	kranker Seelen, den zweiten Gang im Gastmahl der Natur, das nährendste Gericht beim Fest des Lebens«.
2	neu, sodass sie Eigenschaften erhält, die von der Natur niemals vorgesehen waren. Zum Beispiel können wir
3	– haben ihr eigenes Das Verschlüsselungssystem der Natur Bezeichnet man ein Gen – ein DNA-Stück mit dem
4	der Redaktion. Normalerweise kombinieren sich in der Natur nur je drei Quarks zu Baryonen oder je zwei Quarks
5	arbeiten, dank dessen sie Dinge tun würden, die in der Natur nie da gewesen waren: Die synthetische Biologie
6	zwei unserer Maschinen funktionieren, ist wiederum der Natur entlehnt: eine Änderung in der Konformation der DNA
7	Gleichungen auftreten und die Eigenschaften der Natur festlegen, nicht mehr beliebige feste Werte. In der
8	effektive Theorie ist eine Beschreibung eines Aspekts der Natur, deren Eingabedaten - zumindest im Prinzip - mithilfe
9	vermuten, dies seien die fundamentalsten Bausteine der Natur. Doch die Wechselfälle eines Jahrhunderts
10	M-= eorie sei (siehe »Strings – Urbausteine der Natur?« von Pierre Ramond, Spektrum der Wissenschaft
11	Gegensatz zwischen den Furcht einflößenden Kräften der Natur und den »harmlosen« Christbaumkerzen. Die leichte
12	der letzten Base unterscheiden. Außerdem muss man der Natur zugute halten, dass sie im Gegensatz zu den
13	e handelt es sich um so genannte Histone, die Antwort der Natur auf die Frage: Wie bringt man als Zelle 1,8 Meter DNA
14	der vorangegangenen Jahre erschien das von der Natur realisierte System daher vielen Wissenschaftlern als
15	Im Grunde nutzt diese Medizin vor allem Mechanismen der Natur. Schließlich sind Viren im gezielten Töten von Zellen
16	aufgezeichnet worden, sodass wir auch dessen Natur nicht kennen. Skalenfreiheit ist auch nur eine von
17	seine Energie verbrauchende Arbeit verrichten sollte. Die Natur ist nicht computerfreundlich. Um im Freien oder auch
18	beste Lösung im Klaren. Glücklicherweise kommt uns die Natur wieder ein wenig entgegen. Sowohl Millipede als auch
19	sie nicht unbedingt das globale Optimum. Dennoch hat die Natur ihre Sache off enbar gut gemacht. Simuliert man
20	die meisten Wissenschaftler an dem Dogma fest, dass die Natur keine Sprünge macht, sondern sich bis ins Kleinste
21	die wir niemals beobachten können. Warum sollte die Natur so verschwenderisch sein, sich eine unendliche
22	- in großen Mengen erzeugen und eindeutig klären, ob die Natur tatsächlich supersymmetrisch ist. Um das Verhältnis
23	lassen? Und wie steht es um die Zeit. Verändert sich die Natur kontinuierlich oder entwickelt sie sich in winzigen

Figure 2: Listing of examples of the word *Natur* in the German data, once again with the non-metaphorical examples greyed out (WordSmith Tools 4.0)

Given that the texts are not aligned it is necessary to match up the source and target examples by hand, although WordSmith Tools does provide data that makes each line easier to locate. The interesting by-product of this rather painstaking process, however, is that the metaphorical expressions that have been added in translation are revealed: quite obviously, they are the ones that are left once the others have been matched up. In Figure 2, lines 9 and 15, for example, contain metaphorical expressions that have been added by the translator.

The addition of a metaphorical expression is said to occur when there is such an expression in the target text that corresponds to a source text non-metaphor, or to a point in the source text where there is no text at all; as Toury (1995:83) correctly points out these are both eventualities that need to be accounted for in a study of metaphor in translation. In this study the number of added expressions is probably under-reported but the second method used for collecting data at least provides a clear mechanism for such expressions to be identified.

While none of these possible lines of investigation have been explored in the project, it seems that corpus-based methodologies would open up many further opportunities for exploiting your data rather than restricting their use simply to the area of finding examples. For instance, collocation-based research could be used to obtain a range of insights. For example, verbal collocates of central terms – such as *science, evolution* or *nature* – could be analysed to open a window on how these important scientific concepts are metaphorized.

Arguably, however, the only way to conduct a truly exhaustive analysis of all metaphorical expressions is to examine source and target texts separately – and equally thoroughly – before trying to match up individual expressions and their translations. Only in this way would the true extent of metaphor addition become properly apparent. Alternatively, if individual source and target expressions were not paired off with each other the focus of the analysis would move from the word and phrase levels – where it so often resides by default – to that of the text, and the way in which macro-level source- and target-text metaphorical structures contrasted with each other would become truly apparent. As far as I am aware the use of comparable corpora in research into metaphor in translation is hitherto completely unexplored.

In terms of the specific target domains of the metaphorical expressions, 99 concern the area of neurons, 71 that of genes, 47 that of nature, 11 mental illness and 80 can be termed 'miscellaneous' – a category that includes some 'general scientific' metaphors (e.g. *think outside the box, intellectual framework*, etc.) and some that are not specific to science at all (e.g. *trigger, underpin*, etc.). Since the majority of the metaphorical expressions identified relate to the neurobiology and biotechnology subject categories, the metaphorical potential of other disciplines such as cosmology and physics remains almost completely untapped, not least because the only major use of WordSmith Tools involved searching for metaphorizations of nature. If different or more general keywords were to be searched for, then these other areas would also be more fully exploited.

Each of the articles is written by a different author, an expert in his or her field. One of the main advantages of focusing in detail on a small number of articles is that some mappings are represented by large numbers of expressions and in this way it is possible to be sure of capturing them all. This approach was adopted rather than examining extracts from a larger number of articles because it was felt likely to produce a greater number of examples for at least some of the commoner mappings. The main disadvantage is as discussed in the second half of the previous paragraph. The practical result of using the twofold method of data collection described above is that we are effectively left with two corpora: a smaller one, consisting of the six articles analysed in detail, and a larger one that is made up of the full 62. Analysis of the small corpus allows us to carry out a close examination of data, to arrive at an initial list of translation procedures, to provide a source of ready examples and to give us a feel for the general translation approaches adopted by the different language editions. The large corpus, on the other hand, provides a source for further examples that are similar to ones already identified in the small one. This twofold approach to data collection effectively permits a compromise between weighting all one's data towards a particular area (with the concomitant narrowness of coverage) and having it spread too widely (which would have made it harder to collect mappings reflected in a reasonable number of metaphorical expressions).

Candidate expressions that were accepted as metaphorical were added to the master list, stored in an Excel spreadsheet as multilingual examples along with detailed meta-information, and classified according to translation procedure and the seven theoretical parameters.[5] Multiple instances of one-word metaphorical expressions were not listed exhaustively, although repetitions were sometimes recorded to reflect the fact that an expression occurred particularly frequently. In all, the database of examples comprises a total of 308 rows (with one multilingual example occupying each row). Of these, 289 contain an English metaphorical expression along with between three and five translations. The other 19 rows consist of a non-metaphorical English phrase that is translated by a metaphor in one (or occasionally more) target languages. In all, given these two facts, this data gives rise to a total of 1354 target language examples. With a total of 74 columns defined the data set consists of 22,792 data points (although up to 10% of this total are empty for various reasons).

4. Metaphor identification

> Spotting the presence of metaphor is often quite intuitive but producing an infallible test for metaphor is practically impossible.
>
> (Stallman 1999:34-5)

Some progress has in fact been made in automatic and semi-automatic metaphor identification (see Fass 1991, Mason 2004, Berber Sardinha 2006, and Ureña Gómez-Moreno and Faber 2011, for example), although no system is as yet capable of producing a reliable list of candidate metaphors unaided from any discourse type. For this reason most metaphorical expressions have been identified manually in this project. Intuition is indeed involved in this process, and yet it needs to be supported by a set of procedures that are as rigorous as possible, even if infallibility is as stated impossible.

The homing in on, gathering and classification of data is likely to be a complex, multi-staged process, with numerous changes of direction dictated by the need to be selective from the sheer volume of information and one's developing understanding of how to create appropriate methodologies for the study of metaphor systems.

The procedure for classifying all candidate expressions as metaphorical or otherwise is the same regardless of how they were identified and is fraught with difficulties. In many cases it is no easy matter to decide whether or not a linguistic expression should be considered to possess a metaphorical meaning. For instance, is a *population* of glial cells being referred to in terms of a human 'population' through the use of this word? When cocaine *targets* the brain's reward system are we witnessing a (very slight) figurative extension of meaning? The corpus contains a scattering of such marginal cases.

In addition, the articles contain a wide range of metaphorical expressions: not only specific scientific metaphors but also 'general scientific' and others that are not at all specific to science. Expressions can commonly range from single words to phrases – with occasional extended metaphors spanning entire complex sentences. Furthermore, an individual expression can involve more than one metaphor. For example, in *the fundamental laws that govern nature remain the same* we can detect not only NATURE IS SUBJECT TO LAWS but also, and more generally, THE PRINCIPLES THAT GOVERN THE UNIVERSE ARE LAWS. In such instances it is generally only possible to highlight one metaphor at a time, which means that most such examples are listed twice in the spreadsheet.

Although preceding it by a couple of years, the process of metaphor identification that took place was broadly in line with the 'Metaphor Identification Procedure' proposed by the Pragglejaz Group (2007:3). The approach is inductive, in that all mappings and other high-level structures were posited on the basis of the metaphorical expressions that were identified rather than trying to fit the metaphorical expressions into a pre-determined framework of categories (Pragglejaz Group 2007:33–34). In essence, according to the Pragglejaz approach to metaphor identification, if a lexical unit's usage contrasts with a 'more basic contemporary meaning' – one that is more concrete, related to bodily action, more precise or historically older, even if it is not the lexical unit's most frequent meaning (Pragglejaz Group 2007:3) – then the expression is considered metaphorical. While this principle works well for most lexical items, difficult cases such as the two mentioned above still require the exercise of judgement by the researcher.

In the case of the present project, the process involved two people identifying English candidate metaphorical expressions, an individual wording only being included in the master list if agreement was reached: My thanks are due to Prof. Charles Drage. On the other hand, decisions regarding the expressions in the various target languages were generally taken by me alone, but with suitable reference material and/or native-speaker informants being consulted where the need arose.

5. Pilot studies

The purpose of carrying out a pilot study before the research reaches an advanced stage is essentially to ensure that time and effort are not wasted and that you are focusing on the most fruitful lines of investigation, given the nature of your data. Quite simply, in a pilot study you will typically take a small amount of data and carry out a limited investigation on the basis of it. If no interesting results are forthcoming – for instance, because only very few examples of the phenomenon that you are investigating can be found – this will allow you to refocus your research before it is too late to contemplate a major change of direction.

More positively, conducting at least one pilot study will probably help you to see what data your corpus contains that can be easily extracted and analysed and to determine how big your corpus will need to be in order to obtain a sufficient number of concordance lines. This latter aspect is of vital importance as it can save you the time and effort of collecting a corpus that is far bigger than is actually needed, and on the other hand can also help avoid the risk of ending up with too little data to support the kind of research that you are envisaging. Within the present context conducting a pilot study also provides an important opportunity to assign parameter values (see Section 6) on an experimental basis to a subset of the data and to test some of the analysis methodologies that are going to be used.

6. Data classification

As discussed in Section 2, the correspondences between parameter values and translation procedures can be used to identify possible correlations between metaphor type and the preferred translation approach. Section 7.1 presents a brief discussion of how metaphorical expressions with different levels of conventionality are distributed in English and the various different target languages. Any theoretical dimension along the lines of which it is possible to classify a metaphorical expression can potentially be used as a parameter, and there are many of these: Cameron (1999:124–130), for example, provides a list of nine such dimensions. (See also the authors listed in Section 2, and also Goatly 1997 and Knowles and Moon 2006, for further important – and in some cases introductory – statements on metaphor.)

The classification methodology combines the assessment and categorization of large numbers of data points and the detailed analysis of manually selected examples to illustrate the various categories identified. In many cases, even if only a single pass through the data has been made for each parameter in the first instance, any dubious category assignments that come to light at the time of the analysis can be corrected at that point.

7. Data analysis

As suggested by Olohan, a combination of qualitative and quantitative analysis is the most appropriate approach for most data sets (2004:86). For this study, the emphasis is definitely on the former, although the latter also plays an important role. The heart of the analysis entails examining the data once for each of the parameters. At this point the data is looked at from a range of different angles in order to determine what the main points of interest are. Starting from here the attempt is made to identify the main parameter-specific procedures (e.g. a move towards a more abstract form of expression, partial omission, the use of a phrase with a more general meaning, a change of mapping, etc.) that are employed by the translators.

Finally, we know little or nothing concerning the possible overlap between the roles of the translator and the editor. This, combined with the lack of information on who the translators are for most language editions (plus the unresponsiveness of the editorial offices), has done much to determine the kind of analysis that is possible and may even have played a role in shaping the multilingual approach that is being used (which is discussed elsewhere: see Shuttleworth 2011, 2013 and 2014a).

The two subsections that follow are provided as brief examples of the kind of analysis that was conducted in the project. As stated above, the first focuses on one of the seven parameters that were studied, and the second presents an analysis of the expressions that were added during the translation process.

7.1. Metaphorical conventionality

Every metaphorical expression is more or less conventional in nature, or in other words, is either relatively embedded as an accepted expression in the language or else stands out as something new or original. As expected, this parameter also undergoes modifications in the translation process. Metaphorical expressions may be omitted or removed, of course, or may retain, acquire or lose a particular conventionality type. The different levels of conventionality are represented in the English data as follows:

conventionalized	230
innovative	39
grammaticalized	10
dead	8
historical	2

In other words, the range of frequencies is vast, with conventionalized expressions accounting for around three-quarters of the total number of examples and being approximately six times commoner than the next most frequent category, that of innovative expressions. At the other end of the spectrum, there are only two examples of a historical metaphorical expression.

Of the 289 rows, 48 contain at least one modification to this parameter, as set out below:

conventionalized	28
innovative	10
grammaticalized	5
dead	4
historical	1

What is immediately noticeable is that, while the frequency order is retained, conventionalized expressions are modified much less often in relation to their total number. The second point that should strike the reader is that, while only about 12% of conventionalized expressions are modified in at least one target language, this proportion increases to around 26% for innovative and to exactly 50% for grammaticalized, dead and historical. In other words, the rarer the conventionality type the more likely it is to undergo modification in translation. What this means at the bottom end of the spectrum is unclear (and in any case, here the numbers are too small to have any statistical significance), but at the top end – i.e., in the case of conventionalized metaphorical expressions – there is a much more marked tendency to keep such an expression as conventionalized rather than shifting it into one of the other categories.

We will now take a brief look at one example, for illustrative purposes only. In this example, the original grammaticalized expression is modified in each of the five target languages:

English: **Nature's version** [of the genetic code] looked less elegant than several of the theorists' hypotheses.

German: **die Lösung, welche die Natur gefunden hatte**, erschien weniger elegant als einige theoretische Vorschläge.
[**the solution found by nature** appeared less elegant than a number of theoretical proposals.]

Russian: **То, что придумала природа**, выглядело гораздо менее изобретательным, чем многие гипотезы ученых.
[**What nature thought up** seemed much less inventive than many scientists' hypotheses.]

Polish **Wariant, którym posłużyła się przyroda**, okazał się znacznie mniej elegancki niż niejedna z hipotez.
[**The version that nature used** was significantly less elegant than a number of hypotheses.]

French: **la méthode choisie par la nature** était moins élégante que certaines des hypothèses qui avaient été proposées.

[**the method chosen by nature** was less elegant than certain of the hypotheses that had been proposed]

Italian: **La versione elaborata dalla natura** sembrava meno elegante di molte delle ipotesi formulate dai teorici.
[**The version elaborated by nature** seemed less elegant than many of the hypotheses formulated by the theorists.]

The expression *nature's version* is only considered metaphorical because of its grammatical form: convert the possessive construction to a different one (*the natural code*, for example) and the (albeit weak) entailment that nature has created this genetic code vanishes. This is what happens in each of the translations as this form is nowhere retained. Yet in the German, Russian, French and Italian versions the metaphoricity is made more explicit, the resulting expression being classified in each case as conventionalized. The Polish translation, on the other hand, is considered to be an example of innovation; what is different about this example is that it represents a mapping – NATURE IS A USER OF CODE – that is presumed to be rare and is certainly not found elsewhere in the data.

In the Chinese translation, which was obtained sometime after the rest of the analysis had been completed, we see a structure that appears to be parallel to that of the English:

Chinese: 自然的密码规则看上去远不如一些理论家的模型精巧。
[The rules of **nature's code** are considered to be much less ingenious than the models of a number of theorists.]

The Chinese 的 structure is potentially ambiguous as it could be taken to mean either *nature's* or *natural*, which means that the presence or absence of even a marginal, grammaticalized metaphor should to some extent be considered to be a matter of interpretation. Yet given the grammatical parallelism that exists within the sentence ('nature's code' vs. 'the ingenious models of a number of theorists', both of which involve the 'of' character 的), and given that in the latter case the possessive interpretation is the only possible one (since 'theorists' cannot here be reduced to an adjective) it would seem that this particular metaphorical expression has retained its metaphoricity as well as its level of conventionality.

7.2. Added expressions

A special section on expressions that have been added in translation is being included because this is a phenomenon that has tended to be underplayed in studies of metaphor in translation, in large part because analyses normally take the source-text expressions as their starting-point.

Many of the metaphorical expressions that are added in translation serve a purely discoursal function:

English: most of the ion channels that enable neurons to fire action potentials

French: des canaux ioniques qui **permettent** aux neurones de produire des potentiels d'action.
[ion channels that **permit** the neurons to produce action potentials]

Italian: la maggior parte dei canali ionici che **consentono** ai neuroni di scaricare i potenziali d'azione.
[the greater part of the ion channels that **consent** to the neurons discharging action potentials.]

Interestingly, however, the greater number of added metaphors introduce significant new conceptual elements:

English: Under these 'real world' conditions, the natural code's error value appeared orders of magnitude better still, outperforming all but one in a million of the alternatives.

Polish: Po zastosowaniu tych elementów z „prawdziwego świata" współczynnik błędu kodu zmniejszył się nawet o kilka rzędów wielkości. **Rozwiązanie przyrody** okazało się gorsze od zaledwie jednej możliwości na milion.
[After using these elements from the 'real world', the degree of error in the code was reduced by as much as several orders of magnitude. **Nature's solution** was worse than barely one possibility in a million.]

English: This new paradigm in evolutionary biology is certain to penetrate many more mysteries.

Russian: Такой подход наверняка поможет нам разгадать и многие другие **тайны природы**.
[This approach will surely help us to solve many more of **nature's secrets**.]

As can be seen, each of these examples contributes to the metaphorical picture of nature that is built up in the corpus, even if the two mappings to which the examples relate – NATURE IS A SOLVER OF PROBLEMS and NATURE IS A KEEPER OF SECRETS respectively – are new contributions in that they are not represented in any source language examples. Importantly, the last example also demonstrates that strong as well as weak metaphorical meanings can be added by translators.

Finally, there are a number of examples available in the corpus of Toury's procedure of adding a metaphor in the translated text when there is no 'linguistic motivation' for it in the original (1995:83):

Polish: **Prezent od natury**
[A present from nature]

This expression forms a title in the Polish text which comes at a point where there is no equivalent title in the original.

There have been few if any previous studies that have looked at the phenomenon of adding a metaphorical expression where there is no linguistic motivation in the source text, and it is interesting to see that this eventuality is not just a theoretical possibility. In general, no exhaustive search for metaphorical expressions added in translation was conducted, so in all probability there will be far more instances than the relatively few that have been reported in this brief section.

8. Conclusion

This paper has aimed to reflect on a major interdisciplinary research project designed to investigate patterns of metaphor translation and to demonstrate to some extent how concepts taken from one discipline can be linked with methodologies native to another. The paper has looked in some detail at text selection, corpus design, metaphor identification and data collection. The kind of research envisaged is text-based and involves, among other things, examining how the specific characteristics of metaphorical expressions can influence the approach adopted by the translator, and this has been seen to be a highly suitable way of linking up the disciplines of cognitive linguistics and translation studies. The sample analyses presented have briefly demonstrated the kinds of close examination of data that this approach makes possible.

Notes

1 Interestingly enough, most studies of specialised translation have up to now failed to reveal any deliberate manipulation of metaphors by translators, or indeed any clear evidence that such expressions present translators with a high level of difficulty.
2 There is an increasing tendency in contemporary translation studies research to distinguish between procedures and strategies: the former term refers to solutions to specific textual features while the latter denotes the general translation approach adopted (see van Doorslaer 2007:226–7 and also Munday 2012:22–24).
3 These languages are Arabic, Brazilian Portuguese, Chinese (with separate editions for the People's Republic and Taiwan), Czech, Dutch, French, German, Hebrew, Italian, Japanese, Polish, Russian and Spanish.
4 The process of metaphor identification will be discussed in Section 4.
5 These were mapping, typological class, purpose, level of categorization, richness, provenance and conventionality: see Shuttleworth (2013).

References

Al-Harrasi, A. (2001). *Metaphor in (Arabic-into-English) Translation with Specific Reference to Metaphorical Concepts and Expressions in Political Discourse.* Unpublished PhD thesis, Aston University.

Berber Sardinha, T. (2006). "A Tagger for Metaphors", paper given at the Sixth Researching and Applying Metaphor (RAAM) Conference, Leeds University.

Bowker, L., and J. Pearson. (2002). *Working with Specialized Language: A Practical Guide to Using Corpora.* London, New York: Routledge. http://dx.doi.org/10.4324/9780203469255.

Cameron, L. (1999). "Identifying and Describing Metaphor in Spoken Discourse." In *Researching and Applying Metaphor*, ed. Lynne Cameron and Graham Low, 105–132. Cambridge: Cambridge University Press. http://dx.doi.org/10.1017/CBO9781139524704.009.

Chan, M. L. (2011). *How Can Idioms be Translated? An Analysis of English to Chinese Translation in "Scientific American".* Unpublished MSc dissertation, Imperial College London.

Charteris-Black, J. (2004). *Corpus Approaches to Critical Metaphor Analysis.* Basingstoke: Palgrave Macmillan. http://dx.doi.org/10.1057/9780230000612.

Ding, Yan, D. Noël, and H. Wolf. (2010). "Patterns in Metaphor Translation: A Corpus-based Case Study of the Translation of FEAR Metaphors between English and Chinese." In R. Xiao (ed.) *Using Corpora in Contrastive and Translation Studies*, 40–61. Newcastle upon Tyne: Cambridge Scholars Publishing.

Fass, D. (1991). "Met*: A Method for Discriminating Metonymy and Metaphor by Computer." *Computational Linguistics* 17 (1): 49–90.

Gibbs, R. W. (1994). *The Poetics of Mind: Figurative Thought, Language, and Understanding.* New York: Cambridge University Press.

Goatly, A. (1997). *The Language of Metaphors.* London, New York: Routledge.

Harding, S.-A., G. Saldanha, and F. Zanettin. (2013). *Translation Studies Abstracts Online*, Manchester: St. Jerome Publishing. https://www.stjerome.co.uk/tsa.

Holmes, J. S. (2004). "The Name and Nature of Translation Studies." In L. Venuti (ed.) *The Translation Studies Reader*, 2nd ed., 180–192. London: Routledge.

Hoorickx-Raucq, I. (2005). "Mediating the Scientific Text. A Cultural Approach to the Discourse of Science in some English and French Publications and TV Documentaries." *Journal of Specialised Translation* 3:97–108. http://www.jostrans.org/issue03/ art_hoorickx_raucq.pdf.

Ilisei, Iustina (2012). *A Machine Learning Approach to the Identification of Translational Language: An Inquiry into Translationese Learning Models*. Unpublished PhD thesis, University of Wolverhampton.

Knowles, M., and R. Moon. (2006). *Introducing Metaphor*. London: Routledge.

Kövecses, Z. (2005). *Metaphor in Culture: Universality and Variation*. Cambridge: Cambridge University Press. http://dx.doi.org/10.1017/CBO9780511614408.

Kövecses, Z. (2006). *Language, Mind, and Culture: A Practical Introduction*. New York, Oxford: Oxford University Press.

Kövecses, Z. (2010). *Metaphor: A Practical Introduction*. 2nd ed. Oxford: Oxford University Press.

Lakoff, G. (1987). *Women, Fire and Dangerous Things: What Categories Reveal about the Mind*. Chicago, London: University of Chicago Press. http://dx.doi.org/10.7208/chicago/9780226471013.001.0001.

Lakoff, G. (1993). "The Contemporary Theory of Metaphor." In A. Ortony (ed.) *Metaphor and Thought*, 2nd ed., 202–251. Cambridge: Cambridge University Press. http://dx.doi.org/10.1017/CBO9781139173865.013.

Lakoff, G., and M. Johnson. (1980). *Metaphors We Live By*. Chicago, London: University of Chicago Press.

Lakoff, G., and M. Johnson. (1999). *Philosophy in the Flesh. The Embodied Mind and its Challenge to Western Thought*. New York: Basic Books.

Lakoff, G., and M. Turner. (1989). *More Than Cool Reason: A Field Guide to Poetic Metaphor*. Chicago, London: University of Chicago Press. http://dx.doi.org/10.7208/chicago/9780226470986.001.0001.

Liao, Min-Hsiu. (2007). 'The Translation of Interaction in the Genre of Popular Science: The Case of *Scientific American*', in *Proceedings of Corpus Linguistics Conference 2007, University of Birmingham, 27–30 July 2007*, http://ucrel.lancs.ac.uk/publications/CL2007/paper/23_Paper.pdf.

Liao, Min-Hsiu. (2010). "Translating Science into Chinese: An Interactive Perspective." *Journal of Specialised Translation* 13:44–60. http://www.jostrans.org/issue13/art_liao.pdf.

Liao, Min-Hsiu. (2011). "Interaction in the Genre of Popular Science." *Translator* 17 (2): 349–68. http://dx.doi.org/10.1080/13556509.2011.10799493.

Liu, Ting. (2011). *The Translation of Articles in Popular Science Magazines: A Case Study of Huanqiu Kexue (Global Science) – the Chinese Version of* Scientific American. Unpublished MSc dissertation, Imperial College London.

Mason, Z. (2004). "CorMet: A Computational, Corpus-based Conventional Metaphor Extraction System." *Computational Linguistics* 30 (1): 23–44. http://dx.doi.org/10.1162/089120104773633376.

Mauranen, A. (2008). "Universal Tendencies in Translation." In Gunilla Anderman and Margaret Rogers (eds) *Incorporating Corpora: the Linguist and the Translator*, 32–48. Clevedon: Multilingual Matters.

Mauranen, A. (ed.) 2004. *Translation Universals: Do they Exist?* Amsterdam, Philadelphia: John Benjamins Publishing Company. http://dx.doi.org/10.1075/btl.48.

Munday, J. (2012). *Introducing Translation Studies: Theories and Applications*. 3rd ed. London, New York: Routledge.

Olohan, M. (2004). *Introducing Corpora in Translation Studies*. London, New York: Routledge.

Pragglejaz Group. (2007). "MIP: A Method for Identifying Metaphorically Used Words in Discourse." *Metaphor and Symbol* 22 (1): 1–39. http://dx.doi.org/10.1080/10926480709336752.

Rey, J. (2000). "La traduction des textes scientifiques: Structure textuelle et processus cognitifs." *Target* 12 (1): 63–82.

Sharkas, H. (2009). 'Translation Quality Assessment of Popular Science Articles: Corpus Study of the *Scientific American* and Its Arabic Version'. In *trans-kom* 2:1, 42–62, http://www.trans-kom.eu/bd02nr01/trans-kom_02_01_03_Sharkas_Translation_Quality_Assessment.20090721.pdf.

Shuttleworth, M. (2011). "Translational Behaviour at the Frontiers of Scientific Knowledge: A Multilingual Investigation into Popular Science Metaphor in Translation." *Translator* 17 (2): 301–23. (Special Issue: Science in Translation.)

Shuttleworth, M. (2013). *Metaphor in Translation: A Multilingual Investigation into Language Use at the Frontiers of Scientific Knowledge*. Unpublished PhD thesis, University of London.

Shuttleworth, M. (2014a). "Scientific Rich Images in Translation: A Multilingual Study." JoSTrans 21, 35–51. http://www.jostrans.org/issue21/art_shuttleworth.pdf.

Shuttleworth, M. (2014b). 'Translation studies and metaphor studies: Possible paths of interaction between two well-established disciplines', in Donna R. Miller and Enrico Monti (eds) *Tradurre Figure / Translating Figurative Language*. Quaderni del Centro di Studi Linguistico-Culturali, Atti di Convegni CeSLiC - 3. Bologna: AMSActa, 53-65. http://amsacta.unibo.it/4030/.

Stallman, B. (1999). *Divine Hospitality in the Pentateuch: A Metaphorical Perspective on God as Host*, Unpublished PhD thesis. Philadelphia, PA: Westminster Theological Seminary. http://eagle.northwestu.edu/faculty/bob-stallman/files/2012/02/Stallman_Divine_Hospitality_.pdf.

Toury, G. (1995). *Descriptive Translation Studies and Beyond*. Amsterdam, Philadelphia: John Benjamins Publishing Company.

Ureña G.-M., J. Manuel, and P. Faber. (2011). "Strategies for the Semi-Automatic Retrieval of Metaphorical Terms." *Metaphor and Symbol* 26 (1): 23–52. http://dx.doi.org/10.1080/10926488.2011.535415.

van Doorslaer, L. (2007). "Risking Conceptual Maps: Mapping as a Keywords-related Tool Underlying the Online Translation Studies Bibliography." *Target* 19 (2): 217–33. http://dx.doi.org/10.1075/target.19.2.04van.

Williams, J., and Andrew C. 2002. *The Map: A Beginner's Guide to Doing Research in Translation Studies*. Manchester: St. Jerome Publishing.

The foreign and *the domestic* in translations: combining reception and corpus-based analysis

Hannu Kemppanen and Jukka Mäkisalo
University of Eastern Finland, Joensuu

1. Introduction

Domestication and foreignization as theoretical and empirical concepts

Translation studies have a long tradition of dividing translation strategies into dichotomies (Schleiermacher 1992 [1813], Nida 1964, House 1977, Newmark 1981, Berman 2000 [1985] among others). One of the most discussed dichotomies since the 1990s is the one between *foreignization* and *domestication*, introduced by Venuti (1995). During the last two decades these concepts have been used in dozens of articles and books that analyse empirically various translation strategies in literature and audiovisual translations. The concepts *foreignization* and *domestication* are used to refer to translation strategies that either change the text and information or leave them as they are in the original. In foreignisation the target text stays as close to the source text as possible, whereas in domestication the target text is changed when compared to the source text in order to make it more understandable for target language readers. The strategies refer as much to the whole translation task, or the text overall, as to a solution to a translation problem concerning an individual expression. For instance, Mazi-Leskovar defines the concepts explicitly as follows:

> "Foreignisation denotes in this context the conservation of a significant amount of what is alien and unusual in the reading context of the new target audience but common, unique, distinctive or typical for the source culture. The foreign, strange or even the exotic retained in the text is expected to be a stimulus to reading." (Mazi-Leskovar 2003, 254)
>
> "Domestication, on the other hand, is a strategy of translation which intervenes when the foreign and the odd is considered to represent a hindrance or barrier to the understanding of the text. However, even if there were no conscious decision for domestication, there is a certain degree of it in every translation because of the differences between the languages of the source and the target text. Domestication refers to all changes performed on various levels of the text in order to enable the target readers, the members of another nation, living in another geographical reality, with a specific socio-historical experience and a unique cultural background to fully grasp the text." (Mazi-Leskovar 2003, 254–255)

In empirical analyses, the concepts have been used referring to preservations or shifts of personal names (Pascua-Febles 2006, Rossi 2003), historical events and setting (Evans 2008, Paloposki and Oittinen 1998), food items and measures and units (Vid 2008), style, e.g. slangy expressions (Parini 2008) and syntactic patterns (Paloposki and Koskinen 2004), just to mention a few. The Venutian meaning of the terms is also worth mentioning here, since he uses them to refer to the treatment of cultural values that are either preserved or changed in translations (see, for instance Venuti 2009).

Although the division foreignization–domestication has been used as a methodological basis in several studies, it has been criticized as well, mainly because of its vagueness. A sharp dichotomy for analysing translation strategies has not been accepted by everyone. Boyden (2006), for instance, criticizes the dichotomy explicitly and insists that there are mixed forms in translations. He points out (Boyden 2006, 134) that, for a translation, it is actually impossible to oppose the target language culture if it does not belong, at least partially, to the culture. Thus, the dichotomy is questionable in the first place. Furthermore, Tymoczko (2000) criticizes Venuti for giving too much power to translators. For her, translators and translations are part of, or reflections of, the ideological, political and social environment – not as leaders or victims of change, but necessarily just part of it. Thus, translation theory is not the place to discuss ideological values or political choices.

Some researchers have attempted to concretise the two contradictory categories by dividing them into more detailed ones. For instance, Pedersen (2007) poses a continuum from foreignized to domesticated strategies based on an analysis of "extralinguistic culture bound elements" in film translations. He suggests seven phases in the continuum, from retention and specification to explicitation, addition, direct translation, generalization and substitution.

Unlike Venuti's macro-level approach, studies like these examine the question of foreignization and domestication in a restricted area of language use, such as screen translation or the translation of children's literature. A more specific approach reveals the importance of, for example, media- or audience-related constraints that have influence over choosing the translation strategy.

Amidst the several aspects in the structure of the two concepts, one is of utmost importance in regard to research interest, and that is the fact that the concepts as Schleiermacher (1992 [1813] defined them – "Either the translator leaves the writer alone as much as possible and moves the reader toward the writer, or he leaves the reader alone as much as possible and moves the writer toward the reader" – are actually literary metaphors. It is worth noting that no-one has dealt with this methodological issue, so far. As metaphors, they do not easily bend to the needs of empirical research. The problem of operationalization appears to take place at least at two levels. At the theoretical level, one is supposed to find the proper theoretical concepts that define foreignization and domestication empirically, that is in texts (that are translations). It is possible, for instance, that the concepts are mostly attached to the features of language, or, to be more specific, to the syntactic structure or to the lexical choices of the target text. It is also possible that they are attached to different features of the target text – for example, domestication to fluent style and lexical choices, and foreignization to personal names and historical setting. At the moment, any systematic analysis remains undone.

At the empirical level, one is supposed to find methods to recognize foreignness and, possibly even, measure the amount of it in translated texts. Of the two, the problem at the theoretical level is more acute, since the actual foreign and domestic features of translations appear to vary vastly in the research literature, and since, before measuring anything, it has to be known what to measure. In this paper, we touch on both of these issues. First, the qualitative analysis of the evaluation (reception) test is intended to indicate features that are empirically attached to the concepts. Second, the corpus-based analysis of the target texts is aimed at measuring some specific features.

There are a few studies that have asked subjects to evaluate texts as being either translated and non-translated Finnish texts, for instance Vehmas-Lehto 1989, Tirkkonen-Condit 2002, Jantunen 2004, although this has not always been the main objective of these studies. None of them have focused their questionnaires specifically on domestication or foreignization. Beside identifying foreign and domestic features, we also asked subjects to evaluate the texts as being translated and non-translated for comparison to earlier studies. In Tirkkonen-Condit (2002) and Jantunen (2004), the accuracy of guessing a text to be translated or non-translated is between 60 and 70% (cf. chapter 3).

The idea of the present study is based on the results of former corpus analyses (Kemppanen 2004, 2008) where translated and non-translated texts were compared by generating keyword lists with a corpus analysis tool (WordSmith Tools, Scott 1998). In Kemppanen's (2008) findings, Finnish translations had different kinds of word lists compared to word lists of texts originally written in Finnish. Kemppanen suggested that in translations there is some interference from the foreign source text, or language. These analyses show that these elements tend to take a high frequency position in keyword lists. Here, we infer the hypothesis that those keywords have a high correlation with the readers' intuition of what is regarded as foreign in translations.

Objectives

Thus, this study aims at operationalizing the concepts of foreignization and domestication. We test whether certain rather general features of texts such as keywords or sentence length in any way correlate with the features of foreign or domestic experienced in the same texts by readers. We do not argue by default, or a priori, that the features used are examples of domestication or foreignization, because methodologically there are no grounds for such a claim. We study empirically, whether they a posteriori are such. The more specific objectives are as follows: 1) to conduct a blind evaluation test in order to classify translated and non-translated texts on a scale of domesticated/foreignized translations; 2) to find out by means of corpus analysis, whether translated texts have statistical features which reflect the use of domesticating or foreignizing strategy; 3) to compare the results of the corpus analysis and the evaluation test to find out whether there is statistical correlation between the two. To put it in other words, the rationale of our study is to rank translated texts according to their status as foreign by using an evaluation test, and then to try to find statistical correlations between this ranking and other rankings that are based on various statistical and textual features of the texts.

The material in both analyses consists of text extracts from four Russian–Finnish translations (see Kemppanen 2008, Mauranen 2000), labelled as Bartenjev, Baryshnikov, Holodkovskij and Komissarov by their authors, and from two originally Finnish texts, labelled as Apunen and Tarkka. Both the translations and the non-translations represent non-fiction literature on the political history of Finland. The extracts contain 1,000 words and are collected from the beginning of each text. The use of extracts instead of whole texts is justified by the first part of the study, where the text excerpts are used for the evaluation test. It is, of course, also justified by the fact that it is not possible in practice to conduct a test that requires dozens of people to read six books. The material in the corpus-based study consists – in addition to the text extracts mentioned above – of a reference corpus of Finnish newspaper texts (1 million words of Karjalainen newpaper corpus), which was considered to reflect general frequency distributions of language use. Based on the finding by Kemppanen (2008), mentioned on the previous page, it was hypothesized, that compared to translations, history texts originally written in Finnish would show linguistic features which are closer to the frequency norms of reference corpus.

2. Characteristics of translated texts

Features of translated and non-translated texts and language have been studied extensively during the last two decades within translation studies. In the early 1990s, it was dressed in the conceptual and theoretical form of (translational) universals. Today, the theoretical standpoint seems to be that "universal" features – very often empirically hypothetical – are to be considered as possible and statistical trends among translated texts, where the variation within language pairs, textual genres and usage functions is vast (see Toury 2004, and later on, for instance, Becher 2010, 22–23).

Adapting the definition of language universals by Greenberg (1966) that they "are by their very nature summary statements about characteristics or tendencies shared by all human speakers," we want to state our theoretical objective to be characteristics and tendencies shared by translated texts compared to non-translated texts. We deliberately leave the theoretical issue of (translational) universals behind, and say nothing more than Greenberg: that they should be, by their very nature, summary statements – made after a vast amount of empirical studies.

Fortunately, we may say that most empirical investigation into so-called translation universals has focused on linguistic characteristics, and that there are a few studies on Russian-Finnish translations, too. Thus, we focus here in the theoretical introduction to translated language mainly on the empirical studies in Finnish, and textually on non-fiction.

In her text book on translating from Russian to Finnish and vice versa, Jänis (2010, 87–92) adopts contrastive methods, and she lists several linguistic and textual differences between Russian and Finnish, as well as features characteristic to translated language. We refer here to those that characterize translated Finnish.

1. The verb systems of Russian and Finnish differ from each other. First, Finnish does not have the aspectual morphology that Russian has, and second, whereas Finnish has two inflectional tempus categories (present and past tense) plus two analytic tempus categories (perfect and pluperfect), Russian has three inflectional ones (future, present and preterite). This contrastive difference causes tempus deviations in translated texts.
2. Russian texts use deverbal nominalizations whereas Finnish uses active verbs. Through interference, this causes heavy nominalized constructions in translated Finnish texts.
3. The neutral position of temporal adverbials is most often before the predicate in Russian, whereas in Finnish their position is after the predicate.
4. In the Russian language, copula verbs are nearly always omitted, whereas in Finnish they may never be omitted.
5. Since Finnish and Russian are languages with rich morphology, they both have several synthesizing structures that pack predications into syntactic constructions with a non-finite verb form. However, the constructions in Finnish and Russian differ structurally and functionally, which causes either interference or pressure to use paraphrases in the target language.

Eskola (2002) has studied the hypothesis that translations from Russian and English into Finnish show untypical frequencies of synthesizing syntactic constructions. Her original hypothesis that "synthesizing structures would be used more in translations than in original Finnish texts as a kind of strategy to pack and compress information" (Eskola 2002, i) did not find any evidence. It turned out that various synthesizing structures of the target language behave differently, depending on the source language and on the construction as a stimulus. For instance, the referative construction in Finnish (see example 1) does not have a functional and grammatical correspondent in Russian (see example 2), or in English either (Eskola 2002, 258, 77).

1 Tiedän hänen tulleen.
know+1SG he+GEN come+PC+POS
'I know (that) he has come.'

2 Я знаю что она пришла.
I know+1SG that she come+PST
'I know (that) she has come.'

When the functional correspondent is missing in the source language, the construction will be under-represented in translations. However, in the opposite case, that is when there is a direct correspondent of a source language construction in the target language, the construction will be over-represented (Eskola 2002, 264). The temporal construction in Finnish, Russian and English is a good example of this (see 3 and 4, which are from Eskola 2002, 78).

3 Luettuaan kirjan - -
read+PC+POS book+GEN - -
'Having read the book'

4 Прочитав книгу - -
ASP+read+* book+ACC
'Having read the book'

In cases of interference, and from the viewpoint of the target language, we might expect qualitatively untypical constructions in translations. For instance, Russian has a construction of agent participle that has frequent use and very little semantic restrictions, like example 5 (which is from Eskola 2002, 204) in Boris Pasternak's novel Доктор Живаго (*Doctor Zhivago*).

5 Озареннаямесяцемночьбылапоразительна - -
lighten+PC moon+INSTR night was wonderful - -
'The night lightened by the moon was wonderful'

However, in Finnish the actual translation of this sentence (see 6) in *Tohtori Živago* has a grammatical correspondent with an untypical and highly formal flavour and that is a violation against the semantic restrictions of the agent participle in Finnish: the use of the agent participle in Finnish prototypically needs a human subject.

6 Kuun valaisema yö oli ihmeellinen - -
moon+GEN lighten+PC night was wonderful - -
'The night lightened by the moon was wonderful'

Due to differences in constructions between Russian and Finnish, we first expect, since there is a need for paraphrasing, translated sentences to be longer than sentences in original Finnish. This tendency lends itself easily to measurement, since sentence-length is a standard statistical value given for a text in several corpus analysis tools, including WordSmith Tools, which is used here.

Second, we expect translated Finnish texts to have untypical frequencies of specific syntactic constructions. This tendency might become concrete in two ways in the keyword function of WordSmith Tools (see chapter 4 for the representation in details). The function generates a word list which shows statistically significant differences in word frequencies between the target text and reference texts. The programme carries out a comparison of the two frequency lists (target and reference texts) and calculates the keyness value of each word. Finally, the function presents a ranking list of the words that are over-represented in the target text compared to the reference text.

Because of the small number of words (1000) in the target texts compared to the reference corpus (1 million), there will seldom be any trace of under-represented constructions in the keyword lists of translated texts. In this case there are hardly any keywords that appear in the reference corpus that would be more infrequent in the target text. However, the over-represented constructions should appear as keywords in the ranked keyword list, especially when the corpus is not lemmatized, which means that the programme is dealing with (grammatical) word forms and not with (semantic) lemmas. For instance, if a text translated from Russian to Finnish has significantly more constructions of agent participles compared to reference texts originally written in Finnish, the word forms of agent participles should appear in the keyword list of the translated target text.

Overall, in this piloting and experimental work in progress, we end up using measures of sentence-length and various keyword values to throw light on possible statistical differences between translated and non-translated texts.

3. Evaluation test

Questionnaire

The classification of translations into foreignizing vs. domesticating was conducted by using a questionnaire where the four Russian–Finnish translations and two Finnish texts were evaluated on a 1–5 scale (domestic–foreign). The material consisted of the same extracts that were used for the corpus analysis (see later). There were 18 subjects in the evaluation test, all translation students at the MA level, and they were given three tasks: (1) Judge whether the text is originally written in Finnish or a Finnish translation; (2) Score the text as domestic or foreign on a scale 1–5; (3) Name at least one domesticating or foreignizing feature in each text. None of them knew any Russian. It is worth noting that the subjects were translation students who regularly encounter the concepts of foreign and domestic in their studies. So, the subjects had to base their impression about the translations only on observations about the features of the target text, not on their assumptions about the influence of the source text.

Results: the median of evaluations

As mentioned in the introduction, earlier evaluations of whether Finnish texts were translated and non-translated (Tirkkonen-Condit 2002, Jantunen 2004) reached a level of more than 60% accuracy, to be precise, 63.1% (Tirkkonen-Condit 2002, 211) and 62.6% (Jantunen 2004, 561). Our results show a clear difference between translated and non-translated texts, that is the subjects could tell with an accuracy of 79% whether a text is a translation or not (see Table 1, where the numbers of right and wrong guessing sums up to 85 against 23; $p < 0.001$ and $F = 1492$ in Chi-square with Yates correction). The result of this analysis is the most convincing one in our questionnaire.

Table 1. The quantitative results of the evaluation test.

Text	Transl. / non-transl.	Median of evaluations	Mean of evaluations	SD of evaluations	Judged as T/Non-T
Holodkovskij	T	4	3.8	1.0	16/2
Baryshnikov	T	4	3.7	1.2	15/3
Komissarov	T	4	3.5	1.2	13/5
Bartenjev	T	3	3.2	1.4	13/5
Apunen	Non-T	2	2.4	1.0	4/14
Tarkka	Non-T	2	2.2	1.2	4/14

The six history texts were also ranked according to the median of evaluations (see Table 1). Here, it is difficult to form finer categories between various translated texts, since within them there is a continuum from Holodkovskij to Bartenjev without any clear cut-off point; between the two non-translated texts it would be impossible, anyway. The analyses showed that the median and the mean of evaluations varied to quite an extent (2–4 and 2.2–3.8, respectively), although the full range 1–5 was applied to all texts. The small values of standard deviations (1.0–1.4), also, show that there is a clear accumulation of evaluations around the mean and that the use of the full range of 1–5 does not invalidate the differences between the texts.

The main objective, however, was fulfilled; i.e., to distinguish between translated and non-translated texts and to rank the texts according to the continuum from foreign to domestic, where Holodkovskij is regarded as the most foreignized and Tarkka as the most domesticated text.

Results: qualitative comments on foreignization/domestication

The qualitative features of domestic and foreign labelled in the comments proved to be more interesting than the quantitative judgements for the purpose of defining and operationalizing the concepts. The subjects made altogether 134 comments (see Table 2) on domesticated or foreignized features, and there is a clear difference in the distribution of the two, quantitatively and qualitatively.

Table 2. The number of various qualitative comments on foreignisation/ domestication.

Feature	Domestic	Foreign
Syntactic structure	6	23
Perspective	6	18
(Occasional) word choice	5	15
Orthography	1	9
Word order		7
Style (fluent/non-fluent)	21	6
Collocations, idioms	4	5
Sentence length	2	4
Paraphrases		1
Citation use		1
Total 134	45 (34%)	89 (66%)

Foreignization outnumbered domestication, since it accounted for two thirds (66%) of the comments. The difference in the distribution of the two is highly significant ($p < 0.001$ and $\chi^2 = 14.448$ in one way Chi-square test). We interpret this to mean that foreign features and *foreign* as a concept are more prominent than domestic features and *domestic*.

The most commented features in foreignization concerned the perspective and attitude of the text (18 times), for instance comments like *sisältää sellaista tietoa mitä ei historian tunnilla opetettu* 'consists of information that was not taught in history lessons at school' and *hyvin vahva NL-näkökulma* 'very strong Soviet perspective'; or its linguistic features like syntactic structure (23), for instance *outo lauseenrakenne* 'strange sentence structure' and *pitkähköt lauseet* 'longish sentences'; or occasional word choice (15), for instance *entinen vesivärimaalari* 'ex watercolour painter'. These three features accounted for 63% of the comments on foreignization.

The most commented feature (21 times) on domestication was, however, the style and fluency in non-translated texts, for instance *sujuvaa, vaikka osa välimerkeistä puuttuu* 'fluent, although some punctuation is missing', and this accounted for 47% of the comments on domestication, whereas the feature was mentioned only six times regarding foreignization. The fluency or non-fluency of the text is the focal feature of translations discussed by Venuti (1995, 4–5); our results strongly suggest, however, that it is the central feature of domesticated texts.

For instance, in the class of (occasional) word choices (five times as domestic and 15 times as foreign), the use of foreign or 'fancy alien' words was most often mentioned; on the contrary, the use of familiar or colloquial Finnish words was mentioned by only a few subjects. Again, we interpret this to mean that at the level of words and phrases foreignness is more prominent than domestic elements.

It is worth noticing that for most features the number of comments varied considerably between domestication and foreignization in our questionnaire. Exceptions to this are collocations and idioms and sentence length, where the distributions are 4 to 5 and 2 to 4, respectively. A few subjects found the use of familiar or foreign idioms and collocations similar both in translated and non-translated texts. There were four comments on long sentences as foreignized features in translated texts; it is somewhat strange that the very same feature of long sentences was regarded as domestic, too, by other subjects, because they thought that "it is a feature of Finnish non-fiction." These marginal comments do not challenge the main results, namely that domestication and foreignization collect different qualitative features and that foreign features are more prominent in texts.

4. Corpus-based study

The second part of the study consists of a corpus-based analysis, carried out by using the *WordSmith Tools* (Scott 2008) corpus analysis program. For the analysis, a word list was generated for each extract of the translated and non-translated texts. Then the word list of each text extract was compared with the word list of the reference corpus by using the *keywords* function. This generates a keyword list which demonstrates statistically significant differences in word frequencies between the target corpus and the reference corpus. The program automatically carries out a comparison of the frequency lists, cross-tabulates the frequencies and performs statistical tests (Chi-square and log-likelihood tests) for calculating the *keyness value* of each word. The keywords function provides lists with varying numbers of keywords and ranks the words in each list according to their keyness value.

We assume that the degree of foreignness or domesticity as a feature of a text can be defined by examining the keyness or non-keyness of the lexical elements in it. In other words, the concepts of foreignness and domesticity are operationalized by using a research method which is able to reveal deviation from a frequency norm. The frequency-based defining of the norm is derived from the ideas of Mike Scott (1998: 69), who created the *WordSmith Tools* corpus software. He uses the concept of frequency norm in defining the focal notion of our study – keywords. According to Scott "keywords are those whose frequency is unusually high in comparison with some norm." We used three different keyword features for describing the phenomenon of foreignness vs. domesticity: number of keywords, maximum keyness value and the mean of keyness value.

It is hypothesized that a high number of keywords in a list reflects a high level of foreignness of the lexical elements in a certain text compared to the frequency norm given by the reference corpus. This assumption is based on earlier studies on comparison of translated and non-translated texts, where keyword lists functioned as a starting point for further analysis of lexical features of translations (Kemppanen

2004, 2008). These studies show that translated texts, at least in this specific category of texts – Russian-Finnish translations of non-fiction on political history of Finland – differ from non-translated texts of the same genre as far as frequencies of lexical elements are concerned. In other words, keyword lists retrieved from each text can reveal the level of deviation from the frequency norm represented by the reference corpus.

The maximum keyness value can be found at the top of a keyword list. This variable introduces a keyword representing the most deviant lexical element in this certain text. The role of the maximum keyness value in recognizing foreignizing features has not been examined in corpus-based translation studies yet. Nevertheless, earlier analyses have shown that the number one word in a keyword list indicates some specific, norm-braking feature of the text – or the mass of texts (Kemppanen 2004, 2008).[1]

The mean of keyness value is a notion for describing statistical features of a text, derived for the purposes of this study. It can be generated by calculating the mean of all the keyness values given for the words in a keyword list. It is assumed again that this notion indicates the level of foreignness/domesticity of a text. A high mean refers to foreign and a low mean to domestic features of the text. A high mean of keyness can be composed by the occurrence of one or several keywords with a high keyness value. In other words, a large number of keywords does not necessarily generate a high mean value if the words show only a slight deviation from the frequency norm.

In addition to the features described by the statistics of the keyword lists, the analysis deals with two issues depicted in the word list statistics – the standardized type/token ratio (STTR) and the mean sentence length. Low STTR was one of the first features found to characterize translated language (Laviosa-Braithwaite 1996). It indicates that fewer different words are used in translations compared to non-translated texts. This means that translators express themselves with less varied lexical elements. In general, long sentences have been considered as an index of text difficulty (see, for instance, Mikk 2008). The issue of sentence length has been examined in translation studies as well – in respect to one of the translation universals, namely simplification. However, no difference between translated and non-translated texts was found (Corpas Pastor, Mitzkov, Afzal and Pekar 2008). It is assumed that type/token ratio and sentence length can be used to measure the distance of the translated text from the frequency norm represented by the reference corpus.

Results: the statistical features of the texts

The five statistical features (sentence length, STTR, number of keywords and the maximum and mean of keyness) in four translated and two non-translated Finnish history texts were compared, with the newspaper corpus as the comparable corpus. Overall, the analysis showed that the translated and non-translated texts differed in sentence-length, only, and that all other statistical features correlate with each other only weakly (see Figure 1). These features will be discussed separately in the following.

First, sentences are longer in translations than non-translations, since the range of the sentence length within translated texts is 14.68–18.89 and within non-translated texts 12.12–13.33 (in *t*-test the difference is significant, $p = 0.050$; see also Figure 1). We may thus infer that translations are felt to be more difficult to read. Second, in respect to other features, there is no difference between translated and non-translated texts. For instance, the STTR is highest in Apunen, which means that the text is characterized by great lexical variation. The author uses a large number of different words. However, after Apunen the ranking goes down in the following order: Komissarov, Baryshnikov, Tarkka, Holodkovskij and Bartenjev. In this respect we have to conclude that non-translations do not differ from translations. This is also the case with the indexes of keywords.

Most of the statistical features do not correlate with each other. The correlation between the STTR and the mean keyness is strongest (Pearson $r^2 = -0.62$), but negatively, that is 62% of all the word forms satisfy the relationship that the higher the STTR, the lower the mean value of keyness. This is natural, since the more lexically varied a text is, the fewer times each word is used and the smaller the probability for each word to end up in the keyword list. In other words, there is nothing specific about the result regarding either history texts or translations. The second strongest correlation (Pearson $r^2 = 0.51$) is the correlation between a high number of keywords and a high keyness maximum value. Hence, a text with a large number of keywords probably has a word with a higher keyness maximum value than a text with a small amount of keywords.

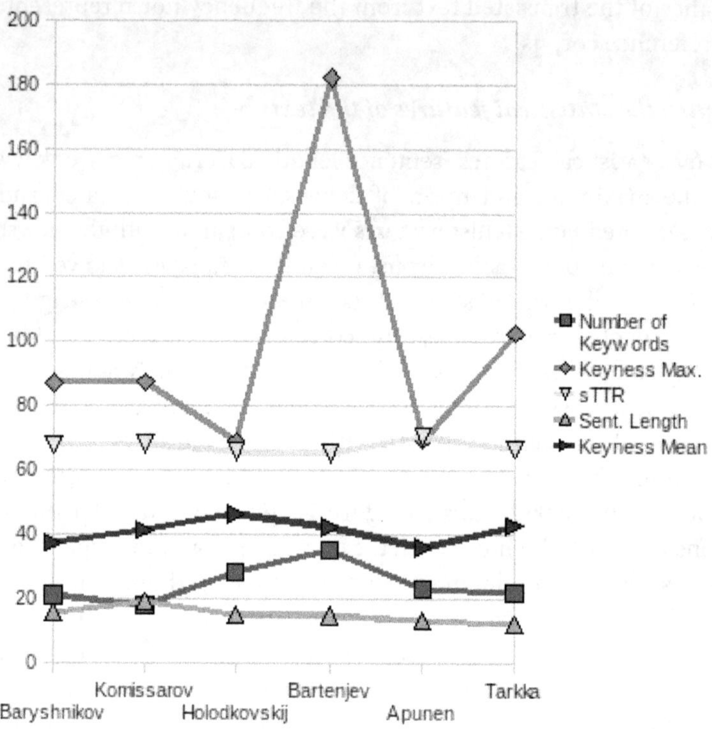

Figure 1. Correlation of the statistical features in the material.

Correlation between the results: statistical features and the evaluation test

The comparison of the results from the corpus-based analysis and the evaluation test (see Figure 2) indicate that the hypothesized statistical features of foreignness do not correlate with the ranking of translations as foreign or domestic. The evaluation ranking correlates best (Pearson $r^2 = 0.59$) with the sentence length: the longer the sentences, the higher the probability that the text will be judged as a translation. This finding confirms the similar result mentioned in the corpus-based analysis: the sentence length is the only statistical feature which shows significant difference between translated and non-translated texts.

Again, we have to conclude that the STTR or various values of keywords do not correlate with the evaluation test at all.

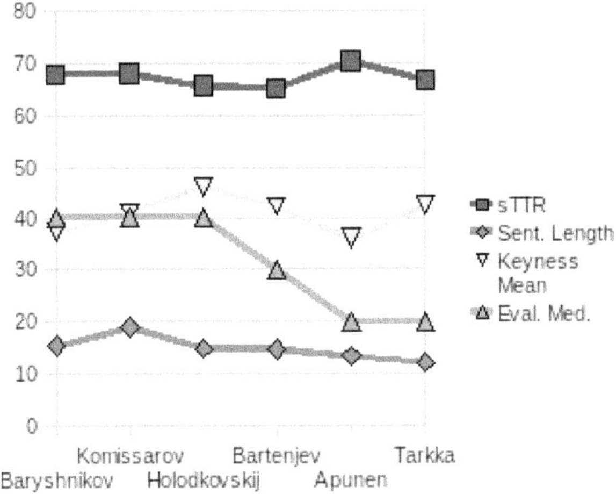

Figure 2. Correlation between statistical features and the evaluation test.

5. Conclusions and discussion

The rationale of our study was to rank translated texts according to their degree of foreignness by using an evaluation test, and then to try to find statistical correlations between this ranking and other rankings that are based on various statistical and textual features of the texts.

The study showed that, for the most part, statistical features of the texts did not correlate with the results of the evaluation test. Nevertheless, several statistical features attached to the keywords and generated by the corpus analysis were in line with each other, but the analysis showed that the translated and non-translated texts differed in sentence-length. The fact that sentences in translations are longer than in non-translated and comparable target language texts is in line with the idea that the need for paraphrasing when translating actually leads to differences in language structures, not only when compared to the source language, but also when compared to other and original target-language texts. This would be worth further study.

We may ask whether it is possible to distinguish translated and non-translated texts from each other, and on these grounds our answer is "yes," it is possible if you consult subjects (who have some expert knowledge), but "so far, no," if you use those statistical corpus-based methods that were chosen here. It seems to be especially difficult to find valid statistical corpus measurements for differences in various syntactic structures between the source and target language.

The evaluation test revealed the subjectivity of ranking the translations as domesticated / foreignised. Although the full range 1–5 was used for all the texts in evaluations, the evaluations accumulated well enough to differentiate translations as foreign from non-translations as domestic. Furthermore, the test results suggest that the subjects pay attention to the use of individual words and phrases, not to those textual (and statistical) features that are reflected in the word frequency lists. The subjects' comments clearly indicate that they mainly react to the foreignizing rather than to the domesticating elements (66% to 34%, respectively) of the texts. This suggests that foreign elements in translations are a marked category compared to domestic, unmarked features; it is easier to recognize the untypical than the typical. Furthermore, there is also a clear qualitative difference between the two categories.

The findings clearly indicate the difference between quantitative and qualitative methods. In a qualitative examination even individual linguistic elements may draw the attention of the subject. From the statistical point of view such features may prove irrelevant. A qualitative analysis seems to highlight occasional word choices, syntactic features, such as sentence length, as well as such qualitative features as the attitude or the perspective of the text, which can be evaluated in the reception process quite easily, even in a short text extract. It is, however, clear that when examining longer texts the results of statistical analyses become more reliable.

An issue worth considering is the use of lay readers as subjects. It would be possible to ask them, whether a text is translated or non-translated Finnish text. However, we had a strong impression that it would be impossible to use them here, since we would have had to teach them first what is meant by the concepts *domestic* and *foreign* in texts. Moreover, that would ruin the methodological validity of the questionnaire, since the subjects would answer as they were taught. It is important to understand that the issue of lay readers is a sociological one, and it is not as crucial here, where the main objective is to operationalize the concepts.

The results of the study suggest that the concepts of domestication and foreignization are more attached to individual reception of translations than to statistical features. There is a clear need for more extensive and methodologically varied studies on the reception of translations.

Although the results of this study showed no correlation between the statistical features of the texts and the evaluation test, it is encouraging to see that in the reception process the subjects mostly seem to pay attention to marked, i.e., foreignizing, elements. The keyword method also generates elements that are marked. It is obvious that further research in this area of marked elements may shed new light on operationalizing the notions of foreignization and domestication.

Material

Translation extracts taken from *The Comparable Corpus of History Texts* (see Kemppanen 2008), a corpus related to *The Corpus of Translated Finnish* (see Mauranen 2000).

Reference corpus: *Karjalaisen korpus. 1990-luvun suomen sähköinen tutkimusaineisto.* ['Karjalainen newspaper corpus. The 1990's Finnish computerised database.'] Available at: Kielipankki-palvelin, CSC – Tieteellinen laskenta Oy. https://www.csc.fi/kielipankki.

Note

1 Kemppanen (2004, 2008) found out that keyword lists show ideology-bound lexical elements, which can be regarded as norm-breaking features of translations. Several keyword lists based on a comparison of translations and non-translated texts on the political history of Finland were surprisingly topped by one of the most common grammatical words in Finnish, namely *ja* 'and'. A closer analysis of the contexts of the word revealed that it is often used untypically in translations for building the collocation *Suomi ja Neuvostoliitto* 'Finland and the Soviet Union'. This collocation labels the co-operating actors in translated texts. In non-translated texts Finland is acting alone, so the collocation is not needed. Russian (and especially Soviet) discourse of history stresses the importance of friendship and co-operation between the neighbouring countries after the Second World War. Finnish history scholars emphasize the role of the fight for independence during the war.

References

Berman, A. (Original work published 1985). (2000). "Translation and the Trials of the Foreign." [La Traducion comme épreuve de l'étranger]. In *The Translation Studies Reader*, ed. L. Venuti, trans. L. Venuti, 284–297. London, New York: Routledge.

Becher, V. (2010). "Abandoning the notion of "translation-inherent" explicitation: against a dogma of translation studies." *Across Languages and Cultures* 11 (1): 1–28. http://dx.doi.org/10.1556/Acr.11.2010.1.1.

Boyden, M. (2006). "Language politics, translation, and American literary history. *Target." International Journal of Translation Studies* 18 (1): 121–37. http://dx.doi.org/10.1075/target.18.1.07boy.

Corpas Pastor, G., Mitzkov, R., Afzal, N., and Pekar, V. (2008). Translation universals: do they exist? A corpus-based NLP study of convergence and simplification. *Conference Proceedings, 8th AMTA Conference, Hawaii, 21–25 October 2008.* http://www.mt-archive.info/AMTA-2008-Corpas.pdf.

Eskola, S. (2002). Syntetisoivat rakenteet käännössuomessa. Suomennetun kaunokirjallisuden ominaispiirteiden tarkastelua korpusmenetelmillä. [Synthesising Structures in Translated Finnish. A Corpus-based Analysis of the Special Features of Finnish Literary Translations.] University of Joensuu Publications in the Humanities, 30. Joensuu: University of Joensuu.

Evans, J. (2008). When Domestication is an Estranging Effect: Adriana Hunter's Translation of Beigbeder's 99 Francs. In Hyde Parker, R. and Guadarrama García, K. (eds) 87–94. *Thinking Translation: Perspectives from Within and Without. Conference Proceedings, Third UEA Postgraduate Translation Symposium*. Boca Raton: BrownWalker Press.

Greenberg, J. (1966). *Universals of Language*. 2nd ed. Cambridge, Mass.: MIT Press.

House, J. (1977). *A Model for Translation Quality Assessment*. Tübingen: TBL Verlag Gunter Narr.

Jantunen, J.H. (2004). "Suomennosten kieliasu puntarissa." [Rethinking the Language of Translations.] *Virittäjä* 108 (4): 559–72.

Jänis, M. (2010). *Venäjästä suomeksi ja suomesta venäjäksi*. [From Russian to Finnish and from Finnish to Russian.] Aleksanteri Series 4/2010. Helsinki: Aleksanteri-instituutti.

Kemppanen, H. (2004). "Keywords and Ideology in Translated History Texts: A Corpus-Based Analysis." *Across Languages and Cultures* 5 (1): 89–106. http://dx.doi.org/10.1556/Acr.5.2004.1.5.

Kemppanen, H. (2008). *Avainsanoja ja ideologiaa: käännettyjen ja ei-käännettyjen historiatekstienkorpuslingvistinen analyysi.* [Keywords and Ideology: A Corpus-Based Analysis of Translated and Non-Translated History Texts]. University of Joensuu Publications in the Humanities, n:o 51. Joensuu: University of Joensuu.

Laviosa-Braithwaite, S. (1996). *The English Comparable Corpus (ECC): A Resource and a Methodology for the Empirical Study of Translation*. Department of Language Engineering, Volume I. A thesis submitted to the University of Manchester Institute of Science and Technology for the degree of Doctor of Philosophy.

Mauranen, A. (2000). "Strange Strings in Translated Language. A Study on Corpora." In *Intercultural Faultlines. Research Models in Translation Studies I. Textual and Cognitive Aspects*, ed. M. Olohan, 119–141. Manchester: St. Jerome Publishing.

Mazi-Leskovar, D. (2003). "Domestication and Foreignization in Translating American Prose for Slovenian Children." *Meta* 48 (1–2): 250–65. http://dx.doi.org/10.7202/006972ar.

Mikk, J. (2008). "Sentence Length for Revealing the Cognitive Load Reversal Effect in Text Comprehension." *Educational Studies* 34 (2): 119–27. http://dx.doi.org/10.1080/03055690701811164.

Newmark, P. (1981). *Approaches to Translation.* Oxford, etc.: Pergamon Press.

Nida, E.A. (1964). *Toward a Science of Translating. With Special Reference to Principles and Procedures Involved in Bible Translating.* Leiden: E.J. Brill.

Paloposki, O., and K. Koskinen. (2004). "A thousand and one translation. Revisiting retranslation." In *Claims, Changes and Challenges in Translation Studies.* Benjamins Translation Library, 50, ed. G. Hansen, K. Malmkjaer, and D. Gile, 27–38. Amsterdam: John Benjamins. http://dx.doi.org/10.1075/btl.50.04pal.

Paloposki, O., and R. Oittinen. (1998). The domesticated foreign. In *Translation in Context. Selected Contributions from the EST Congress, Granada 1998.* Benjamins Translation Library, 39, ed. Chesterman, A., Gallardo San Salvador, N. and Gambier, Y, 373–390. Amsterdam: John Benjamins.

Parini, I. (2008). Domesticating or Foreignizing Texts? Case Study: Niccolo Ammaniti's Ti prendo e ti porto via translated into English. In Hyde Parker, R. and Guadarrama García, K. (eds.) *Thinking Translation: Perspectives from Within and Without. Conference Proceedings, Third UEA Postgraduate Translation Symposium*. Boca Raton: Brown Walker Press. 135–155.

Pascua-Febles, I. (2006). "Translating Cultural References. The Language of Young People in Literary Texts Children's Literature in Translation." In *Challenges and Strategies*, ed. J. Van Coillie and W.P. Verschueren, 111–121. Manchester: St. Jerome.

Pedersen, J. (2007). How Is Culture Rendered in Subtitles? In Nauer, S. (ed.) *Challenges of Multidimensional Translation*. Proceedings of the Marie Curie Euroconferences *MuTra: Challenges of Multidimensional Translation* – Saarbrücken 2–6 May 2005. http://www.euroconferences.info/proceedings/proceedings.php.

Rossi, P. (2003). "Translated and Adapted – The Influence of Time on Translation. *META*." *XLVIII* 1–2:142–53.

Scott, M. (1998). *WordSmith Tools Manual. Version 3.0.* Oxford: Oxford University Press; http://www.lexically.net/wordsmith/version3/manual.pdf.

Scott, M. (2008). *WordSmith Tools version 5.* Liverpool: Lexical Analysis Software; http://www.lexically.net/wordsmith/index.html.

Schleiermacher, F. (Original work published 1813) (1992). "On Different Methods of Translating." In *Theories of Translation*, ed. R. Schulte and J. Biguenet, trans. W. Barscht., 36–54. Chicago, London.

Tirkkonen-Condit, S. (2002). "Translationese – a myth or an empirical fact? A study into the linguistic identifiability of translated language." *Target* 14 (2): 207–20. http://dx.doi.org/10.1075/target.14.2.02tir.

Toury, G. (2004). "Probabilistic explanations in translation studies: Welcome as they are, would they qualify as universals?" In *Translation Universals? Do they exist?*,

15–32. Benjamins Translation Library 48, ed. A. Mauranen and P. Kujamäki. Amsterdam: John Benjamins. http://dx.doi.org/10.1075/btl.48.03tou.

Tymoczko, M. (2000). "Translation and Political Engagement. Activism, Social Change and the Role of Translation in Geopolitical Shifts." *Translator* 6 (1): 23–47. http://dx.doi.org/10.1080/13556509.2000.10799054.

Venuti, L. (1995). *The Translator's Invisibility. A History of Translation.* London, New York: Routledge. http://dx.doi.org/10.4324/9780203360064.

Venuti, L. (2009). "Translation as cultural politics: Régimes of domestication in English." In *Critical Readings in Translation Studies,* ed. M. Baker, 65–80. London: Routledge.

Vid, N. (2008). Domesticated translation: the case of Nabokov's translation of Alice's Adventures in Wonderland. *Nabokov Online Journal,* Vol. II. http://libraries.dal.ca

Part II

Stylistic Approach to Translation

A corpus-assisted stylistic analysis of metaphor through the prism of translated poetry

Iraklis Pantopoulos

1. Metaphor and Translation: A complicated relationship

1.1 Parallelisms

It is not hard to make the claim that metaphor and translation have, in many ways, been living a parallel existence. This notion can be traced back even to the etymological origins of the two terms (and what they tell us about these concepts themselves). Guldin (2010) offers a comprehensive view of the structural analogies and dialogical relationship between the two, based mostly on earlier work by Cheyfitz (1991). As part of his evaluation of the nature of metaphor and translation in relation to each other, he notes the centrality of the notion of 'transfer(ence)' for both concepts ('metaphora' the ancient Greek word for metaphor and its Latin equivalent 'translatio'). On a fundamental level, then, both concepts are immediately concerned with 'transfer' (ibid.: 170). What is more, our view of translation (even as an established discipline) is still largely determined by this relation. This is evident in such pivotal terms in translation studies as source-text (ST) and target-text (TT). These indicate a profoundly metaphorical understanding of translation, with ST implying originality and direction towards a TT similar to the course of a river towards the sea. Furthermore, Guldin (2010) claims that this relationship is reciprocal and defines our understanding of, and approach to, both metaphor and translation.

However, despite this fundamental link (and other facets that will be touched upon later), Boase-Beier (2006: 96) rightly notes that metaphor has been conspicuously absent from a number of major recent works on translation studies, while overall there appears to be a division of opinion regarding the marginal/central status of metaphor in the study of translation.

1.2 The 'Problem' of Metaphor

What is beyond doubt, however, is that the treatment metaphor originally received in the vast majority of translation studies literature, even when the translation of metaphor is regarded as the "most important particular problem" as by Newmark (1995:104, see also 1980, Snell-Hornby, 1988) is precisely that of a problem (for a more detailed timeframe see Samaniego Fernández, 2011). As a result a considerable percentage of works on metaphor and translation are in essence treatises and guidelines on breaking down the problem and drawing up lists of possible solutions 'according to case'. The best known and most widespread are those proposed by van den Broeck (1981) and Newmark (1981) which are in essence a series of procedures for the translator to choose from. There is, however, a substantial difference in the underlying approach here: while van den Broeck's list is meant to be a starting point for a descriptive observation and analysis of the translation of metaphor, Newmark offers his list of translation procedures as a set of rules and guidelines aiming for better practice and training of translators.

1.3 Linguistic Approaches and Implications

The common ground between the above-mentioned approaches (and others such as Snell-Hornby 1988: 55) is that metaphor is either regarded as a linguistic phenomenon (in the traditional sense) that presents particular difficulties for translators, or is marginalised. These outlooks are based mainly on what is now regarded as the traditional view of metaphor, which is more clearly evident in the perspective that Black (1962) terms the "substitution view of metaphor." This view, reflected in his claim that: "a metaphorical expression is used in place of some equivalent literal expression" (Black 1962: 31), is characteristic of the linguistic approach to metaphor in both language and literature. It is also relevant, and noteworthy, that in this view, (linguistic) metaphor in essence is a form of (linguistic) translation, as exemplified by the use of the loaded term 'equivalent' that was prevalent in earlier theoretical approaches to translation.

Overall, linguistic approaches epitomised by the substitution theory regarded metaphor as a largely ornamental stylistic feature, mostly encountered in literary/poetic language. Metaphoric meaning, then, despite often being complex and elaborate can be 'translated' back to its literal form. There are distinct similarities here with linguistics-based early approaches to translation. These have mostly to do (as Guldin also notes) with a hierarchic point of view, according to which the literal or the original precedes and supersedes the metaphorical and the translational. Furthermore, Tabakowska (1993: 66) points to an effect of this when she claims that with "the advance of [...] linguistics metaphor was reduced to a marginal phenomenon" in translation studies. In other words, as the above linguistic-based approach came to dominate translation studies, the study of metaphor found itself increasingly at the fringes of the discipline.

Accordingly, there are numerous attempts to classify metaphor, either from a prescriptive or a descriptive outlook, so as to facilitate a better analysis and the most appropriate solution in translation. A related common tendency of these approaches is a strong source-oriented perspective which provides the basis for the classification of metaphor and/or of the proposed translation procedures. Even in those approaches, such as van den Broeck's, that are not prescriptive, the ST metaphoric expression is the 'yardstick' against which the TT expression is measured. From the point of view of translation studies, then, the linguistic view of metaphor is, historically, closely related to the view of metaphor as mainly a translation problem.

1.4 The Cognitive Turn and Implications

The advance of cognitive approaches to metaphor, postulated by, among others, Lakoff and Johnson (1980), Sweetser (1991), and Turner (1993) has had a fundamental impact on the understanding of metaphor and its embodied and experiential foundations. According to this 'cognitive turn', metaphor is no longer regarded as merely a literary stylistic feature tied to fundamentally linguistic concerns. This outlook sees metaphor as a phenomenon common in everyday language that is inextricably tied to our cognitive processing and understanding of the world. More specifically, "[t]he essence of metaphor is understanding and experiencing one thing in terms of another" (Lakoff and Johnson 1980: 5).

Inevitably, this turn redefines the relationship between metaphor and translation, and offers not only a different perspective on metaphor but also on translation. Crucially, Conceptual Metaphor Theory (CMT) differentiates between 'linguistic metaphor', which is the verbal aspect of metaphor, and 'conceptual metaphor' which is a direct product of the human experience and conceptualization of the world. Both of these, comprise information structures which are processed by language users as they process and understand metaphor. This applies to readers of literature as much as to everyday users of language. According to Lakoff and Johnson (as quoted by Steen) "the verbal aspect of metaphor ought to be regarded as dependent on, or derived from, conceptual metaphor" (Steen, 1994: 7).

What this means in practice is that (verbal) metaphor is no longer widely regarded as merely "a violation of selection restrictions" (Boase-Beier 2006: 96) or a linguistic peculiarity that mainly characterizes literary language but, conversely, a linguistic manifestation – that may or may not be literary – of a fundamental function of human thinking. Schäffner rightly observes that the translatability of metaphors seen from such a perspective takes on a completely new dimension: "Translatability is no longer a question of the individual metaphorical expression, as identified in the ST, but it becomes linked to the level of conceptual systems in source and target culture" (Schäffner 2004:1258). In other words, the focus appears to shift from each particular linguistic expression to the underlying conceptual mapping.

The shift introduced by CMT can therefore, from a translation studies point of view, radically change the outlook on metaphor and transform it from a 'problem' – regardless of the significance attributed to it – to a unique opportunity for linking individual linguistic expressions to deeper lying conceptual structures. This, in turn, presents an ideal area for researching the core issue of the interaction between the individual, the culturally specific and the universal in translation. This paper ventures in this direction by means of a case study, in an attempt to explore and highlight the benefits of studying metaphor in translation from a cognitive perspective. To this end, it adopts Steen's (1994: 7) outlook that "[t]here are various ways in which the linguistic expression of a conceptual metaphor can affect the appearance of the conceptual metaphor in question." This realization is crucial and, furthermore, places style, regarded here as "the perceived distinctive manner of expression" (Wales, 2001: 371), in a pivotal role in the whole process. Any approach to metaphor and/in translation that "is not only interested in possible equivalences between an unwavering ST and a supplementary TT but also in the *creative power of all translational procedures* lies then in the common idea that any transference [...] always implies *interpretative transformation* and renewal" (Guldin (2010: 187, my emphasis). This "interpretative transformation" inevitably brings the translator to the foreground and, approached from a cognitive perspective, "is determined by both universal features of the brain and cultural influences" (Boase-Beier 2006: 96).

2. Cognitive Poetics and Translational Stylistics

2.1 Re-locating Style in Translation

Style has been playing an increasingly important role in translation studies over the course of recent years, and its place in the discipline can be claimed to have been steadily shifting from the periphery towards the centre. What is crucial in this development is that this increasing interest in, or awareness of, the importance of style in the study of translation appears to coincide with a parallel shift in interest from the style of the ST, as an overriding factor, to the style of the TT or, to be more precise, the style of the translator(s). A number of seminal works such as Baker (2000) and Boase-Beier (2006) have adopted and advocated the importance of such a shift which, of course, does not neglect the presence of the ST and author, but dislodges them from their formerly dominant position. In other words, style is no longer used in the study of translation with the sole purpose of analysing the ST so as to best translate it, nor as the means of comparing source and target in search of 'equivalence' and 'loss' in the process of translating. In notably mirroring the move away from strictly linguistic concerns in the study of metaphor and translation, a 'cognitive turn' in the study of style places it at the very core of the translation process.

This turn, originating from the field which has come to be known as 'cognitive linguistics', is what has come to be known as cognitive poetics. According to Turner:

> An important aspect of cognitive poetics is that it sees the literary mind not as something that only comes into play when a literary text is to be read, but as the mind itself. In other words, not only are elements of style such as metaphor or ambiguity ways of thinking, but they are ways of thinking that are central to our cognitive functioning. (1996: 4–5)

2.2 Cognitive Style and the Translator

This focus on style as a cognitive construct, has of course implications for the study of translation on a very fundamental level: it reconfigures the status of the translator and their place within an overall theoretical model. Boase-Beier (2006: 54) notes that, when translating a text or author "the translator is attempting to reconstruct states of mind and thought processes, always with the awareness that the individual states of mind are affected by social and cultural influences." This attention paid to the social and cultural factors involved in the production, reception and translation of literature is a key element that cognitive linguistics bring to the study of style in translation through their pragmatic concern with what goes beyond the strictly textual elements. In fact, they were such text-restricted approaches that have, as far as they infiltrated early TS, hindered the development of models to replace the traditional – ST focused – views of style in relation to translation.

Thus, the concern that developed in cognitive stylistics regarding the aspects of language and meaning that go beyond the strictly linguistic is instrumental in the conception of a broader notion of style in the study of translation. This convergence, that affords a range of possibilities, is achieved through the notion of 'context' as a cognitive construct which according to Stockwell's (2002: 60) definition is "the psychological and social circumstances under which language is used." In this way, through the interest in context, cognitive stylistics takes into account the cultural (social and historical) aspects of the production and understanding of texts. This means that attention is paid not only to the role of the writer (author or translator) but also to that of the reader, in the way meaning is created according to the reader's inferences. This naturally applies to the translator also, and sees him/her as the – inferred – reader and writer of literature. Semino (1997: 160) adopts the notion of 'schemata' or pre-existing knowledge structures that each individual has and activates during the process of interpretation of a literary text. These schemata are, of course, different for each reader and are acquired through "repeated exposure to similar objects and situations." Accordingly, meanings "are not 'contained' within a text but are constructed in the interaction between the text and the interpreter's background knowledge" (ibid.: 124).

The active role of the reader in the construction of meaning and the emphasis on context make the cognitive outlook on style and translation a broader one, able to relate "linguistic choices to cognitive structures and processes" (Semino and Culpeper 2002: ix). In this sense, to translate style is indeed to translate a state of mind, and if the ST is the product of the author's mind, then traces will be also evident in the TT, intertwined with those of the translator's own. It should then be expected that the style of the ST will act as a constraint on the choices the translator will make in attempting to recreate it, and these choices, in turn will establish the style of the TT. So, in the case of more than one translation of the same ST (as in the case study reported here), the style of the ST that will be the source of constraint is the same for all translators. Yet, the way each translator will perceive these constraints, and the stylistic choices s/he will make in attempting to re-create the style of the original, are subject to the translator's own perception of language (as a reader and as a writer) as this perception is shaped by his/her own personal experience and context. As a consequence, the study of translation: "will need to be concerned with stylistic figures and devices, with the cognitive counterparts of textual stylistic elements and with poetic effects." (Boase-Beier 2011)

2.3 Translating Metaphor as a Cognitive Stylistic Feature

There are two overarching factors in approaching the translation of metaphor from a cognitive point of view: the very notion of the translatability of metaphor needs to be reviewed and, the distinction between conceptual metaphor and its linguistic manifestation(s) foregrounded. Tabakowska (1993: 67) touches upon both issues when she notes that accepting that metaphor is rooted in one's experience can lead to the conclusion that it is thus culture specific by default. This outlook, in turn, can present obvious problems when contemplating the translatability of metaphors within a cognitivist framework: if metaphors are culture specific by nature, due to their close link with perception, then they must be untranslatable by default.

And yet, it is this very link with human perception that can be seen as the basis for an opposing argument concerning the culture specificity of metaphors: "[S]ince the nature of perception, rooted in the process of human cognition, is by definition universal to all people [...] there must exist some regular patterns of meaning extension, which will repeat themselves in different languages" (ibid.). In other words, the conceptual nature of metaphor is common across different languages and cultures. Stienstra (1993) applies this outlook specifically to translation studies by making a distinction between universal, culture-overlapping and culture-specific metaphors, while Schäffner (2004: 1265) expands this classification, which is based on the view that a large amount of human experience is universal, to argue that: "conceptual metaphors may be culture-specific at a more specific level, but culture-overlapping (or maybe universal) at a more abstract level." There is a crucial implication in this distinction, pertaining to the study of metaphor and its relationship with translation: perhaps it is not the conceptual metaphor that is culture-dependent, but its linguistic realization. The case study reported in this paper seeks to investigate both the validity and the implications of this premise.

In the end, it is not possible to discuss metaphor as a cognitive feature and its implications for translation without considering the notion of 'equivalence'. It is telling that, despite its decline in terms of theoretical 'currency,' and the scepticism with which it is regarded, the concept of equivalence is taken up in the argumentation of a number of prominent studies on the relationship between cognitive metaphor and translation (cf. Schäffner 2004, Tabakowska 1993, Guldin 2010, Boase-Beier 2006, Samaniego Fernández 2011). This, as Samaniego Fernández (2011: 274) points out, is mostly in response to a perceived relation between a ST and a TT which is close in nature. What is common ground between these approaches is that "equivalence is a formula that has to be enlarged to cover the multiplicity of translational answers given by translators" (ibid.).

What all of the above considerations, regarding the cognitive/experiential nature of metaphor and its implications for translation, point to is the pivotal position of metaphor for the study of intercultural communication, on the one hand, and, crucially, the unique affordances of translation for the study of the nature and function of metaphor, on the other. As Schäffner (2004: 1266) observes: "[d]ifferent perspectives and/or aspects of a common conceptual metaphor are made explicit in the texts" and "translations can make differences in conceptual metaphors, and/or metaphorical expressions explicit, and that they may indeed trigger controversial debates in intercultural communication." What is also clear, is that the fulcrum between a conceptual metaphor, with its multiple aspects, and its linguistic 'reincarnation' is the translator:

> That is precisely what most approaches to a cognitive theory of metaphor translation ignore: the translator decides what is transferred and how it is transferred on the basis of some factors that may be said to be general (relatively common to some genres, text types, metaphor types, etc.) and some factors which may be said to be individual or ad hoc (translator choices, etc.). Some of them may be cultural and some of them may have a different nature. (Samaniego Fernández: 268)

It is, of course, clear that this outlook and its implications throw into relief the importance of style, as the distinctive manner of expression, in the understanding of the relationship between metaphor and translation. Different aspects of a conceptual metaphor can be (and are) foregrounded in translation, a fact that constitutes a manifestation of the complexity of metaphorical processes, the proliferative capacity of (literary) language, and the role of the translator as reader/writer. In short, the universality, cultural specificity and particularity that are inscribed in both the notions of style and translation are encapsulated in the case of metaphor as a cognitive stylistic feature. The case study that follows will look into this relationship in great detail by focusing on the exploration of a single metaphor.

3. Methodological Considerations

3.1 Metaphors, Dead Metaphors and Translatability

The focus of the case study reported here will be on a metaphor that is recurring in the poetry of Greek Nobel prize winning poet, George Seferis. This is the ST linguistic metaphor "μαρμαρωμένος," which can be back translated as "marble-fied," an adjective that denotes someone/thing is "turned-into-marble." This specific metaphor was selected as the focus of the study taking into account both the nature and function of metaphors and its particular overall importance in Seferis's work. The main aim of the study is to exploit and explore the relationship between metaphor and translation through interaction between the universal, culturally determined and individual in translated literature. While the juxtaposed 'constituents' of a linguistic metaphor can, in theory, be easily translated as lexical items, the cultural, conceptual elements involved can help foreground the intricacies involved in the process. Furthermore, as will be seen, their cumulative effect beyond the level of the individual text (poem), and how it is affected by translation, is another factor that needs to be considered.

"Μαρμαρωμένος" in Greek is also a 'dead' or 'lexicalized' metaphor, a metaphorical expression whose use is "conventional, unconscious, automatic and typically unnoticed" (Lakoff and Turner 1989: 80). A further reason that makes it an interesting focus for the study is the fact that within the multitude of classifications for metaphors in terms of their translatability, "in general it is stated that dead metaphors are more readily translatable" (Samaniego Fernández 2011: 266). The validity of such a hypothesis and its implications for the relationship between metaphor and translation will be considered.

3.2 Data-handling: A Corpus-assisted comparative approach

In terms of an overall method, the study adopts a comparative approach, looking at two different translations of Seferis's poetry and the way all occurrences of "μαρμαρωμένος" in the ST are treated by the translators. The translations are by Friar (1973) and by Keeley and Sherrard (working in collaboration) (Seferis 1995). This comparative element comprises the core of the study, as it is intended to direct focus precisely at the point where the universal, the culturally dependent and the individual interact, namely at the translator adopting the dual role of reader/writer across cultural frontiers. To this end, the corpus analysed includes only those selections of Seferis's poetry that have been translated by both Friar and Keeley and Sherrard. Closely considering different translations of the same source text allows the study to contemplate the question of what there is between a source text and a target text, beyond the words of either language, as the ST is refracted into two different texts of equal status/footing.

The study adopts a corpus-assisted approach for the basic handling of data. Accordingly, the texts have been converted to a digital format, forming a small corpus of 16,000 words in total (approximately 5,300 words for each sub-corpus). For technical and methodological reasons, the orthographic word is often pivotal in corpus approaches to language. Corpus analysis software accesses data and retrieves and sorts results mainly via word forms. As a consequence, corpus-based studies of translations, in most cases, also take the word as a focal point around which analyses are built. At first glance, this does not make a corpus approach the ideal research tool for the investigation of metaphor, as metaphorical mappings cannot be uniquely identified by particular words or formal properties (cf. Koller et al. 2008).

However, it is the precision facilitated by such an approach and not the scope that this study wishes to highlight, so the small size of the corpus is not an issue. At the same time, the decision to focus on a single lexical metaphor, circumvents some of the limitations of the methodology. In addition, the software used[1] facilitates the search using 'regular expressions'. Regular expressions, generally, are used to indicate what characteristics a text must have to fit a certain pattern, when performing searches of large strings of text. A corpus search using regular expressions[2] is much more precise than using simple wildcards. Using regular expressions to investigate this particular linguistic metaphor allows for a much more streamlined search through the corpus variations of "μαρμαρωμένος" and its different possible versions in English translation. This will be detailed in the following section.

Overall, this study constitutes a response to calls for an approach to the investigation of metaphor in translation (Schäffner 2004, Samaniego Fernández 2011) that uses natural unrestricted text, rather than constructed or selected illustrative examples. It focuses on the patterns and/or variations in the recognition, interpretation and rendering of metaphor, as they are realized in the translated texts, and on how these patterns reflect each translator's distinct identity as well as illustrate the cognitive workings of metaphor from an intercultural perspective.

4. Case Study: The Metapoet Among the Statues

4.1 Some Context

4.1.1 The Translators

There are a number of significant analogies (especially between Friar and Keeley) in the translators' backgrounds that go beyond their contemporaneity. Apart from the fact that they both spent periods of their childhood in Greece, the most notable link is the academic positions that they held in literature departments of North American universities (both in the Northeast) for a large part of their lives, thus ensuring that their background puts them in the same "interpretative community" – a term used in cognitive poetics to refer to "a group who can be said to share a similar way of understanding and reading" (Stockwell, 2002: 33).

Regarding Keeley and Sherrard and their method of collaboration, it was based on a process of exclusion rather than inclusion, meaning that, during the early stages, they did not yet have a sense of direction to go by, but had drawn up a list of things that they felt should be avoided. Among such things were any expressions that were too explicitly British or American, "archaisms, inversions, personal idiosyncrasies, and rhetorical flourishes" (Keeley, 2000: 33). It sums up the Keeley and Sherrard approach that after a collaborative career of some 35 years (the course of which entailed constant and sometimes radical revision) there are still lines in their last versions of both Cavafy and Seferis that Keeley (personal communication) admits he would revise again, if he had the chance.[3]

4.1.2 The Poet

George Seferis (1900–1971), born in Smyrna, Asia Minor, studied Law in Paris and soon afterwards entered the Greek diplomatic service holding a variety of posts throughout the world until his retirement in 1962, his last post being that of Ambassador to the United Kingdom. During his stay in Paris he familiarised himself with the symbolist and surrealist movements of the time that were to inform his poetry until the end. For his own symbols Seferis used the rich tradition of Greek mythology, and particularly Homer and the theme of the Odyssey, as a resource. In his early collections he established some of the symbols that were to stay with him throughout his career by incorporating them into some of the traditional forms of Greek poetry. During the latter part of his career his economy of expression reached its highest level, and the different parts of the poems are intricately connected through images and symbols that he had developed throughout his work. As a natural consequence of the fame and recognition that came with the Nobel Prize in 1963, he was abundantly translated, thus providing good grounds for a comparative examination of style-related issues in the resulting TTs.

4.1.3 The Metaphor

"Μαρμαρωμένος"is a metaphor which has its roots in Greek mythology and the myth of Perseus. The use of the adjective "μαρμαρωμένος" (turned-into-marble) signifies what happened to those that beheld Medusa in the aforementioned myth. This is a conventional metaphor in Greek that, apart from its visual significance, has come to mean a status of immobility, and also the stopping of time. It has no direct linguistic equivalent in English even though a number of analogies can be proposed.

4.2 Analysis

Example 1 comprises the essence of the corpus-driven part of the case study. The results presented in the concordance table provide a very useful starting point. The example was compiled using *CasualConc* and by means of a search using regular expressions. The specific expression used was: marbl|μ[α|ά]ρμ. It uses both Latin and Greek characters (the software allows for searches using more than one different scripts) to search for the root for '*marble*' in both ST and the two translations. Consequently, the search returns all relevant hits containing this root, but that also, crucially, include all the various prefixes and suffixes.

	Concordance
1	we will see the almond trees blossoming the **marbl**e gleaming in the sun
2	d our privation and plunged into the sun like a crow beyond **marbl**e ruins, without hope of enjoying our reward.
3	her and taken her back, mother and child. Her feet remained **marbl**e still
4	There still remains the blond **marbl**e youth, summer,
5	n glistens in the last declining light the captain stands en**marbl**ed in his
6	There still remains the blond en**marbl**ed youth, summer,
7	the **marbl**es shining in the sun the sea breaking in waves
8	εικόνα μορφής που **μαρμ**άρωσε με την απόφαση μιας πίκρας παντοτιν
9	Τα πόδια της μείναν ακόμη **μαρμ**αρένια
10	θισε μέσα στον ήλιο σαν κοράκι πέρα απ' τα **μάρμ**αρα,
11	τα **μάρμ**αρα να λάμπουν στον ήλιο
12	κοίταζα τα πετούμενα πουλιά, κι ήταν **μαρμ**αρωμένα
13	Μένει ακόμα ο ξανθός **μαρμ**αρωμένος έφηβος το καλοκαίρι
14	ο καπετάνιος μένει **μαρμ**αρωμένος μες στ' άσπρα και στα χρυσά.

Example 1.

Even though the concordance search performed here is a very basic function of corpus approaches, it is a very common feature in corpus-based studies of translation (see for example Malmkjær 2003, Bosseaux 2007, Pantopoulos 2012). In this instance, apart from a speedy and thorough manner of searching the available data, it allows for examining every occurrence of the metaphor under investigation in the context in which it occurs. Consequently, a number of very interesting observations are immediately apparent. Prominent among these is the realization that no translator has been consistent in their rendering of the linguistic metaphor in question. This can be seen as inevitable to a certain extent, considering the very nature of metaphor and since no direct equivalent is available in English. Yet, further investigation is warranted.

On two occasions Friar opts for the adjective "enmarbled" that seems the closest in linguistic terms to the ST. The connotations, however, are different and, in the case of "enmarbled," more limited than those of the ST metaphor. This is manifest in Friar's choosing of "turned to stone" for the other two instances of "μαρμαρωμένος" where, he may have decided that the "immobility" connotation was stronger in that particular ST context, and therefore opted for an appropriate TL expression to emphasize it. Keeley and Sherrard also use both "marble" and "stone" in translating this particular metaphor, but employ them in a wider variety of expressions than Friar. This indicates an attempt on their part to capture the nuance of each instance as accurately as possible on the semantic level. A consequence of this is an inevitable loss of the repetitive use of the same metaphor throughout Seferis's poetry, especially in the case of Keeley and Sherrard who have translated the vast majority of his poetry in one volume. This is significant in terms

Table 1.

ST	**Ο καπετάνιος μένει μαρμαρωμένος μες στ' άσπρα και στα χρυσά.**
Back Translation (BT)	the captain remains marble-fied in the white and the golden (clothes).
Friar	[Now as night falls on the Piraeus the ships whistle they whistle and keep on whistling but not a single capstan stirs not a single wet chain glistens in the last declining light] the captain stands enmarbled in his white and gold.
Keeley and Sherrard	[The ships hoot now that dusk falls on Piraeus, hoot and hoot, but no capstan moves, no chain gleams wet in the vanishing light,] the captain stands like a stone in white and gold.

of the overall importance of the metaphor in Seferis work and will be discussed below. It also serves to illustrate the complexity of meanings that can be encompassed even in a dead metaphor, and the difficulties it can present to the translator who, in this case seems resigned to transferring only a fraction – according to each particular context – of the blend of meanings of the original metaphor, and, consequently, of the original mental process.

In this occurrence the linguistic metaphor is in the form of an adjective and located in the object/complement position. Coming directly after the verb, which also contributes to the overall effect, this fairly straightforward use of the metaphor in the source language, has induced diverse approaches in the two translations. While both translators opt for the same verb "stands," Friar's is clearly the most marked of the two translations of the adjective. "Enmarbled" is a very unconventional, archaic choice of adjective, a striking and certainly not lexicalized linguistic metaphor. Keeley and Sherrard, on the other hand, do appear to opt for a conventional expression in their translation. In addition, their translation of "μένει μαρμαρωμένος" by means of a simile as "stands like a stone" draws attention to the implications of translating different types of metaphor in different ways. Boase-Beier (2006: 98–100) elaborates on this issue, following Stockwell's (2002: 105) suggestion that different types of metaphor involve "different levels of processing difficulty" and therefore different cognitive values. It follows that a stylistic choice – as in this example – of translating a metaphor into a simile would have the effect of involving the TT reader (through available inferences) far less than the ST (Table 2).

Table 2.

ST	**Μένει ακόμα ο ξανθός μαρμαρωμένος έφηβος το καλοκαίρι**
BT	Remains still the blonde marble-fied adolescent the summer
Friar	There still remains the blond enmarbled youth, summer, [a little salt dried up in the hollow of a rock a few pine needles after the rain scattered and red like tattered fishing nets.]
Keeley and Sherrard	There still remains the blond marble youth, summer, [a little salt dried in the rock's hollow a few pine needles after the rain scattered and red like broken nets.]

A very similar instance comes from a poem titled "A Word for Summer," where the linguistic metaphor is in the form of the same adjective as in the previous example. This time it is found in the pre-modifier position, modifying the noun "youth," which, in turn, is used as a metaphor for "summer." It is immediately noticeable that Friar is consistent, using "enmarbled" again, with similar stylistic implications. In the Keeley and Sherrard translation, "marble" is used as the adjective pre-modifier. Again, this is a much more conventional, unmarked, stylistic choice, as "marble" is also found in this slot in non-metaphorical expressions in English (e.g. marble table).

Finally, Table 3 shows an instance where both translations use similar linguistic expressions. This is a particularly interesting example, as the entire verse foregrounds one of the pivotal connotations of the "μαρμαρωμένος" metaphor in the source language, namely the concept of arrested motion and/or immobility. In order to reflect this Friar uses the phrase "were turned to stone" while Keeley and Sherrard opt for "stopped stone-dead." Both translations seem to convey the concept of immobility that is essential here, and is also relevant to the examples analysed above. What is most interesting, however, is that both translators have used expressions that contain the element of "stone" rather than "marble" as the basic image. In fact, a careful look back at the cumulative concordance search results in Example 1 shows that for a total of seven occurrences of the "μαρμαρωμένος" metaphor in the ST, there are only seven hits in the English sub-corpus which contains both translations. A more detailed search then reveals that this is because in a total of five instances the translator has opted for a TL linguistic expression that uses "stone" rather than marble as an image. The possible reasons and significance of this shift need to be explored further (Table 4).

Table 3.

ST	**Άξαφνα περπατούσα και δεν περπατούσα κοίταζα τα πετούμενα πουλιά, κι ήταν μαρμαρωμένα κοίταζα τον αιθέρα τ' ουρανού, κι ήτανε θαμπωμένος κοίταζα τα κορμιά που πολεμούσαν, κι είχαν μείνει κι ανάμεσό τους ένα πρόσωπο το φως ν' ανηφορίζει.**
BT	Suddenly I was walking and not walking I was looking the flying birds, and (they) were marble-fied I was looking the air of-the sky, and (it) was dim I was looking the bodies that were fighting, and they had remainedand between them a face the light to be ascending.
Friar	Suddenly I was walking and did not walk I looked at the flying birds, and they were turned to stone I looked at the air of the sky, and it was full of dazzling wonder I looked at bodies that had been struggling, and they stood stilland among them a face ascending in the light.
Keeley and Sherrard	Suddenly I was walking and did not walk I looked at the flying birds, and they had stopped stone-dead I looked at the sky's air, and it was full of wonder I looked at the bodies labouring, and they were stilland among them a face climbing the light.

Table 4.

Source-Text	**Friar**	**Keeley & Sherrard**
Μαρμαρωμένος (x3) marble-fied (adj./part.)	Enmarbled	like a stone
	Enmarbled	Marble
	turned to stone	stopped stone dead
μαρμάρωσεturned-into-marble (v.)	turned to stone	turned to stone
μάρμαρα (x2) marbles (n.)	Marbles	marble
	marble ruins	ruins
μαρμαρένιαmarble (adj.)	Marble	adamantine
+statues	x4	x4

This last table presents a summary of every ST hit returned by the concordance search (in the left hand column) along with both translations. The first four rows contain the examples examined in context in the tables above. What is most interesting in the remaining instances (two occurrences in the form of a noun, one as an adjective) are the two translations of the plural ST noun "μάρμαρα" (marbles). Friar uses the noun phrase "marble ruins" with marble as a pre-modifying adjective, while Keeley and Sherrard simply use the noun "ruins." This is a case of metonymy from a cognitive perspective, where the noun "marbles" is related to a possibly salient feature[4] (in this context) as ruins. Or, at least, both translators appear to have read it at such. In other words, there appears to be a case of 'translation by metonymy'. The overall image infusing both translations, by extension, is that of marbles as ruins scattered in a Greek landscape. And this overall inference, which, importantly is maintained over the whole corpus examined, and not in a specific poem, is further reinforced with four references to "statues" found in the corpus.

4.3 Metaphorical Poetic Blend: Image and Conceptual Levels

In trying to use the results of the analysis in order to illuminate the workings of the metaphor under investigation on the cognitive level, on the one hand, and their implication for translation, on the other, the claim can be made that there are two different levels on which this particular metaphor operates. And they both contribute to the way the metaphor works in the poetry and is read/re-written by the translators.

4.3.1 Conceptual Level

On the conceptual level, the detailed analysis above shows that "μαρμαρωμένος" operates as a linguistic manifestation of such basic conceptual metaphors as IMMOBILITY IS SOLID (e.g. steady as a rock), MOVEMENT IS LIQUID (e.g. "A crowd flowed over London Bridge ..." or even TIME IS LIQUID (e.g. the flow of time). Perhaps the most appropriate conceptual metaphor, that follows from the above and applies to all occurrences in the corpus is ARRESTED MOMENTUM IS A CHANGE INTO SOLID. The most widely used linguistic manifestation of this conceptual metaphor in English is the verb "freeze" and its participles, used in expressions such as: "As soon as he saw her face, he froze." In fact all of the previous examples could have been linguistically expressed using "frozen" with the possible exception of "A word for summer". So, if we see all the different linguistic metaphors as translations of this core conceptual metaphor, in all of the above examples the conceptual metaphor has in fact been retained in all instances by both translators. This, however, has been achieved through the use of different and varying linguistic expressions.

4.3.2 Image Level

There is, however, also another level at which the metaphor seems to work in the poetry. As a stylistic feature and expression used repeatedly, it contributes to the overall imagery of the poetry and the way it generates inferences in the mind of the reader. This can be illustrated, and the significance of translation in this respect highlighted, by revisiting Example 1. If we consider the effects of Keeley and Sherrard's translation "the captain 'stands like a stone'..." in this context, there is a noticeable and significant shift in the inferences induced by the ST expression and the translation. On the other hand, the "turned-into-marble" metaphor of the ST, invokes a contrast of the image of a man turned into marble, a combination that easily infers the picture of a marble statue. This in turn, adds to the overall imagery of Seferis's poetry, in the form of metaphorical and actual statues encountered often in his verse. By contrast in the Keeley and Sherrard translation, as well as in similar TT expressions that were elaborated on in the previous section, the inferred image is radically shifted to that of a "standing stone" or similar.

4.3.3 Megametaphor

Close analysis, then, reveals that the metaphor investigated operates in Seferis's poetry by means of a 'blend' of the conceptual and image levels, contributing at once to the semantic and stylistic make up of his work, beyond the boundaries of specific poems. In cognitive poetics terms, the recurring instances of a metaphoric expression constitute 'micrometaphors' whose cumulative effect in turn comprises a 'megametaphor'. According to Stockwell:

> Megametaphor is a conceptual feature that runs throughout a text and can contribute to the reader's sense of the general meaning or 'gist' of a work and its significance. Specific realisations of the numerous metaphors that occur in the text and that accumulate into the sense of a megametaphor are, by contrast, micrometaphors. (2003: 111)

The significance of "μαρμαρωμένος" as a megametaphor in Seferis's work, in combination with the recurring reference to statues, is encapsulated in the verse from the poem "Mythistorima": "the statues are not the ruins / we are the ruins" (Seferis 1995). It reflects a central pre-occupation in Seferis's thought and work with the relation of modern man to history, and, more specifically, the relationship of Greek history, and language, to the present. Accordingly, it contributes to, and shapes the inference that the past remains in suspended animation within the Greek present; it is not dead but not exactly living either.[5] The discussion above highlights how the recurring use of this megametaphor in Seferis helps shape the reader's inferences in this direction.

4.4 Metaphor and Translation Through Style

4.4.1 Translator's Stylistic Patterns

If we concentrate focus on the different stylistic choices made by the translators, it is clear that no one is significantly consistent in translating the metaphor on the linguistic level. Out of the two translations, Friar manifests the greater consistency throughout. This is achieved through the use of the unusual and archaic adjective "enmarbled" and the expression "turned to stone" both of which are used twice in the corpus examined. Keeley and Sherrard, on the other hand, use four distinct linguistic expressions for each of these occurrences of the ST metaphor. Overall, they opt for more conventional expressions to render the ST dead metaphor, avoiding the use of archaic terms, for instance, and opting instead for such lexicalized expressions as "stone dead" or the use of "marble" as a pre-modifying adjective. They also manifest a certain tendency, often considered as a 'norm' in translation, for making things that are implicit in the ST explicit in their translation. This is encountered in the use of the verb "stopped" before "stone dead" to emphasize the focus on immobility, and in the addition of the noun "ruins" after "marble."

4.4.2 Stylistic Patterns beyond the linguistic level

The translators' choice of linguistic 'counterparts' for a particular conceptual metaphor, on the one hand, is especially – but not only – important when considering the use and function of metaphor in poetic texts. The important role of inferences in reading a literary text that is highlighted by cognitive poetics, is foregrounded even further in poetry. Poetry, more so that most other types of writing relies on 'implicatures' for its function. Implicatures, based on Sperber and Wilson (1995: 193–202) are implications intended by the speaker (1995: 182), but not made explicit. According to Boase-Beier (2011) style is a set of weak implicatures, and therefore translation should pay equal, if not more, attention to what is being left unsaid to that which is being expressed. This is especially the case when translating metaphors with their direct link between the conceptual and the linguistic. Accordingly, Keeley and Sherrard's choices to translate a metaphor using a simile ("stands like a stone") or enhancing a particular aspect of a ST metaphor (as with "stopped stone dead") or clarifying the "marbles as ruins" can be claimed to constitute a stylistic pattern. This pattern works beyond the linguistic level and can be characterized as "cognitive explicitation".

4.4.3 Beyond the Marbles

In attempting to draw more general conclusions from the results of the analysis, it is noticeable that both translators read the conceptual metaphor, but chose to use different linguistic metaphors in their texts. Despite this variety in linguistic expressions, however, which results in five different linguistic metaphors, the core conceptual metaphor behind them appears to remain the same. In other words, as readers they seem to have reacted to the ST metaphor in fundamentally similar ways. This applies even to the extent to which they both appear to either overlook, or relegate somewhat the significance of the image level on which the metaphor contributes and the importance of its recurrence in Seferis's poetry. The fact that they clearly chose different and varying images in their translations, resulting in distinct TL representations indicates that, even as they read the ST metaphor in the same manner, their reactions to it as writers are distinct, resulting in a variety of linguistic expressions. The precise reasons behind this, are beyond the scope of this study, but are certainly worthy of further investigation. Different strategies adopted by the translators or their different affinities and the way they manifest themselves are among possible topics for further exploration. In the light of this analysis, in particular, it is feasible to see the links between the shifts in the key element of the metaphor from marble to stone, and Venuti's (1995) concepts of domestication and foreignization in translation.

Furthermore, the "marble" constituent of the metaphor can be related to its experiential basis. It is through experience that the relevant images are acquired that are then used in metaphors. In this sense there is a strong connection between these images and cultural models encapsulated in the metaphors. This, in turn, relates directly to the translator's intercultural function and provides a direct link between the universal (often conceptual) level of metaphor, the culturally dependent (image) level and the personal (linguistic) choices of each translator. This is a reflection of Stienstra's (1993, cited in Schäffner 2004: 1264) claim that "a large amount of human experience is universal, or at least shared by several cultures; thus it is not the conceptual metaphor that is culture-dependent, but its linguistic realisation."

So, overall, as the metaphor is fully retained on the conceptual level but the key image is shifted in a number of the linguistic metaphors used in the English translations, thus making different perspectives and/

or aspects of a common conceptual metaphor explicit in the texts, the cruciality of the notion of style when contemplating the relationship between metaphor and translation is thrust into relief. Stockwell (2002: 107) highlights this importance of style in contemplating metaphors from a cognitive poetics perspective when he notes that:

> The stylistic detail can foreground different parts of the source domain, so that the target domain is understood in different ways in different forms of expression. The connotations and associations, the resonances and textures of the metaphor, and perhaps even the denotational meaning itself can vary the structure of the mapping, which traits in the cognitive model are mapped, and how the target model then comes to be structured.

In an analogous manner, and in considering the implication of stylistic approaches to metaphor in relation to translation, Schäffner (2004: 1267) points out that: "the expression in the TT reflects a different aspect of the conceptual metaphor." The results of the present study, then, reaffirm both the benefits of considering metaphor and translation from a stylistic perspective, and the effect that stylistic choices on the part of the translator have in the intercultural dissemination of metaphor on the cognitive level.

5. Conclusions

5.1 Metaphor, Translation and Style: Fundamental similarities

What the case study presented here essentially illustrates, is how a careful study of metaphor in translation can thrust into relief the tripartite relationship between the universal, the culturally dependent and the individual, that is a pivotal concern of linguistics as well as translation studies. By looking beyond traditional concerns regarding the typology and translatability of metaphor, at what the different approaches followed by translators can reveal, metaphor's ability to provide a link between the cognitive/conceptual and the linguistic can be utilised. In the particular instance studied here, the conceptual level of the metaphor (ARRESTED MOMENTUM IS A CHANGE INTO SOLID) can be claimed to operate on a universal level and is present in both ST and TT linguistic metaphors. The image level, however, of the ST metaphor appears to be culturally/experientially conditioned and, therefore, a notable issue in translation. The diverse ways in which the translators rendered the linguistic metaphor relate the above two levels directly, through the concept of style, to the individual, embodied in the translators. A means of expanding the study in this direction can entail a detailed look at which factors influence the strategies adopted and choices made on the linguistic level. Furthermore, and as detailed in section 4.4, above, a close and careful analysis of metaphor in translation from a cognitive perspective, makes it possible to revisit the translator as a reader/writer of texts, in manner that derives from Holmes' (1968 reprinted 1988) model of the metapoet and has received renewed attention by scholars such Boase-Beier (2011).

Overall, the usefulness and validity of metaphor as a tool for investigating translation (and vice versa), rather than as a translation problem, is highlighted, with style as the fulcrum in such an approach. Within this framework, and despite the somewhat limited scope of the study presented here, the unique affordances and merits of a corpus-driven approach cannot be overlooked. The very premise of using natural, unrestricted text rather than constructed or selective illustrative examples as the basis of research constitutes an irresistible possibility. Even when accounting for the documented limitations of corpus-based approaches because of the crucial role played, for technical and methodological reasons, by the orthographical word, the very capability to search for and investigate megametaphors, for example, directly ties corpus approaches with the cognitive poetics toolkit. It is also feasible to use corpus-assisted methods to look for stylistic patterns beyond the linguistic level, such as cognitive explicitation in translation. This crucial affordance of corpus approaches in identifying patterns, has seen some recent applications in translation studies (see for example Bosseaux 2007; Pantopoulos 2012), limited, mostly, to the search for orthographical words. Other methodologies such as the use of regular expressions utilized here, or much more promisingly, the use of semantic tagging (as utilized for instance in Hardie et al. 2007) offer many exciting options and possibilities in this direction.

Notes

1 The CasualConc suite for Mac (version 1.9.6) by Yasu Imao.

2 Regular Expressions are defined as: a sequence of symbols and characters expressing a string or pattern to be searched for within a longer piece of text. For more see Friedl (2006)

3 For more see Pantopoulos 2012: 98–99
4 Lakoff and Johnson define (conceptual) metonymy as the act of "using one entity to refer to another that is related to it" (1980: 35).
5 Keeley Paris Review (No. 50, Fall 1970) Interview http://www.theparisreview.org/interviews/4112/the-art-of-poetry-no-13-george-seferis

References

Baker, M. (2000). "Towards a Methodology for Investigating the Style of a Literary Translator." *Target* 12 (2): 241–66. http://dx.doi.org/10.1075/target.12.2.04bak.

Black, M. (1962). *Models and Metaphors.* Ithaca, NY: Cornell University Press.

Boase-Beier, J. (2011). *A Critical Introduction to Translation Studies.* London: Continuum.

Boase-Beier, J. (2006). *Stylistic Approaches to Translation. Translation theories explored.* Manchester: St. Jerome.

Bosseaux, C. (2007). *How Does It Feel?: Point of View in Translation; The Case of Virginia Woolf Into French. Approaches to translation studies.* Amsterdam: Rodopi.

Cheyfitz, E. (1991). *The Poetics of Imperialism: Translation and Colonization from the Tempest to Tarzan.* Oxford University Press.

Friar, K. (1973). (compiler). *Modern Greek Poetry: From Cavafis to Elytis.* New York: Simon & Schuster.

Friedl, J. E. F. (2006). *Mastering Regular Expressions.* 3rd ed. Farnham: O'Reilly.

Guldin, R. (2010). "Metaphor as a Metaphor for translation." In *Thinking Through Translation with Metaphors,* edited by James St Andre, 161–191. Manchester: St. Jerome.

Hardie, A., V. Koller, P. Rayson, and E. Semino. (2007). "Exploiting a Semantic Annotation Tool for Metaphor Analysis." In Proceedings of the Corpus Linguistics *2007 Conference,* edited by M. Davies et al.

Holmes, J. (1986). *Translated!: Papers on Literary Translation and Translation Studies.* Amsterdam: Rodopi (reprinted 1988).

Keeley, E. (2000). *On Translation: Reflections and Conversations.* London: Taylor & Francis Ltd.

Koller, V., A. Hardie, P. Rayson, and E. Semino. (2008). "Using a Semantic Annotation Tool for the Analysis of Metaphor in Discourse." *Metaphorik.de* 15:141–60.

Lakoff, G., and M. Johnson. (1980). *Metaphors We Live By.* Chicago: University of Chicago Press.

Lakoff, G., and M. Turner. (1989). *More Than Cool Reason: A Field Guide to Poetic Metaphor.* Chicago: University of Chicago Press.

Malmkjær, K. (2003). "What Happened to God and the Angels. An Exercise in Translational Stylistics." *Target* 15 (1): 37–58. http://dx.doi.org/10.1075/target.15.1.03mal.

Newmark, Peter. 1980. "The translation of metaphor." *Babel* 26 (2): 93–100. http://dx.doi.org/10.1075/babel.26.2.05new.

Newmark, P. (1981). *Approaches to Translation.* Oxford: Pergamon Press.

Newmark, P. (1995). *A Textbook of Translation.* London: Phoenix.

Pantopoulos, I. (2012). "Two Different Faces of Cavafy in English: A Corpus-assisted Approach to Translational Stylistics." *International Journal of English Studies* 12 (2): 93–110.

Samaniego Fernández, E. (2011). "Translation Studies and the cognitive theory of metaphor." *Review of Cognitive Linguistics* 9 (1): 262–79. http://dx.doi.org/10.1075/rcl.9.1.12sam.

Schäffner, C. (2004). "Metaphor and translation: some implications of a cognitive approach." *Journal of Pragmatics* 36 (7): 1253–69. http://dx.doi.org/10.1016/j.pragma.2003.10.012.

Seferis, G. (1995). *Complete Poems*. London: Anvil Press Poetry.

Semino, E. (1997). *Language and World Creation in Poems and Other Texts. Textual explorations*. London: Longman.

Semino, E., and J. Culpeper. (2002). Cognitive Stylistics: Language and Cognition in Text Analysis, vol. 1569–3112. In Sonia Zyngier and Joanna Gavins (eds) *Linguistic Approaches to Literature*. Amsterdam: John Benjamins Publishing. http://dx.doi.org/10.1075/lal.1.

Snell-Hornby, M. (1988). *Translation Studies: An Integrated Approach*. Amsterdam: John Benjamins Publishing. http://dx.doi.org/10.1075/z.38.

Sperber, D., and D. Wilson. (1995). *Relevance: Communication and Cognition*. 2nd ed. Oxford: Blackwell.

Steen, G. (1994). *Understanding Metaphor in Literature: An Empirical Approach*. London: Longman.

Stienstra, N. (1993). *YHWH is the Husband of His People. Analysis of a Biblical Metaphor with Special Reference to Translation*. Kampen: Kok Pharos.

Stockwell, P. (2002). *Cognitive Poetics: An Introduction*. London: Routledge.

Sweetser, E. (1991). *From Etymology to Pragmatics: Metaphorical and Cultural Aspects of Semantic Structure*. Cambridge University Press.

Tabakowska, E. (1993). *Cognitive Linguistics and Poetics of Translation. Language in performance*. Tübingen: G. Narr.

Turner, M. (1993). *Reading Minds: The Study of English in the Age of Cognitive Science*. Princeton: Princeton University Press.

Turner, M. (1996). *The Literary Mind. The Origins of Thought and Language*. New York: Oxford University Press.

van den Broeck, R. (1981). "The limits of translatability exemplified by metaphor translation." *Poetics Today* 2 (4): 73–87. http://dx.doi.org/10.2307/1772487.

Venuti, L. (1995). *The Translator's Invisibility: A History of Translation. Translation studies*. London: Routledge. http://dx.doi.org/10.4324/9780203360064.

Wales, K. (2001). *A Dictionary of Stylistics*. 2nd ed. Studies in language and linguistics. Harlow: Longman.

Normalization in Translating Personal Collocations: *A Corpus-Assisted Study of Chinese Translation of* Ulysses[1]

Qing Wang, Defeng Li and Yuanjian He

1. Introduction

Many would agree that translation involves a balance between the loyalty demands of the source language and the acceptability norms of the target language and culture, but to achieve such a balance requires efforts, even talents, of the translator, especially in cases where the two languages and cultures are vastly different, entrapping the translator in a dilemma between loyalty and acceptibility. The result will often be a compromise, more or less inclined to one side or the other. Prior to the advent of computer technology, such an inclination or rather tendency could be more felt than proved. In recent years, scholars of corpus-assisted translation studies have found some tendencies in translated texts (e.g. Baker 1993:243–245; 1995:236; 1999, Johansson et al. 1996; Laviosa 1997:315; Bernardini 2003:2). Such tendencies are generally known as "translation universals," among which three major ones have been claimed, namely, "explicitation," "simplification" and "normalization." "Explicitation" relates to the tendency in translations to "spell things out rather than leave them implicit" (Baker 1996: 180). "Simplication" refers to "the tendency to simplify the language used in translation" (*ibid*: 181–182). The hypothesis of "normalization," originally proposed as "conservatism" by Baker (*ibid*: 183), is defined as the tendency of the translator to "conform to patterns and practices typical of the target language, even to the point of exaggerating them." Some studies have supported the existence of such universals in translated texts (e.g. Munday 1998; Øverås 1998), but in other projects (e.g. Kenny 2001; Xiao et al. 2010) contrary evidence has been found, making translation universals an even more complicated and contentious issue in translation studies.

This study is to further expound on "normalization." We want to explore those linguistic expressions that typically represent the authorial style, how they are translated into the target language and what may be the reasons behind the changes? We venture a corpus-based research project on the Chinese translation of the English novel *Ulysses* by James Joyce (1882–1941) [1986], who was regarded by T. S. Eliot as "the greatest master of the English language since Milton" (Jin 2001: 225). Our purpose is to investigate how the translator, Qian Xiao (1910–1999) deals with Joyce's personal collocations. Our primary research question is whether the author's novelty in word collocation is "normalized" by the translator into commonplace phraseology. There are several Chinese versions of *Ulysses* produced by different translators.[2] We choose to examine the translation by Qian Xiao mainly for two reasons. First, Xiao, working together with his wife Jieruo Wen, was the first to translate the complete novel of *Ulysses* into Chinese, publishing his first translation in 1994 and the revised edition in 2005. Second, his translation has been considered as exemplar, hence awarded the national prize for foreign literature by the Press and Publication Bureau of China. In this project, we also compare Xiao's translation with his original Chinese writings. As Xiao is a renowned man of letters in Chinese, we consider it useful to compare his translation with his creative writing, to see whether intellectual creativity is displayed in both categories.

2. Design of the Corpus of Xiao's Translation and Writing (COXTAW)

Research on translation universals is conducted typically by comparing corpora of translated and non-translated texts in the target language; in other words, by relying on a comparable corpus. In our study, the texts in the comparable corpus are produced by the same person, Qian Xiao. We think, however, a parallel corpus is also indispensable because in this way more can be revealed of the translator's behaviour in handling the two languages and cultures. The finished Corpus of

Table 1. The Corpus of Xiao's Translation and Writing (COXTAW)

CORPUS	TEXTS	SIZEWords/ Characters
Parallel Corpus	Joyce's *Ulysses*	300,000 Words
	Xiao's Chinese translation of *Ulysses*	500,000 Characters
Comparable Corpus	Xiao's Chinese creative writing	230,000 Characters
	Xiao's Chinese translation of *Ulysses*	500,000 Characters

Xiao's Translation and Writing (COXTAW) consists of two subcorpora, as shown in Table 1.

The bilingual parallel subcorpus contains the source text of *Ulysses* and Xiao's Chinese translation, and the monolingual comparable subcorpus is made up of Xiao's Chinese translation of *Ulysses* and his Chinese writings, which include all his 23 short stories and one novel[3], written in the 1920s and 1930s and collected in Xiao (2005b). While the fact that Xiao's translation of *Ulysses* and creative writings were produced in different periods of time might undermine the comparability of the two corpora, we would like to argue that as the result of the New Cultural Movement starting in 1919, the 1920s and 1930s were a critical period in which the Chinese language began to take the present shape. And for that reason, we believe that Xiao's creative writing in this period is comparable to his translation of *Ulysses* in the 1990s. The finished corpus totals 1,530,000 words/characters. The COXTAW does not include the last chapter of the original and translated *Ulysses*, an unpunctuated eight-paragraph-long passage difficult for sentence alignment. The translator's notes are also excluded from the text body in the corpus and stored elsewhere. The bilingual texts in the parallel corpus are aligned at sentential level and the Chinese texts in both corpus are tokenized into words with the software ICTCLAS, a lexical analysis system developed by the Institute of Computing Technology of Chinese Academy of Sciences. The corpus processing tools that facilitate the retrieval and analysis of data from the corpus is WordSmith Tools 5.0 developed by Mike Scott. In the present study the "concord" function of WordSmith is frequently used, as the software will find all instances of the search word, or node, in the corpus, with the immediate co-text of each instance displayed.

3. Joyce's personal collocations and their translations in Chinese

Firth (1957: 195) classifies collocations into two types. One is general or usual collocation. The other is technical or personal collocation, which typically occurs in a special genre or a particular writer's habitual use of language. In *Ulysses* we find Joyce describing the activity of playing the piano as "Bob Cowley's outstretched talons gripped the black deep-sounding chords." (*U*11.998–99).[4] The word *talon*, usually co-occurring with a bird, is transplanted to refer to the hand of the pianist, and to tap the piano keys is to *grip the black chords*, alluding to a bird's talons gripping its prey. Such personal collocations of an author are invested with stylistic features and become objects of interest in translational stylistics.

Newmark summarizes three high-frequency collocations that usefully affect translation (Newmark 2001:212): (1) adjective plus noun; (2) noun plus noun; (3) verb plus object. But in this study we focus on another form of collocation: verb plus adverb. We choose three verbs LAUGH, SMILE and SAY as nodes, and for the sake of convenience, we limit the adverbs to only those immediately following the head verbs and ending with *-ly*. With the help of WordSmith Tools, all collocates of the three verbs that meet the requirements are retrievable. We get 13 instances for LAUGH and 11 for SMILE. The lemma SAY occurs 1,444 times in the novel, and its collocation with an *-ly* ending adverb totals 101 occurrences (see the appendix for concordance lines of the three lemmas). The personal collocations are mostly found in episode 9 "Scylla and Charybdis," in which Stephen, in a playful manner, airs to other "intelligentsia" in the library office his views on Shakespeare, the playwright's relationship with his wife Ann Hathaway, and his tragedy *Hamlet*. We cite six instances in this episode as illustrations of Joyce's personal collocation of SAY.

We find that Joyce has the tendency to use adverbs of pejorative implications to go with LAUGH and SMILE, the two verbs that are usually used to express happiness. Of the 13 instances of LAUGH, only three adverbs *heartily*, *richly* and *kindly* are appreciative, the neutral adverb *loudly* occurs three times, and the rest of the adverbs – *guardedly*, *nervously*, *derisively*, *mockingly*, *emptily*, *immoderately* – all have pejorative implications. The collocation *laughing guardedly* (as shown in [1a] in Table 2) seems especially unusual, because it runs counter to one's normal experience in socio-cultural communication. To test whether this collocation is unusual, the frequency of *laughing guardedly* is checked against Corpus of Contemporary American English (COCA) and British National Corpus (BNC). By inputting "[laugh].[v*] *ly," we are able to get all collocates of the verb *laugh* with an *-ly* ending word. Among all the collocates, there is no hit of this the collocation *laughing guardedly* in the 100-million-word BNC and only one hit in the 400-million-word COCA. Joyce uses this collocation to depict Haines, an English student at Oxford University who has been staying for a while at the Martello Tower to study Irish people and culture and, having brought unspeakable annoyance to Stephen, is relegated by the latter as "an intruder." By using a queer adverb *guardedly* to modify the verb *laugh*, Joyce intends to express his disdain on the duality of Heines's response to Mulligan's "blasphemous" song, "*The ballad of Joking Jesus*." Similarly, Joyce uses pejorative adverbs such as *joylessly, credulously, superciliously, uneasily, yellowly, boldly* and *desirously* to collocate with SMILE. Such deviant collocations have their stylistic significance. By using unusual collocates such as *guardedly* and other pejorative adverbs, Joyce intends the laughter and smile in these contexts to carry an overtone of mockery, and Gibson even argues that the laughter and smile in the novel are one of the "ways of managing political and cultural contradictions in *Ulysses*" (Gibson 2002:19).

What seem unusual among the collocations are *smiled tinily* and *smiled daubily* ([2a] and [3a] in Table 2), which have never been used by other authors, as confirmed by our search in the corpora of COCA and BNC. A study of the contexts of the collocation reveals Joyce's playful use of the words. He creates the unusual collocation through a clever lexical cohesion, namely, synonyms in the immediate context. For example, in [2a] Joyce uses the word *small* twice to describe the lady before she "*smiled tinily*". Such a semantic chain works out a humorous and satirical effect.

Joyce's playful manoeuvre is also found in his way of saying, which is exemplified by the six instances of the collocation of SAY as shown in Table 2. In [4a] *said shrewdly* is apparently used to rhyme with the word *shrew*. In [5a], [6a] and [7a], the adverbs *forgetfully, youngly* and *gently* seem to be used more for fun than for the earnest sense of the words, as they are used as an echo of themselves. In [8a], the author flirts with the words *best, secondbest, Mr Best* and finally uses a synonym *finely* to match the manner of Mr Best's speech. Finally in [9a] the words *brightly* and *gladly* simply repeat themselves.

Table 2. Joyce's Collocations and the Chinese Translations

	Joyce [a]	**Xiao [b]**
1	Haines, who had been laughing guardedly, walked on beside Stephen and said: … (U 1.603–04)	海恩斯一直谨慎地笑着,他和斯蒂芬并肩而行,说:……
2	She raised her small gloved fist, yawned ever so gently, tiptapping her small gloved fist on her opening mouth and smiled tinily, sweetly. (U 10.125)	她举起戴着手套的小拳头,十分文雅地打了个哈欠,用戴了手套的小拳头轻轻碰了碰启开的嘴,甜甜地泛出一丝微笑。
3	A charming soubrette, great Marie Kendall, with dauby cheeks and lifted skirt smiled daubily from her poster upon William Humble, earl of Dudley, … (U 10.1220–22)	专演风骚角色的妩媚女演员 – – 杰出的玛丽•肯德尔,脸颊上浓妆艳抹,撩起裙子,从海报上朝着达德利伯爵威廉•亨勃尔,……嫣然笑着。
4	– A shrew, John Eglinton said shrewdly, is not a useful portal of discovery, one should imagine. (U 9.232–33)	– – 很难想象,约翰•埃格林顿卓有见识地说,泼妇会是个有用的认识之门。
5	– But Ann Hathaway? Mr Best's quiet voice said forgetfully. Yes, we seem to be forgetting her as Shakespeare himself forgot her. (U 9.240–41)	– – 可是安•哈撒韦呢?贝斯特先生像是心不在焉似地以安详的口吻说,是啊,我们好像忘记了她,正如莎士比亚本人也把她遗忘了。
6	– Yes, Mr Best said youngly, I feel Hamlet quite young. (U 9.387)	– – 是啊,贝斯特先生兴致勃勃地说。我觉得哈姆莱特十分年轻。
7	– Gentle Will is being roughly handled, gentle Mr Best said gently. (U 9.793)	– – 温和的威尔遭到了粗暴的对待, 温和的贝斯特先生温和地说。
8	– It is clear that there were two beds, a best and a secondbest, Mr Secondbest Best said finely. (U 9.714–15)	– – 他显然有两张床,一张最好的,另一张是次好的,次好的贝斯特先生乖巧地说。
9	– Ryefield, Mr Best said brightly, gladly, raising his new book, gladly brightly. (U 9.263–64)	– – 裸麦地,贝斯特先生欣喜快活地说,并且欣喜地、快活地高举着他那本新书。

With only two exceptions (instances [7] and [9] where Xiao retains the repeated words in the original), Xiao ignores the stylistic effect, the touch of mockery created by Joyce's personal collocations and translates them into normal, and somewhat mediocre Chinese expressions, and therefore lost is the luster of originality characteristic of the Joycean language.

What is most puzzling now is why Xiao has normalized Joyce's stylistic collocations. As a writer himself, Xiao is not likely to be lacking such linguistic capability to do otherwise. A comparison of his translation with his original writings in Chinese should enable us to further testify whether such a normalization is purpose-driven and part of his translation style.

In order to find whether in his own writings Xiao prefers to use personal collocation, collocations of verbs with the noun "微笑" are investigated in Xiao's free writing. The search discloses that the noun "微笑" goes with six verbs: "浮现," "浮满," "挤出," "皱出," "有" and "是." One stylistically creative use is "皱出," as in the following example.

[10] 我只在嘴角皱出一个无意义的微笑. (I wrinkled out a meaningless smile round the corner of my mouth.)

In other cases Xiao makes adaptive use of Chinese idioms to create his artistic collocation. Functioning as a single unit, the components of an idiom is inseparable in most cases, but Xiao's deployment of the components is ingenuous. By transforming the idiom "笑容可掬," he uses the verb "掬" to collocate the noun "笑," as in the sentence below.

[11] 他掬了一脸笑来兜我这笔小生意. (He was all smiles, trying to close the small deal with me.)

Xiao's personal collocation is also found in his use of quantifiers. A quantifier in Chinese is a word used to indicate the unit for a person, a thing or an action. In the Chinese language, the quantifier "座" is usually used to collocate with "山" (a mountain) and "条" with "河" (a river), and the two quantifiers are not interchangeable, because the former is used more frequently with objects of some significant vertical height, such as a mountain "山," while the latter is more often used with objects that cover some significant horizontal length such as a river "河." Therefore the collocation of a quantifier with its head noun is often governed by iconicity, which explains the non-arbitrary relationships between meanings and expressions. In Xiao's *Dreamy Valley*, however, some uncommon quantifiers can be found that render the collocation fresh and striking in stylistic effect. Below are some examples.

[12] 我的眼前已遮蔽一丛扇形的青山了。(I found myself face to face with a cluster of fan-shaped forested mountain.)

[13] 我仰头茫然地看看寥廓的蓝天,天边正游了一程鳞形的白云。(I looked up blankly at the vast blue sky: a trip of white scaly cloud was voyaging across.)

[14] 我好像吸着一鼻古怪气息。(I seemed to be breathing a noseful of eerie air.)

[15] 我索性把那只包袱背在肩头了,这样我才像一个虔诚的朝香者,负了一肩伤感的祭品,向着梦之谷踱去了。(Finally I carried my bundle on the shoulder, thus making me look like a devoted pilgrim with a shoulderful of sentimental sacrifice, and made my way towards the Dreamy Valley.)

The nouns "青山," "白云," "气息," and "祭品" in these instances usually collocate with quantifiers such as "座," "朵" (or "片"), "股," and "份" respectively. Xiao uses unusual quantifiers, but not without reason and effect. When "丛" (a cluster) is used in combination to represent a fan-shaped mountain, the reader can easily envision the trees atop it. When "程" (a trip) is used as a modifier of the white cloud, the reader can conjure the passing cloud in the sky in his mind's eye. When "鼻" (a noseful) is used to refer to the unit of odor, it correlates well with the reader's senses. When "肩" (a shoulderful) is used as a measure word for sacrifices, the reader feels the character's burden as well.

4. Discussion

The study on Xiao's own creative writing portrays a gifted writer who avails himself of the Chinese characters in a number of innovative ways. However, when translating Joyce, an author who values creativity above anything else, Xiao becomes conservative towards stylistic innovation, levelling out personal collocations in Joyce's *Ulysses* into mediocre phraseology. It seems that one can be less innovative in language use in translation, though s/he may be quite confident in experimenting with unusual ways of expression in his/her own creative writing.

Such a difference may be attributed to the divergent roles the writer/translator envisions for himself in different contexts. Compared with creative writing, translation has always been given a "marginal status" and "is degraded by prevalent concepts of authorship" (Venuti 1998:1–2). Besides, as Levý maintains, translation involves a series of decisions, or "moves, as in a game." How the readers will judge the formal closeness to the original style will affect how the translator determines which "move" to make (Levý 2000:148). Working at once under the linguistic and cultural constraints of the foreign texts, and the acceptability of the target text by the readers, the translator has to make a decision between form and content, especially in cases where an authorial style is not readily in conformity to the target-language norms. The struggle often ends with the sacrifice of authorial originality in style for the surer conveyance of meaning. A mechanism that is working its effect on this decision-making process is the translator's self-awareness of his role as a translator rather than an author, which bestows upon him more a fetter than freedom.

Another reason why Xiao did not retain Joyce's originality of expressions may be traced back to the significance the translator attached to the authorial style. Xiao, at heart, did not approve of Joyce's experimental writing style, although he regarded Joyce as a genius. In the preface to his translation of the novel, Xiao wrote that in the 1940s he thought "it is hard to say whether Joyce had employed his talent and knowledge to explore a pathway towards the acme or he had wasted his gift upon taking the road of an impasse" (Xiao 2005a:4). Later in the 1980s Xiao still held that western modernist literature was only to be acquainted with, but not to be followed by Chinese writers (ibid). This attitude determines Xiao's strategy in translating *Ulysses*. When he predicted that Joyce's experimental way of writing was likely to cause unnecessary confusion to the reader, he chose to translate the *sense* at the cost of the *style*. In the preface he explained "we did our utmost to disentangle all the knotty abstruse points in the novel and make the translation as fluent and colloquial as possible" (ibid:16). The high readability is the reward for Xiao's "disentanglement." What he created for the Chinese reader is a *Ulysses* which is normalized in many stylistic aspects, as the current study has revealed.

Normalization of the unique features of the source text may also be attributatable to the vast differences between the source and the target language. As known to all, unique items are difficult, if not entirely impossible, to translate. Failure to find similar formal correlation, for instance, may result in a loss of that feature in the target text. Joyce is known for his unique language. It is, therefore, not surprising that Xiao, when faced with the challenges, chose to normalize them in his Chinese translation.

5. Conclusion

Based on the self-built Corpus of Xiao's Translation and Writings, this study examines how one form of Joyce's creativity, namely the personal collocation as exemplified in the pattern of "verb + adverb," was represented in Xiao's Chinese translation. It is found that the author's novelty in lexical collocation was "mediocrized" by the translator into commonplace phraseology. This mediocrization may be attributed to the unique linguistic features of the two languages involved, which makes it impossible to render some stylistic features of the source text into another language, but the translator's prioritization of "matter" over "manner" may also account for his conformity to the norms of the target language. The comparison of the translator's translation with his own creative writings reveals a more deep-rooted reason for the loss of authorial creativity in the translated text, that is, the translator assumed a marginalized and subjugated role as a translator, in contrast to the creative and dominating role he assumed as an author.

Notes

1 This project is sponsored by Key Project of National Social Science Funds of China, "Large-Scale English-Chinese Parallel Corpus The Building and Processing of"(Project No 10zd&127), National Social Science Funds of China," A Study on the Interactivity between Translation and Modern Chinese Based on Diachronic Corpora (Project No.10BYY008) and by Social Science Funds of Ministry of Education of China, "A Corpus-based Diachronic Study on Normalization in Translated Novels in Chinese" (Project No.10YJC740108).
2 These translations are done by Qian Xiao (1994), Di Jin (1997), Hong Li (2001), Jin Li (2001), Yingguang Zhang (2001), Jianghong Jin (2001), and Gang Wu et al. (2010).
3 The creative writings of Xiao included in the corpus are Pear Peels (1929), After the Banquest (1930), Silkworms (1933), Little Jiang (1934), Stamps (1934), Spotty Doggie and Old Huang (1934), Deng Shandong (1934), A Scandal (1934), The Destine of the Rickshaw (1934), The Captivated (1934), Under Others'Roofs (1934), Exile (1934), Rainy Twilight (1934), Conversion (1935), Epiphyllum (1935), Roadside (1935), Shen and Shang (1935), Chestnuts (1935), Low Eaves (1936), The Wedding Day (1936), Promising Prospect (1936), Black and White (1937), Sunset (1937), Dreamy Valley (1938).
4 This index refers to the episode and line(s) of the quotation in *Ulysses.*

Bibliography

Baker, M. (1993). "Corpus Linguistics and Translation Studies: Implications and Applications." In *Text and Technology: In Honour of John Sinclair*, ed. Mona Baker, Gill Francis, and Elena Tognini-Bonelli, 233–250. Amsterdam, Philadelphia: John Benjamins. http://dx.doi.org/10.1075/z.64.15bak.

Baker, M. (1995). "Corpora in Translation Studies: An Overview and Some Suggestions for Future Research." *Target* 7 (2): 223–43. http://dx.doi.org/10.1075/target.7.2.03bak.

Baker, M. (1996). "Corpus-based Translation Studies: the Challenges that Lie Ahead." In *Terminology, LSP and Translation: Studies in Language Engineering, in Honour of Juan C. Sager*, ed. Harold Somers, 175–186. Amsterdam: John Benjamins. http://dx.doi.org/10.1075/btl.18.17bak.

Baker, M. (1999). "The Role of Corpora in Investigating the Linguistic Behaviour of Professional Translators." *International Journal of Corpus Linguistics* 4 (2): 281–98. http://dx.doi.org/10.1075/ijcl.4.2.05bak.

Bernardini, S. (2003). "Corpora in Translator Education: An Introduction." In *Corpora in Translator Education*, ed. Federico Zanettin, Silvia Bernardini, and Dominic Stewart. London: St. Jerome.

Firth, J.R. (1957). *Papers in Linguistics 1934–1951*. London: Oxford University Press.

Gibson, A. (2002). *Joyce's Revenge: History, Politics, and Aesthetic in Ulysses*. Oxford: Oxford University Press.

Jin, D. 2001. *Shamrock and Chopsticks*. Hong Kong: City University of Hong Kong Press.

Johansson, S., J. Ebeling, and K. Hofland. (1996). "Coding and Aligning the English-Norwegian Parallel Corpus". In K. Aijmer, B. Altenberg and M. Johansson (eds), *Languages in Contrast: Papers from a Symposium on Text-based Cross-linguistic Studies*, 87–112. Lund: Lund University Press.

Joyce, J. (1986). *Ulysses*. London: Penguin Books.

Kenny, D. (2001). *Lexis and Creativity in Translation*. Manchester: St. Jerome.

Laviosa, S. (1997). "How comparable can 'comparable corpora' be?" *Target* 9 (2): 289–319. http://dx.doi.org/10.1075/target.9.2.05lav.

Levý, J. (2000). "Translation as a Decision Process." In *The Translation Studies Reader*, ed. L. Venuti, 148–159. London, New York: Routledge.

Munday, J. (1998). "A Computer-assisted Approach to the Analysis of Translation Shifts." *Meta* 43 (4): 542–56. http://dx.doi.org/10.7202/003680ar.

Newmark, P. (2001). *A Textbook of Translation*. Shanghai: Shanghai Foreign Language Education Press.

Øverås, L. (1998). "In search of the third code: An investigation of norms in literary translation." *Meta* 43 (4): 557–70. http://dx.doi.org/10.7202/003775ar.

Venuti, L. (1998). *The Scandals of Translation: Towards an Ethics of Difference*. London, New York: Routledge. http://dx.doi.org/10.4324/9780203269701.

Xiao, R., Lianzhen He, and M. Yue. (2010). *Pursuit of the 'Third Code': Using the ZJU Corpus of Translational Chinese in Translation Studies." In Using Corpora in Contrastive and Translation Studies*. Ed. Richard Xiao, 182–214. Newcastle: Cambridge Scholars Publishing.

Xiao, Q., and J. Wen, trans. (2005a). *Ulysses*. Nanjing: Yilin Press.

Xiao, Q. (2005b). *The Complete Works of Qian Xiao*. Wuhan: Hubei People's Press.

Appendix 1 Corcordance lines of LAUGH

1 of the dreadful present, they both **laughed heartily**, all the spectato
2 s. – I see, the professor said. He **laughed richly**. – I see, he said
3 on who passed it all off as a jest, **laughing immoderately**, pretending
4 other cart for a penny, Dilly said, **laughing nervously**. Is it any good
5 sisters celebrated. Two bridegrooms **laughing heartily** at each other. C
6 irdlike cries. Haines, who had been **laughing guardedly**, walked on besi
7 ping him) Retain your own. STEPHEN (**laughs emptily**) My centre of gravi
8 Parleyvoo! STEPHEN (with head back, **laughs loudly**, clapping himself gr
9 next Lessing says. Thirsty fox. (he **laughs loudly**) Burying his grandm
10 hair is dyed gold and heâ€¦ BELLO (**laughs mockingly**) That's your daug
11 I promise never to disobey. BELLO (**laughs loudly**) Holy smoke! You lit
12 the ear of a blushing waitress and **laughs kindly**) Ah, naughty, naught
13 THE HONOURABLE MRS MERVYN TALBOYS (**laughs derisively**) O, did you, my

Appendix 2 Corcordance lines of SMILE

1 with dauby cheeks and lifted skirt **smiled daubily** from her poster upo
2 tracing her steps by King's windows **smiled credulously** on the represen
3 loved fist on her opening mouth and **smiled tinily, sweetly**. Father Con
4 that knows her own father. Mr Bloom **smiled joylessly** on Ringsend road.
5 his Thursdaymonun. Iagogogo! BLOOM (**smiles yellowly** at the whores) Whe
6 cuddling him with supple warmth. He **smiles uneasily**. Slowly, note by n
7 I may... BEAUFOY (his lip upcurled, **smiles superciliously** on the court
8 flows over her flesh. Bloom stands, **smiling desirously**, twirling his t

9 an elderly female with false teeth **smiling incredulously** and a black
10 IENT FOR THE DAY... J. J. O'Molloy, **smiling palely**, took up the gage.
11 miss, he said. She tendered a coin, **smiling boldly**, holding her thick

Appendix 3 Corcordance lines of SAY

1 him on accordingly. – Yes, Stephen **said uncertainly** because he though
2 asite. Alluding to the encounter he **said, laughingly**, Stephen, that is
3 ge. – Cry you mercy, gentlemen, he **said humbly**. An you be the king's
4 nedy said. When all agog miss Douce **said eagerly**: – Look at the fello
5 ing form. – God's curse on you, he **said sourly**, whoever you are! You'
6 d his left foot. – O, my corns! he **said plaintively**. Come upstairs fo
7 tians they were having, Jimmy Henry **said pettishly**, about their damned
8 ackward. – Boyd? Martin Cunningham **said shortly.** Touch me not. John W
9 – God bless you, Martin Cunningham **said, cheerily**. He signed to the w
10 a few days tell him, Father Cowley **said anxiously**. Ben Dollard halted
11 d here. I smiled at him. America, I **said, quietly**, just like that. Wha
12 s thought and nodded. – I will, he **said gravely**. I looked all along t
13 an that. – Wait awhile, Mr Dedalus **said threateningly**. You're like th
14 cultured allroundman, Bloom is, he **said seriously**. He's not one of yo
15 ut at Glencree reformatory, Lenehan **said eagerly**. The annual dinner yo
16 Crampton court. – He's a hero, he **said simply**. – I know, M'Coy said
17 ith impatience. – Goodnight, M'Coy **said abruptly**, when you two begina
18 st from those sacks, J. J. O'Molloy **said politely**. – No, Ned Lambert
19 the gloom. – Yes, sir, Ned Lambert **said heartily**. We are standing in
20 periamo, the round mustachioed face **said pleasantly**. Ma, dia: retta a
21 owl. Katey, sitting opposite Boody, **said quietly**, as her fingertip lif
22 ng! Boody sat down at the table and **said hungrily**: – Give us it here.
23 onceived a play for the mummers, he **said solemnly**. The pillared Mooris

24 eve your own theory? – No, Stephen **said promptly**. – Are you going to
25 f the Shrew. – You are a delusion, **said roundly** John Eglinton to Step
26 ing roughly handled, gentle Mr Best **said gently**. – Which will? gagged
27 nd a secondbest, Mr Secondbest Best **said finely**. – Separatio a mensa
28 you at that stile. – Yes, Mr Best **said youngly**, I feel Hamlet quite
29 n? When? Come! – Ryefield, Mr Best **said brightly, gladly**, raising his
30 ssiduous. – A shrew, John Eglinton **said shrewdly,** is not a useful por
....
92 you. – Someone killed her, Stephen **said gloomily**. – You could have k
93 hair stirring slightly. – God! he **said quietly**. Isn't the sea what A
94 lder. – God, isn't he dreadful? he **said frankly**. A ponderous Saxon. H
95 care. – Tell me, Mulligan, Stephen **said quietly**. – Yes, my love? –
96 his lips. – The mockery of it! he **said gaily**. Your absurd name, an a
97 wl smartly. – Back to barracks! he **said sternly**. He added in a preach
98 eritable sensation, he might safely **say greatly** adding to her other la
99 drew off his trousers and stood up, **saying tritely**: – Redheaded women
100 d and disrobed himself of his gown, **saying resignedly**: – Mulligan is
101 kneebreeches and broadbrimmed hat, **says discreetly**) He is our friend.

Part III

Quantitative Approach to Translation

Modelling proximity in a corpus of literary retranslations: a methodological proposal for clustering texts based on systemic-functional annotation of lexicogrammatical features

Adriana S. Pagano (Federal University of Minas Gerais, Brazil)
Giacomo P. Figueredo (Federal University of Ouro Preto, Brazil)
Annabelle Lukin (Macquarie University, Australia)

1 Introduction

Exploring the relation holding between two texts which stand as one being the translation of the other is one of the central aims of a linguistic theory of translation, not only in terms of what it is that relates those two texts and how, but also why that relation is considered good or bad,

The present research is funded by the National Council for Scientific and Technological Development (CNPq) under grants No. 308652/2010-0 and 305129/2013-9 and the State Funding Agency of Minas Gerais (FAPEMIG) under grants PPM-00087-12 and PPM-00289-14.

near or distant (Halliday 2001). When the relation spans multiple translations of the same source text, so-called retranslations, the number of questions grows exponentially in search for the reasons underlying each new target text and ways of assessing target text proximity or distance to the source text.

In the field of computational linguistics and corpus linguistics and their interface with the discipline of translation studies, researchers have tried to explore methods that can yield comparative profiles of texts and thus lend more objectivity to a task prone to the bias of human judgement (see contributions in Oakes and Ji 2012). Among these methods, automatic clustering of translated texts is an emergent methodology in translation studies purporting to unveil similarities between texts on the basis of multivariate analysis statistics. Not only does cluster analysis allow for handling raw or unannotated text, but it also offers novel ways of discovering patterns that would otherwise remain unseen if the analyst had to rely on the mere eyeballing of numerical data (Gries and Wulff 2012).

Methods for discovering clusters of texts automatically have for the most part relied on representations of texts by single word or co-occurring words, drawing on frequency of the most frequent words. Alternatively, frequency of n-grams has also been used with substantial success for cognate languages (Oakes 2012). This methodological approach allows for the automatic processing of large numbers of data, yielding results which organize texts in terms of the degree of similarity between them. Successful initiatives are those like the Computational Stylistics Group's in Krakow, which has explored methods for authorship detection or attribution based on stylometry and developed and submitted a package for the R software environment (Rybicki and Eder, 2011; Rybicki 2012; Rybicki and Heydel 2013). With a different aim, Ke (2012) applied cluster analysis to a corpus of translations and found that the clusters obtained reflected the evaluation those texts had received by a board of experts, pointing to a methodology that could be productive to investigate translation quality assessment.

The aforementioned initiatives rely on word-frequency-based methods and machine classification of texts with little or no human intervention. As with all unsupervised machine text analysis, there are shortcomings in the results obtained, which points to the need for further advancement in the methods and resources available as well as complementarity with human supervised text analysis.

Lexical items, both the so-called lexical words and grammatical or stop words, are no doubt more directly accessible by the computer due to their distinctiveness and their automatic retrieval on the basis of type/token computation. However, being the end step in the process of producing meaning, lexical items are not sufficient to explain how language is organized. A lexical item analysis alone may be impaired by the narrow scope of the phenomena it investigates.

When it comes to clustering a translation corpus with a view to comparing translations into different languages between one another and with the source text common to them all, lexical items per se have a limited potential. They can be rich evidence for diachronic studies and offer insights into the genetic critique of translations, allowing in some cases for studies in which phraseology and even grammatical phenomena can be mapped (cf. Ji 2012; Ji and Oakes 2012). For other inquiries, however, word frequency can reveal little about the way a text is organized (Ke 2012) and lexical variation is at times a feature to be done away with, as in the case of word frequency lists for translator authorship detection (see Rybicki and Heydel 2013). Moreover, if the analysis pursued focuses on more generalized patterns of text organization, a corpus needs to be queried, not only in terms of language expression and lexical items, but also of grammar functions realized by expression (lexical items being exponents of grammatical choices) and annotated for that purpose. In that sense, a compromise has to be reached between methodologies relying upon automatic retrieval and other forms of counting and computing frequencies obtained from the corpus, even if the latter still call for human mediation.

Systemic functional linguistics (SFL) as developed by M. A. K. Halliday is a comprehensive theory of language that offers a descriptive and interpretive framework for making informed claims about how texts are organized and what kind of meanings are made through particular language choices.

Since its inception under the Firthian influence, SFL has been developed as a general linguistic theory, or a set of principles *appliable* to the description of all languages. As such, typology and translation are versions of comparative studies within a general linguistic theory. Moreover, SFL analytical methodology permits the annotation of texts and the comparison of patterns therein built regardless of the language texts have been produced in. In this sense, SFL categories used for annotation of text samples (as qualitative variables) can be quantified and computed to obtain a metafunctional profile of each text. Clustering techniques can then be used to examine degrees of similarities between texts and these interpreted in terms of the aim envisaged by the analyst.

This chapter seeks to contribute to a model for quantitative exploration of literary translation by adopting clustering techniques to search for patterns of comparability in a corpus of retranslations. Drawing on SFL as a framework for text analysis, it reports on an exploratory study aimed at investigating source – target text relations as computed through statistical methods for a manually annotated representative text sample. Unlike approaches based on frequency of most frequent words, frequency of values attributed to each text sample for 68 variables is used in order to obtain clusters and map relations of proximity as visualized in a dendrogram.

The corpus used is made up of 10 translations of a source text – a short story written in English by Katherine Mansfield. The set of target texts are retranslations of the original in English into Spanish and Portuguese by different translators over a period of six decades.

The main purpose of our study was to develop a useful analytical framework for comparing source and target texts on the basis of theory-informed categories of functions realized by choices in the grammar of each language system. As the categories refer to functions description under a common general theory, they apply to variation in functional organization across language systems, each language having its particular lexicogrammatical realizations. Thus, comparability is ensured between texts written in different languages to which equivalence is assigned because they stand in a relation of translation between one another.

In addition, our study brings results that can be discussed in terms of the claim that retranslations tend to be more source-oriented than first translations (Berman 1990). Orientation is here interpreted as proximity between texts in a cluster relation or, in other words, distance between source and target text as computed through cluster analysis.

In what follows we will briefly describe the theoretical and methodological framework used for our proposal. Next, the results obtained through cluster analysis are presented and discussed. We conclude this chapter by summarizing our findings and providing future research pointers.

2. Integrating linguistic analysis and computer analysis of data

The methodology provided by corpus linguistics enables the compilation of representative language samples – i.e., corpora – as well as patterning identification of language items. Since corpora are stored in electronic format and investigation steps are carried out mostly by software, corpus linguistics methodology is strongly associated with the use of the computer (Tognini-Bonelli 2010).

During the analysis phase, it is important to distinguish linguistic analysis from computer analysis of language data. The point of this is to avoid using tokens, concordances and computer item frequencies as explanations for language phenomena. Computers can only access and process language indirectly, through a computer-coded version of natural language items into software-readable items (cf. Ke 2012). As a result, natural language items are re-labelled and it is these that are analysed and patterned. For example, a 'word' (grammatical unit constituted by morphemes) is "translated" into a 'token' (software-readable stretch of characters). As much as types, tokens, collocations, concordances, etc. indicate language patterns, they are not. Corpus Linguistics methodology, thus, provides the means so these can be, as it were, "back-translated" into natural language.

From the point of view of corpus studies, Tognini-Bonelli (2010) provides a detailed explanation of the distinction between corpus-based and corpus-driven investigations. While corpus-based studies function as validation/refutation of theory principles, corpus-driven studies generalize findings aiming at building theory step by step. In trying to seek out language patterns which are not overt or explicit in the form of items or structures, the theory approximates the data (cf. Halliday and James 1993).

Thus, moving from a corpus-based towards a corpus-driven approach allows for building a micro-theory of the corpus in order to analyse it. By doing so, software results – i.e., concordances, wordlists, collocates, etc. – are constantly reinterpreted in linguistic terms. Consequently, types and tokens show patterns of word class; collocations of lexical collocation; and concordances of cryptotypic or "hidden" grammar.

From the point of view of language theory, Halliday (1992) explains the distinction between level of organization and level of expression in language. The patterns retrieved from the corpus by software are patterns of language expression (mostly the graphic word and the graphic sentence). In a sense, the level of expression, especially in graphic form, is mostly arbitrary and can be compared to computer-coding. However, expressions are the manifestation of language organization, or lexicogrammar. The organizational level of language can be modelled as a continuum from most general systemic features (e.g. nominal: verbal: adverbial; or past: present: future) to distinct items respectively (e.g. "sun": "shines": "everywhere"; or "shone": "shines": "will shine"). When interrogating the corpus, this view also brings out the language organization encoded by software results.

That being so, it is possible to understand that (i) moving from theory to data [and back to theory] (corpus-based/corpus-driven) and (ii) moving from the level of expression (a set of arbitrary characters) to the level of organization (lexicogrammar) are the steps taken during analysis to retrieve language data from the corpus when using computer tools. If the interest is in grammar organization, then, a further step is taken (iii) moving from the lexical end of specific occurrences to more generalized patterns of organization.

In a sense, the job is "easier" (Halliday 1992, 64) when in (i) one moves from corpus-based to corpus-driven; in (ii) one focuses on the level of expression; and in (iii) one moves from grammar to lexis. However, when a study focuses on grammar, there are other aspects to be considered.

Lexical items, the most delicate end point of grammatical systems, encode the most distinct items. As such, they are almost always unique. They are reserved specific items by the grammar, typically selected from the word rank (less frequently from the group rank). Moreover, they are given equally unique expressions. By definition, that's what a lexical item is: the mapping of one meaning into one grammar item into one expression. While investigating a corpus, lexical items are more directly accessible by the computer due to their distinctiveness. A word list, for instance, takes less parsing steps to obtain than a modal responsibility list or process type list.

Grammar items, however, are resources developed to be deployed in a wider range of situations, involved in the making of many meanings. Except for specific grammar functions morphologically encoded in lexical items – such as plurality or tense – grammar items do not take unique forms or expressions. Their features tend to be realized by different means, being these structures, particulate units, prosodies or even patterns of recurrent features (cf. Halliday 2002).

While investigating a corpus, grammar items are accessible either by concentrating on the few overt exceptions – e.g., analysing plural forms or tense – or "doing a massive job of manual analysis and simply using the [computer] system to crunch the numbers afterwards" (Halliday 1992, 64). Wu (2000) points out that this is a hard, time-consuming work, since it cannot be automated so far. He characterizes the metalanguage user as the linguist/analyst role shared by humans and computers and states:

> intellectually demanding field activities must be carried out by humans while high-volume, repetitive tasks may best be carried out by computers. At the one end of the cline, the computer does all the work with very little human involvement. Such tasks are mostly limited to simple tasks, such as the count of word frequency, the disambiguation of word senses, and the discovery of word classes by clustering words on the basis of their distribution. At the other end, the computer serves as a tool for humans to do their work. The computer is used simply as a tool for editing and sorting out the data, while all the serious data analysis is performed by the human user. (Wu 2000,11–12)

A more sensible approach emerges in the form of a compromise: shared labour between humans and computers on a selection of systems deemed "critical for a probabilistic grammatical theory" (Halliday 1992, 64). In a sense, grammar analysis can be viewed as the controlling process of corpus linguistics not only in the corpus compilation step, but also in the analysis step of language data. The notion of 'corpus' is then broadened to encompass not only language expression and lexical items (strings of characters), but also grammar functions realized by expression (labelled for the purpose of text analysis).

As stated, our proposal is grounded on Systemic Functional Theory and adopts a corpus linguistics methodology. The set of categories used to annotate the corpus and the rationale for their design are explained in the following section.

3 Metafunctional profiles for text comparability across languages

As M. A. K. Halliday himself states in his preface to *An Introduction to Functional Grammar*, systemic functional grammar (SFG) was primarily designed to fulfil the needs of text analysts, enabling them to "say sensible and useful things about any text, spoken or written" (Halliday 1994, xv). As part of a comprehensive theory of language – systemic functional linguistics (SFL) – it accounts for one of the main components in a descriptive and interpretive framework aimed at explicating what meanings are made through particular language choices and how they contribute to text.

Halliday (1978) states that language is a naturally evolved semiotic system, its main purpose being to offer a reservoir of meaning-making resources for humans to interpret and organize both our natural world and our social relations. Language, thus, is not a means for conveying thoughts, or a tool for communication of previously existing ideas. Rather, it is the most powerful resource for symbolic modelling because it has a grammar.

Semiotic systems are bi-stratal. They encompass symbols, which are characterized by the univocal correspondence between their content plane ("semantics") and their expression plane ("phonetics"). Language, however, has evolved to formally organize the content. The content is, as it were, divided into two: the substance of content (semantics) and the form of content (grammar).

Grammar, then, is defined as the formal organization of the language content plane. It is the stratum of language responsible for creating meaning by organizing language items (Halliday 1996). Consequently, the meaning of a linguistic symbol is not given by the univocal correspondence between content and expression; rather, the understanding of content can change depending on its formal organization.

SFL views language as a semiotic system organized as sets of choices. Each choice acquires meaning against the background of choices that could have been made but were not. Since meaning is, in fact, the contrast of paradigmatic features, for any given language subsystem, the job done by grammar is to change (responding to the pressure of new contextual demands) systemic (paradigmatic) organization of features in order to create meaning. Whenever there is need for a reshaping of some aspect of human life – different aspects of symbolic modelling – there is also a contextual pressure for new meanings and new texts. Grammar reorganizes features of systems, changing both their paradigmatic contrast and their probability, thus creating new meanings through variation of text types.

As a result, language is modelled in terms of (Halliday 1991): (i) its relations to the context of culture – the "environment" in which it takes place, in which it is meaningful; and (ii) the process in which language as a reservoir of meaning-making potential (the system) becomes, through grammar operation, language in context (the text).

The modelling of language as a system – i.e., the linguistic system – takes first into account its internal organization (Halliday and Matthiessen 2004, 24). Accordingly, systemic modelling "metaorganizes" language in relation to its internal functions – or metafunctions. Language is structured to make three main kinds of meanings simultaneously – ideational, interpersonal and textual meanings – which are fused together in linguistic units, the clause being "the central processing unit in the lexicogrammar" where the three metafunctional lines of meaning are "mapped into an integrated grammatical structure" (Halliday and Matthiessen 2004, 10).

The interpersonal metafunction responds for the relationship between speaker and listener, as well as the interaction types among interlocutors. Power, politeness, humility, familiarity, expertise relations between interlocutors are organized within language by features of this metafunction.

Grammatically, the systems of mood, modality and polarity enact social interaction through clause types: indicative (declarative/interrogative) and imperative; and evaluation and assessment. These enable the speaker to give/demand the commodities information/services from the listener (Halliday 1978). The Mood Element comprises the functions of Subject (degrees of responsibility, from responsible to impersonal) and Finite (arguability anchored in reference to the speech event as past, present or future). Modality enables assessing propositions according to the degrees of modalization (probability and frequency) or modulation (obligation and inclination). Polarity is realized grammatically by absolute degrees of commitment between speaker and proposition.

The ideational metafunction organizes the experience of the natural world in terms of events and things impacting or impacted by those events (experiential component). In addition it also chains the events in sequences of logical relations among them (logical component). The experiential component of the ideational metafunction is realized by the system of transitivity (nuclear and circumstantial). The logical component is realized by taxis (degrees of dependency between clauses) and logical relations.

Transitivity is the system assigned to represent things and events as grammatical functions of Participant and Process respectively. Transitive representations can be typologized in a general form as Material (representation of the events external to Participants), Mental (internal events to Participants – or consciousness), Relational (relations between Participants), Verbal (symbolic events). Logical relations chain up experiential meanings in sequences of adding (extension), restating (elaboration), focusing on specific aspects (enhancing). Projection sets up a semiotic reality (realis/irrealis) in terms of ideas, desires, wishes, sayings, hypotheses, etc.

The textual metafunction enables interpersonal and ideational meanings by contextualizing them in a specific situation, according to a specific text type. Textual grammatical systems construct texture, or the distribution of information (i.e., enabled/contextualized ideational and interpersonal meanings) along the flow of discourse. The main grammatical system that does this job is Theme. Discursively, Theme rearranges each clause to fit context within text. Its main function is either to keep the arrangement of the discourse flow or shift the arrangement to best fit contextual/text types new phases.

The modelling of "actual" grammar – the grammar that creates meaning functioning in the context of culture – needs to account for (a) the way context is materialized in language (examining the systemic dimension of realization) and (b) the probabilities for a potential grammatical feature to be instantiated as text (the dimension of instantiation) (Halliday 1992).

A metafunctional profile is, then, a descriptive statement retrieved from the modelling of grammar for a given corpus. A metafunctional profile needs to account for grammar choices, resources of organization and frequencies of resources deployment.

An example retrieved from our corpus (Table 1) illustrates this metafunctional profiling. It depicts the fusion of meanings in the clause and what each choice in each particular system entails in terms of other possible choices that could have been made, but were not, and against which that particular choice becomes meaningful. The example is the very opening clause complex in "Bliss."

Interpersonally, language is here used to exchange information and the complex enacts a proposition, that is, a piece of information that can be affirmed or denied (as opposed to an exchange of goods and services through a proposal). The mood for the free clause is indicative:

Table 1. Metafunctional lines of meaning fused in clause units

	Although Bertha Young was thirty	**she still had moments like this**
Interpersonal	bound clause realis responsible non-interactant	free clause declarative realis responsible non-interactant
Textual	Theme: perspective: initial	Rheme
Ideational: Experiential	Relational clause	Relational clause
Ideational: Logical	Hypotactical dependent clause enhancing	dominant clause

declarative (as opposed to imperative or indicative: interrogative). The bound clause does not select for mood, as it is has a lower potential than the free clause to embody a proposition that can be arguable. In an exchange, the free clause is more likely to be challenged first than the bound one: "No, she didn't have moments like that"). Both clauses enact realis meanings, that is, events that have taken (or are taking place), as opposed to irrealis or meanings that are potential or hypothetical (compare "If Bertha Young were thirty"). Events are past as opposed to present or future. In both clauses, modal responsibility is related to the Subject "Bertha Young," vested with the modal responsibility for the proposition. This Subject is a third-person non-interactant, as opposed to first person interactant (speaker "I" or speaker plus "we") or a second-person interactant (addressee "you").

Textually, the complex presents a message, the bound clause functioning as the Theme or point of departure of the clause complex. It is not a default Theme, in the sense that it foregrounds a perspective or angle from which the message should be interpreted. Had the story begun as "Bertha Young still had moments like this, even though she was thirty," the Theme would be a default one and the main clause or free clause would be the one put in the foreground. As this is the first clause in the story, the Theme is an initial one. The main clause operates as the Rheme or remaining part in the message.

As regards the ideational metafunction, experientially the clauses construe two analogous configurations whereby the Participant ("Bertha Young") is the Carrier of two Attributes: she is thirty and has moments like this. These are relational (relationships) processes, as opposed to material (doings), mental (thoughts), verbal (locutions) or existential (statement of existence) processes. The logical configuration of the clause complex is characterized by the interdependence of two clauses in a hypotactical relation where components have unequal status, one clause ("Although Bertha Young was thirty") being dependent upon another ("she still had moments like this), the dominant one. Hypotaxis is chosen as opposed to parataxis, where interdependency is between clauses of equal status (compare "Bertha Young was thirty and she still had moments like this").

There is an explicit logico-semantic relation of expansion, more specifically, enhancement, whereby the dependent clause enhances the meaning of the dominant one, in this case in terms of condition. Enhancement could have been done by reference to time or cause, for instance, as in "When Bertha was thirty" or "Because Bertha Young was thirty."

The above example is meant to provide a brief illustration of the way in which choice is relevant in a systemic-functional approach to language, since every instance of meaning in every system in the grammar is the outcome of an operation of choice within a paradigm of potentially available options in a system. The chosen feature acquires meaning against the background of all the potential features that could have been but were not chosen.

The systemic functional approach to language is particularly useful for comparability across languages, in that features of systems can be compared independently of the way each one is realized in the lexicogrammar of each language system. Thus it is not the particular realization that is being compared, as when lexical items are compared on the basis, for instance, of word frequency lists, but selections of features in grammatical systems.

Table 2 shows the metafunctional analysis of one of the target text renditions for the first clause complex in "Bliss." An interlinear morphemic analysis in Portuguese and a gloss in English are provided in the top rows.

Table 2. Metafunctional analysis of first clause in the target text EV

	Apesar dos	trinta anos	Berta Young	tinha	ainda	momentos	como	aquele
Interlinear morphemic analysis	Apesar de o-s	trinta ano-Ø-s	Berta Young	*t* < inh > -a	ainda	momento-Ø-s	como	aquele-Ø
Interlinear morphemic gloss	In spite of the M-PL	thirty years-M-PL	Berta Young	have < PST. IPFV > –3SG	still	moment-M-PL	like	that-M
Interlinear translation	In spite of her thirty years of age		Berta Young	had	still	moments	like	that one
Interpersonal	free clause declarative realis responsible non-interactant							
Textual	Theme: perspective: initial							
Ideational: Experiential	relational clause							
Ideational: Logical	Simplex							

A comparison of Table 1 and Table 2 clearly shows which features are similar and dissimilar for the choices in the source and target texts. The main feature showing dissimilarity in this particular case is located in the ideational metafunction in its logical component. The target text realizes the clause complex in the source text as a single clause or simplex. This choice has obvious implications for choices at a lower rank, namely that of the group, since the bound clause in the source text ("Although Bertha Young was thirty") is realized in the target text as a unit within the clause, a circumstance of contingency: concession ("In spite of her thirty years of age").

Our analysis is sensitive to features that contribute to similarities and dissimilarities between the texts and quantifies them in order to compute distances and generate dendrograms that show us how texts enter into clades of clusters. This clustering behaviour has been explored in our study in connection to the so-called retranslation hypothesis as explained in the following section.

4. Retranslations

Although retranslation has been used to name different phenomena within translation studies (cf. Baker and Saldanha 2009), the term is most frequently chosen to refer to the phenomenon whereby a work has been translated more than once into the same language and by different authors over a period of time.

The phenomenon of retranslation has been approached from various perspectives within translation studies. Antoine Berman (1990) was one of the most influential voices in pointing out the particular conditions within which retranslations operate: they are produced within a space, as Berman notes, where besides a source text there is also a first, and possibly more than one, translation of that source text, which conditions the work of the hence called retranslator. Berman ascribes to retranslations an ideal position in that they are born after a first translation of the original and can thus improve that first attempt at rendering the source text.

Vanderschelden (2000, 4–6) lists five reasons for retranslations to be produced:

1. The existing translation is unsatisfactory and cannot be revised efficiently [...]

2. A new edition of the source text is published and becomes the standard reference [...]
3. The existing target text is considered outdated from a stylistic point of view [...]
4. The retranslation has a special function to fill in the target language [...]
5. A different interpretation of the source text justifies a new translation [...]

As Vanderschelden remarks, not all translated texts are retranslated and the probability for a text to be retranslated is directly proportional to the status gained by that text in the target culture in terms of being the object of analysis and critique. While reason number 3 above has to do with the need felt for producing a new translation of a source text due to the development of the target language, reason number 5 is more clearly connected to the wish to improve a first translation in the sense of positing a new reading and interpretation of the source text. These two main motivations are conceptualized by Pym (1998) as 'passive retranslation', which responds to the need for updating a previous translation; and 'active retranslation', which comes into being due to conflicting views on the source text within the target culture, themselves related to 'translation norms' and 'poetics' usually imposed by the commissioner of the texts (cf. Lefevere 1992).

Still in connection with retranslation, the role of retranslators has also received attention from translation studies scholars. Venuti (2003) highlights the fact that there may be an individual drive on the part of a translator to produce a new translation of a previously translated source text. However, individual initiatives, the author stresses, need to be framed within the social situation in which individuals operate.

In the corpus selected for our study, as will be shown below, there are indeed statements by some of the translators pointing to idiosyncratic reasons why they chose to (re)translate the short story "Bliss," though little historiographical documentation is available regarding publishing commissioners and remain thus open to speculation.

Retranslations have mostly been investigated as a case of rewriting clearly showing the impact of variables such as patronage and target audience and as an example of norms at work in the production of literary translation (Gambier 1994). The idea of a retranslation improving an existing translation has been developed in relation to the claim that retranslations tend to be more source-text oriented than first translations, a claim frequently referred to as the retranslation hypothesis. This claim builds on Berman's conception of retranslations as subsequent moves, after a first translation, towards a better approximation to the source text. The claim is not without controversies. Desmidt (2009) for one tested the hypothesis in a corpus of German and Dutch versions of a classic Swedish book for children to find that source text orientation was not sufficient to account for the retranslations examined by her. Rather, target culture norms seemed to have the strongest impact upon subsequent translations of the source text, a finding she ascribes partly to the type of corpus – children's literature – which seems to be more sensitive to target culture demands. More recently, O'Driscoll (2010) explored a corpus of retranslations into English of Jules Verne's novel *Le Tour du monde en quatre-vingts jours* and arrived at a similar conclusion regarding the retranslation hypothesis.

Desmidt (2009) based her analysis on the number of pages and words of each version as compared to the source text and the choice of words in the versions, there being little indication as to how proximity to the source text was measured in terms of the words used in the target texts. O'Driscoll (2009) made use of randomly selected samples and analysed them according to interpretive categories he devised building on causes and norms of translation.

For the corpus herein analysed, as will be described in the methodology section of this chapter, a criterion used to compare source and target texts was functions manually annotated for a selected text sample and frequencies of occurrences for features in the systems responsible for those functions, which allowed for quantification of data and the adoption of methods of multivariate analysis, such as cluster analysis.

5. Corpus and methodology

The choice of the corpus for our study was motivated by the fact that the Bliss corpus is a translational corpus made up of a source text, a short story by Katherine Mansfield, written in English and published for the first time in 1918, and 10 of its translations, five of them into Portuguese and five into Spanish, their publication date ranging from 1940 to the year 2000. Table 3 shows details about the source and the translated texts.

Table 3. The Bliss corpus

File	Status	Lang.	Title	Date	Place	Author	Words
KM	Source	Eng.	Bliss	1918	England	Katherine Mansfield	4,774
EV	Target	Port.	Felicidade	1940	Brazil	Érico Veríssimo	4,854
ACC	Target	Port.	Êxtase	1980	Brazil	Ana Cristina Cesar	4,652
EVS	Target	Port.	Infinita Felicidade	1984	Brazil	Edla van Steen and Eduardo Brandão	4,574
JC	Target	Port.	Felicidade	1991	Brazil	Julieta Cupertino	4,752
MS	Target	Port.	Felicidade	1993	Brazil	Maura Sardinha	4,608
JMS	Target	Span.	Felicidad	1945	Chile	Jose Maria Souviron	4,520
EA	Target	Span.	Felicidad	1959	Spain	Esther de Andreis	4,962
JH	Target	Span.	Dicha	1976	Argentina	Juana Heredia	4,793
LGEL	Target	Span.	Felicidad Perfecta	1998	Spain	Lucía Graves and Elena Lambea	4,768
JG	Target	Span.	Éxtasis	2000	Spain	Juani Guerra	4,931

The Bliss corpus is a typical case of retranslation, that is, of a single original text spawning multiple translations by different translators over time.[1] Following Vanderschelden (2000)'s enumeration of reasons and drawing on speculation due to the scarce historiographical documentation available, motivations for the periodic retranslation of the short story can be ascribed to updating target texts in terms of the language used and providing a new interpretation for the source text. Both in Spanish and Portuguese, first translations were published in the 1940s, a decade usually referred to as the Golden Age of translation in Latin America (cf. Pagano 2001) and their subsequent updating through new translations can be accounted for the orthographic reforms implemented in Spanish and Portuguese ever since. Besides, the insights brought by literary criticism regarding Katherine Mansfield's significance in literary Modernism and her craft as an exponent of the so-called 'stream of consciousness' technique can be posited as a further motivation to retranslate her work. In the case of the Brazilian translations, paratextual documents reveal the motivations both for the first translation by Érico Veríssimo and a retranslation by Ana Cristina César. Both respond to the wish by the translators to render Mansfield's short story into Portuguese, a task they describe as challenging in terms of the way in which Mansfield uses language to construe the meanings in the story.[2]

In the case of Veríssimo, Mansfield is part of long list of authors that the writer deemed essential to render in Portuguese, as translation was seen as a form of creating a register in the language. For Cesar, Mansfield was a challenge to render into Portuguese in view of the particular form in which "Bliss" is crafted.

The excerpt chosen as a text sample to be manually annotated is the first move in the story as defined by Pagano and Lukin (2010). This ranges from the opening clause, where the protagonist Bertha is introduced, up to the first exchange in which the she addresses her maid, this being signalled through the use of direct speech.

Drawing on SFL and building on Toolan (2001), who points to the first four paragraphs in "Bliss" as a condensation of the story's intricate play on narrative planes, Pagano and Lukin (2010) explore how narrative shifts are textured in "Bliss" from the viewpoint of selections in the different subsystems of language and how they construct meanings relevant to the theme of the story. The authors analyse all the clauses in the short story by Mansfield in terms of the ideational, interpersonal and textual meanings they construe and enact in order to obtain a metafunctional profile of the text. Also, drawing on SFL, they analyse the story at the stratum of graphology in order to explore sentence boundaries as well as sentence internal punctuation, focusing on punctuation marks such as dashes, ellipses (suspension dots) and parentheses as well as graphological devices such as italicization.

As Pagano and Lukin (2010) point out, the move is characterized by an intricate logical organization. Graphologically, the first four paragraphs are made up by seven sentences. These sentences span 22 ranking clauses, only four of them being simplexes, i.e., clauses made up by one clause. The remaining ones enter into clause complexes in paratactical and hypotactical relations of expansion and projection of locution and ideas. Adding to the intricacy, there are embedded clauses as well.

As an illustration, Table 4 shows the logical organization of the excerpt under analysis, following the notational conventions set up in Halliday and Matthiessen (2004:10). Numerical notation 1 2 3 . . . is used to represent paratactic structures; hypotactic structures are represented by Greek letters, the dominant clause being α and the dependent ones β, γ, etc. Expansion is annotated as = for elaboration, + for extension and x for enhancement; Projection is annotated with double quotes (") for locution and single quotes (') for idea. Double brackets indicate embedded clauses and double angle brackets (<< >>) indicate enclosed clauses.

Table 4. Logical organization of the opening move in Bliss

Clause	Logical structure											
ALTHOUGH Bertha Young was thirty	x	β										
she still had moments like this [[when ...]]		α										
What can you do		α										
if you are 30	x	β		1								
and, < < 2_3_4 > > , you are overcome, suddenly by a feeling of bliss–absolute bliss!–			+	2		α		α				
turning the corner of your own street					x	β						
as though you'd suddenly swallowed a bright piece of that late afternoon sun							x	β		1		
and it burned in your bosom,									+	2		A
sending out a little shower of sparks into every particle, into every finger and toe? ..											x	B
Oh, is there no way [[you can express it // without being "drunk and disorderly"]]												
How idiotic civilisation is												
Why be given a body		α										
if you have to keep it shut up in a case like a rare, rare fiddle	x	β										
No, that about the fiddle is not quite [[what I mean]],	'	1										
she thought,		2		α								
running up the steps			x	β		1						
and feeling in her bag for the key–					+	2		1				
she'd forgotten it, as usual–							=	2				
and rattling the letter-box					+	3						
It's not [[what I mean]], a		α										
Because	x	β										
Thank you, Mary												
–she went into the hall												
Is nurse back?												

Besides logical intricacy, there is the added complexity of interpersonal, experiential and textual meanings in the excerpt. As can be seen in the excerpt in Table 2, interpersonally, from the perspective of Mood, the narrative begins with declarative mood, then shifts to interrogative mood, then shifts back to declarative mood and ends with interrogative mood. These shifts are coupled with shifts in Subject. Thus the story opens with a third person non-interactant "she" (anaphorically retrieved as Bertha, the main character), then shifts to a second person non-interactant "you" (which can be argued to be the character's own reference to herself as an individual "I," but at the same time an impersonal "you") and finally shifts back to the initial third person non-interactant "she." Deicticity is mainly temporal with a shift from past to present and back to past, with a few occurrences of modal deixis.

Shifts in Mood and Subject are coupled with shifts between the two main Participants in the story's opening. The main character, Bertha, is implicated, in relational processes of attribution – intensity ("she was thirty") and possessive ("she still had") – and a mental of process of desideration in the story's opening lines ("she wanted") and a mental process of cognition that projects the content of her thoughts and material processes ("thought"). A second participant is a "you," who is implicated mostly in material processes of doing. Two verbal processes in downranked clauses can be said to provide a link between these two participants ("mean"). The second person participant "you" reproaches herself for not being able to verbalize her thoughts in a more orderly way and Bertha corrects herself for having chosen the wrong wording for what she wants to say. In this sense, even though we are dealing with a narrator outside the story and a character inside it, we are led to believe that the reproach uttered by the narrator is the content of Bertha's thought, who is herself not happy with the way she is verbalizing her ideas.

"Bliss"'s opening move exhibits features that are ascribed to the unplanned, more spontaneous nature of spoken language, such as clause complexing of the kind described above and which helps " 'choreograph' very long and intricate patterns of semantic movement while maintaining a continuous flow of discourse" (Halliday and Matthiessen, 2004, 389). The pattern is reenacted in subsequent moves throughout the short story and is as such representative of the text – a microarray of the whole story and one suitable for comparison between source and target texts and the different target texts themselves.

This interpretation lent support to our decision regarding how to better proceed in order to sample the source text for annotation purposes. Selecting a particular sample corresponding to a whole unit of text analysis outweighed random sampling of the text. This is due to the fact that the excerpt selected to be annotated in terms of grammatical organization had to be a unit of running text throughout which functions were realized through particular lexicogrammatical choices. The rationale for the annotation scheme herein proposed was made based on the assumption that the grammatical organization of a text can be profiled for comparability purposes across language systems.

As regards corpus compilation, the following methodological procedures were taken.

The source text by Katherine Mansfield (1918) was retrieved from the online digital library Internet Archive and saved as a txt file. The 10 translated texts were manually scanned from printed sources, proofread and saved as txt files.

The excerpt of the texts selected for analysis consisted of the first four full paragraphs in the source text in English, totalizing 213 words, and the equivalent text in all 10 translations.

The excerpts were segmented into ranking clauses and pasted onto an Excel sheet for a metafunctional analysis as proposed by Halliday and Matthiessen (2004). Following SFL analytical framework, each clause was analysed in terms of the three metafunctional strands operating at clause rank: ideational, interpersonal and textual. In the case of ideational meanings, both the logical and the experiential components were taken into account. Data regarding the graphology of the text excerpt, such as number of paragraphs, sentences and words, was also considered.

Within each main category of metafunctional analysis, subcategories were designed following clause systems and their features. An Excel sheet was filled out for each text and the resulting files were saved in xlsx format to be imported in R and converted as a single data.frame. This was converted to a numerical matrix, the rows being each of the corpus texts, so that the dist. function in R could compute the distances between the rows of our data matrix. The values for each analytical subcategory (features) were read as variables and the counts for each of them were used for computing the distances using the Euclidean distance measure and the Ward method for cluster linkage. Table 5 shows the 68 features for which counts were computed.

Table 5. Categories for corpus annotation

Metafunction	System	Feature
Interpersonal metafuncion	1. clause_type	[1] "bound"
		[2] "free"
		[3] "minor"
	2. polarity	[4] "negative"
		[5] "positive"
	3. indicative_type	[6] "declarative"
		[7] "interrogative"
	4. interactant_type	[8] "addressee"
		[9] "non.interactant"
		[10] "speaker"
		[11] "speaker.plus"
	5. responsibility	[12] "impersonal"
		[13] "responsible"
	6. tense	[14] "infinitive"
		[15] "past"
		[16] "present"
		[17] "future"
	7. reality	[18] "irrealis"
		[19] "realis"
	8. modality_type	[20] "modalization"
		[21] "modulation"
		[22] "unmodalized"
	9. comment	[23] "comment"
		[24] "unassessed"
ideational metafunction: experiential component	10. process_type	[25] "existential"
		[26] "material"
		[27] "mental"
		[28] "relational"
		[29] "verbal"
		[30] "unrealized_process"
	11. circumstance_type	[31] "location"
		[32] "manner"
		[33] "no_circumstance"
		[34] "purpose"
		[35] "reason"
		[36] "extent"

textual metafunction	12. textual_theme	[37] "no_textual_theme"
		[38] "textual"
	13. interpersonal_theme	[39] "interpersonal"
		[40] "no_interpersonal_theme"
	14. topical_theme	[41] "default"
		[42] "intensive"
		[43] "perspective"
		[44] "wh"
	15. message	[45] "continuity"
		[46] "initial"
		[47] "diversion"
ideational metafunction: logical component	clause complexing	[48] "ranking_clauses"
		[49] "simplexes"
		[50] "complexes"
		[51] "embedded_clauses"
		[52] "two_clause_complex"
		[53] "three_clause_complex"
		[54] "four_clause_complex"
		[55] "over_four_clause_complex"
	taxis and logico-semantic relations	[56] "paratactical_expansion_elaboration"
		[57] "paratactical_expansion_extension"
		[58] "paratactical_expansion_enhancement"
		[59] "hypotactical_expansion_elaboration"
		[60] "hypotactical_expansion_extension"
		[61] "hypotactical_expansion_enhancement"
		[62] "paratactical_projection_locution"
		[63] "paratactical_projection_idea"
		[64] "hypotactical_projection_locution"
		[65] "hypotactical_projection_idea"
graphology	graphological units	[66] "paragraphs"
		[67] "words"
		[68] "sentences"

A script was developed in R in order to obtain a numerical matrix and perform cluster analysis of the data for: (i) each set of target texts for each language; (ii) each set of target texts for each language including the source text in English; and (iii) for the two sets of target texts and the source text. In the following section, the results obtained in the form of dendrograms are presented and discussed.

6. Results

The output of the script run in R for the databank containing the data of the target texts in Portuguese yielded the following dendrogram:

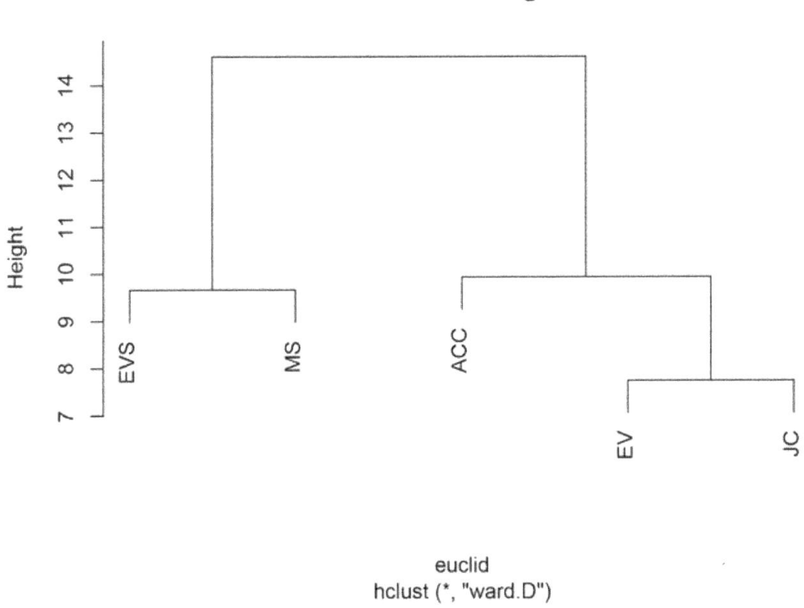

Figure 1. Dendrogram showing hierarchical clustering of target texts in Portuguese (Ward linkage) of Euclidean distances.

As can be seen, in a bottom-up reading, the EV and the JC texts form a first clade, which is the closest link to the bottom of the diagram, thus showing that these two texts are the most similar and join together first. This clade is higher up linked to ACC, the three of them clustering into a clear set. The clade formed by the EVS and MS texts cluster into a separate clade due their mutual similarity and difference from the first group.

When the source text data is incorporated into the databank and the R script run again, the following dendrogram is obtained.

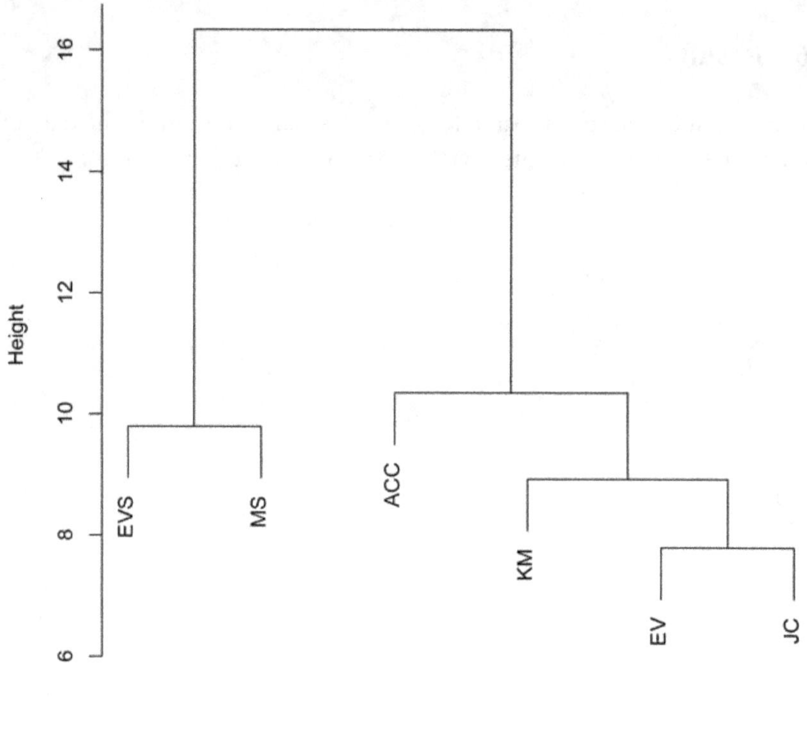

Figure 2. Dendrogram showing hierarchical clustering of source text in English and target texts in Portuguese (Ward linkage) of Euclidean distances.

Figure 2 shows a reorganization of the texts in only one of the clades. While the clusters bear resemblance to those in Figure 1, there is a new clade now joining JC and EV together with KM, the source text in English. This may be interpreted as an indication that of all five translated texts into Portuguese, EV and JC are closer to the source text KM, the three of them bearing similarity to ACC.

In order to discuss these results from the perspective of the so-called retranslation hypothesis, the dates of publication of the target texts need to be taken into account. These have been added to the dendrogram in Figure 3.

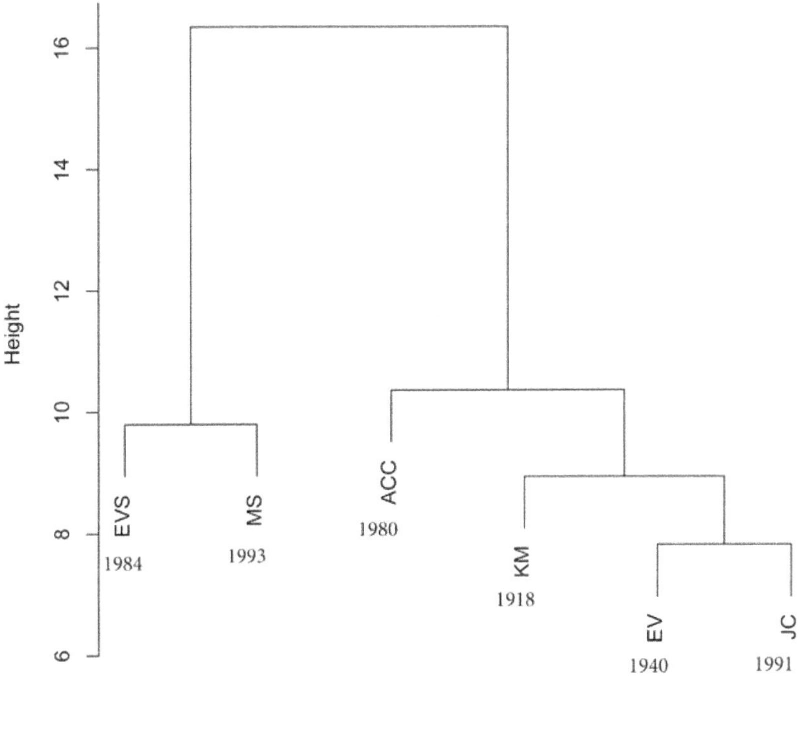

Figure 3. Dendrogram showing hierarchical clustering of source text in English and target texts in Portuguese (Ward linkage) of Euclidean distances annotated for date of publication

As can be seen in the dendrogram, two of the retranslations (EV and JC) seem to be closer to the source text (KM), as they are in the same clade, and another one (ACC) is also close to it in that it is in a clade with the three (EV, JC and KM) on a higher level. These results can be read as challenging the claim that first translations (in this case EV) are further away from the source text than subsequent retranslations. However, as noted by Desmidt (2009) the retranslation hypothesis cannot be held valid in absolute terms, as not all retranslations are closer to the source text than the first translation. In Figure 3, only two of the retranslations (EVS and MS) are actually further away from source text (KM) than the first translation (EV) and two other retranslations (LC and ACC).

Turning now to the target texts in Spanish, Figure 4 shows the dendrogram obtained running the same script in R.

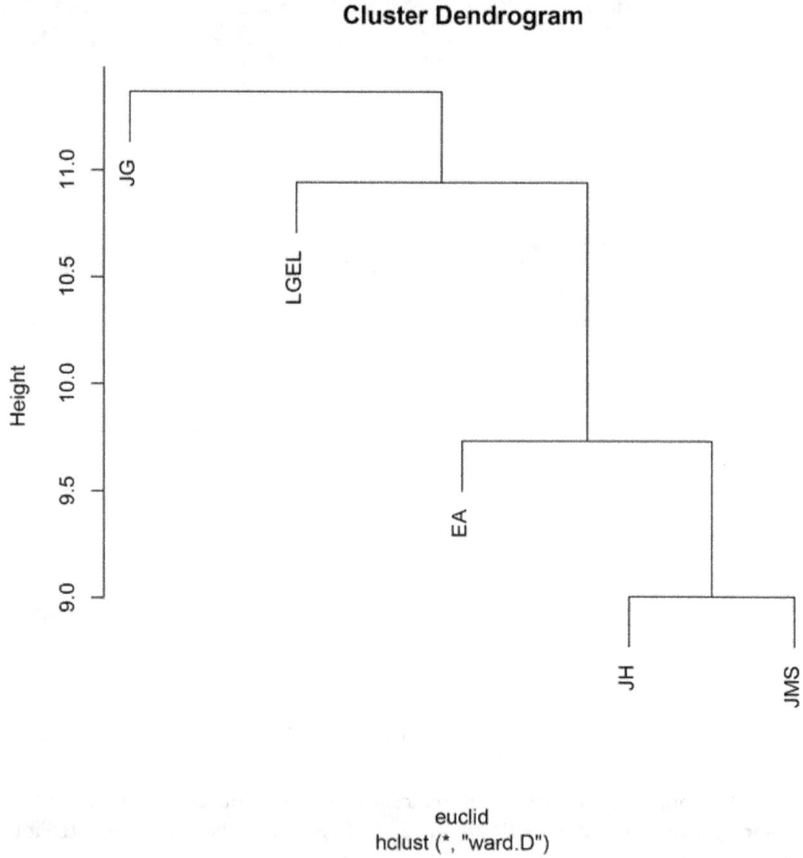

Figure 4. Dendrogram showing hierarchical clustering of target texts in Spanish (Ward linkage) of Euclidean distances.

A bottom-up reading of the dendrogram shows that the JMS and the JH texts form a first clade, which is the closest link to the bottom of the diagram, thus showing that these two texts are the most similar and join together first. This clade is higher up linked to a clade with EA, itself joined to LGEL in a clade higher up. The whole branch is joined to JG at the top of the diagram. Unlike the dendrogram for the Portuguese target texts (cf. Figure 2), the target texts in Spanish seem to show a more homogeneous pattern with all texts ultimately clustering into one single large clade.

When the source text data is incorporated into the databank and the R script run again, the following dendrogram is obtained.

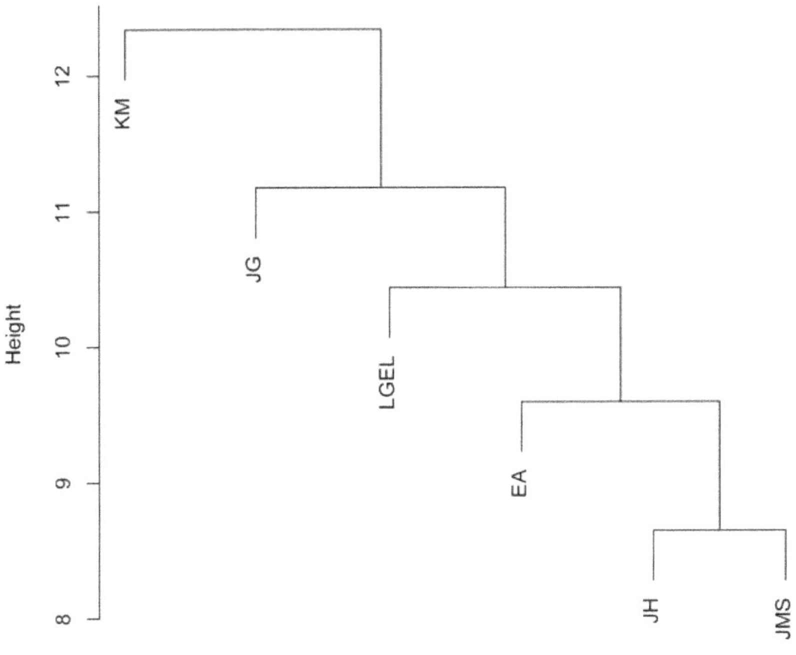

Figure 5. Dendrogram showing hierarchical clustering of source text in English and target texts in Spanish (Ward linkage) of Euclidean distances.

The results in Figure 5 show KM, the English source text, joining the large clade made up by all the Spanish target texts. In Figure 6, dates for each text have been added so that the proximity relations can be interpreted from a temporal perspective.

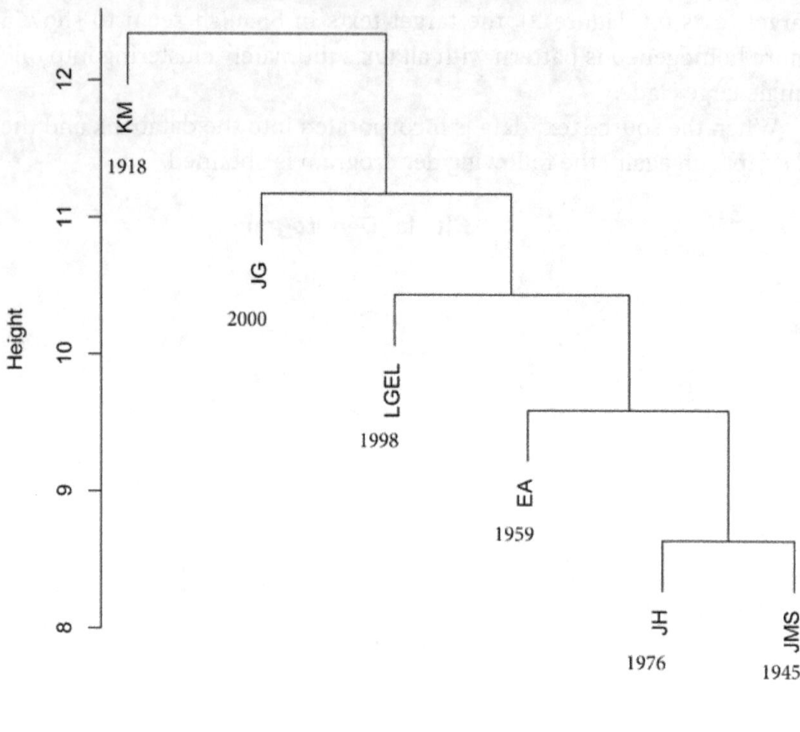

Figure 6. Dendrogram showing hierarchical clustering of source text in English and target texts in Spanish (Ward linkage) of Euclidean distances annotated for date of publication.

JMS, first translation of the short story into Spanish is in a clade further down and away from the source text, which could be taken to support the retranslation hypothesis in that first translations are further away from the source text than subsequent retranslations. Moreover, the results for the Spanish set seem to be more supportive of the retranslation hypothesis than those for Portuguese, since there is a clearer order in the pattern of proximity to the source text for the retranslations. The further away in time is a retranslation from the original short story, the closer the distance of retranslations to the original text.

When it comes to applying clustering analysis to the whole corpus, the following dendrogram is obtained.

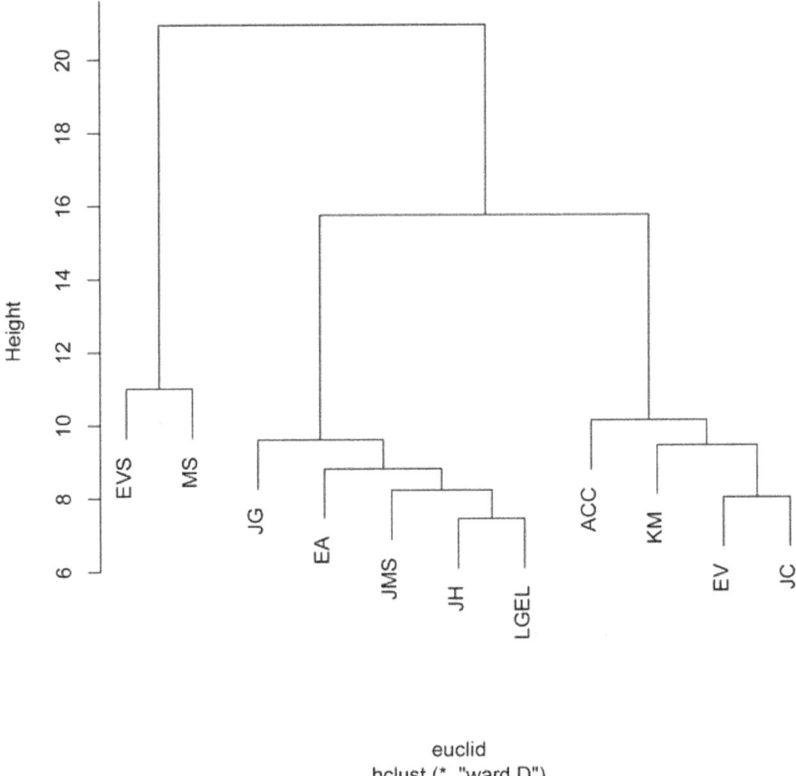

Figure 7. Dendrogram showing hierarchical clustering of source text in English and target texts in Spanish and Portuguese (Ward linkage) of Euclidean distances.

Figure 7 does retain most of the patterns observed when clustering each set of target texts, pointing to a clear difference between the Spanish and the Portuguese subsets. While the target texts in Spanish form a single big cluster, the target texts in Portuguese form two main separate clusters, distanced one from the other, one of them including the source text.

In order to probe the retranslation hypothesis to the whole corpus, dates are added in Figure 8.

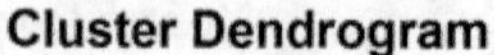

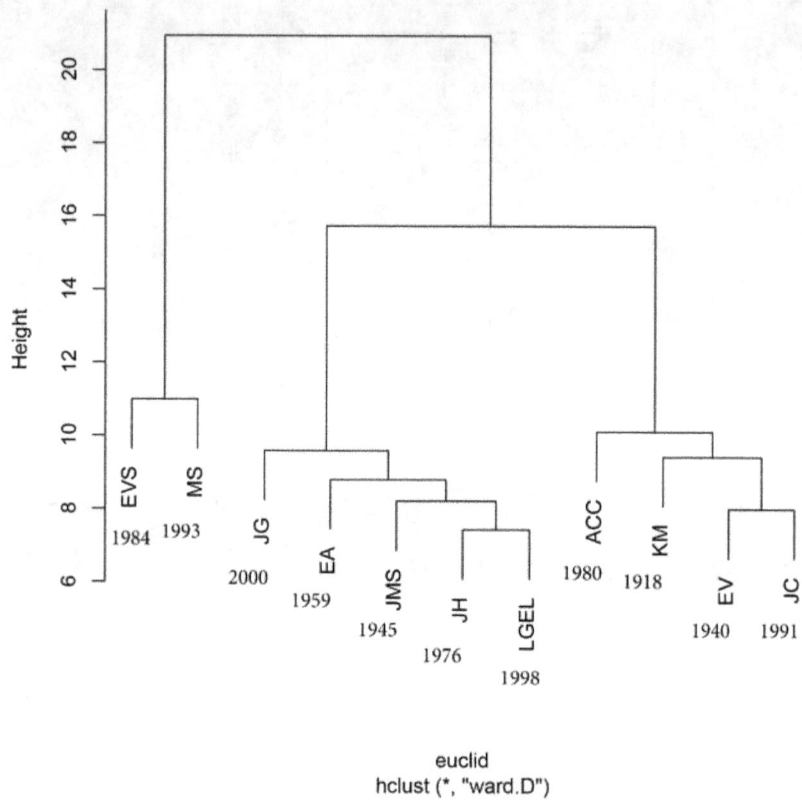

Figure 8. Dendrogram showing hierarchical clustering of source text in English and target texts in Spanish and Portuguese (Ward linkage) of Euclidean distances annotated for date of publication.

The diagram in Figure 8 partially supports the retranslation hypothesis in that the first translation into Spanish (JMS) is further away from the source text than the remaining Spanish retranslations. However, as noted above, this is not the case for the Portuguese subset, where the original, its first translations and two other retranslations cluster into a common clade.

If we take bibliographical data into account, we interpret the proximity between the original text and its three Portuguese translations in the light of those Brazilian translators' motivations for translating Mansfield. As we pointed out above, both Érico Veríssimo (author of the first translation into Portuguese) and Ana Cristina Cesar view their task of rendering Mansfield's short story into Portuguese as a challenge to craft a text in Portuguese which would match Mansfield's use of language to construe the meanings in the story.

The following section presents the concluding remarks of our study and its implications for further research.

7. Conclusions

The clusters obtained at each step in our analysis point to similarities between texts computed on the basis of categories ascribed to the lexicogrammatical choices made by each author within the grammatical systems analysed. These pertain to the metafunctional organization of the meanings construed and enacted, which we argue is relevant to the theme of the short story. In other words, proximity to the source text can be interpreted as choices in the lexicogrammar of each language to realize analogous functions. Unlike word-frequency based analysis, grammatical categories allow us to make more meaningful claims about the lexicogrammatical resources used in each text and to what extend they realize functions which are instrumental to the choreography of meanings designed by Katherine Mansfield.

So far the application of a clustering technique based on grammatical categories is exploratory in nature and its full potential is yet to be investigated, particularly in connection to quality assessment as possibly mirroring proximity. An interesting initiative in that direction is the grouping of the texts, as suggested by Ke (2012), towards investigating whether the similarity shown by the dendrograms could be correlated to scores attributed to each text by a board of expert assessors.

As regards the retranslation hypothesis, our results corroborate the findings of other researchers who have used other approaches and methodologies (Desmidt 2009; O'Driscoll 2009). While they seem to confirm the relative distance of a first translation from the source text, retranslations show varied degrees of proximity to the source text and are sometimes further away from it than first translations. In the case of Katherine Mansfield, from the perspective of norms or the factors conditioning the rewriting of texts, more recent retranslations would be expected to be closer to the source text in that literary criticism has brought rereadings of Mansfield's work and the significance of her use of language to craft her texts. However, as Desmidt (2009) and O'Driscoll

(2009) also point out, there are other factors at play in retranslation (publishing house agendas? target readers?) and the retranslation hypothesis is not sufficiently sensitive to them.

One final concluding remark has to do with our main aim in this study, which was to work towards a methodology for approaching retranslations in a labour division between human annotation and machine computation. The results point to a promising avenue in retranslations research in order to deal with retranslations across languages, as the same methodology can be applied to retranslations of "Bliss" into German, French, Chinese and others and observe clusters that may operate across languages and dates. An increment in the number of annotated samples can certainly be expected to yield insights into the retranslation phenomenon.

Notes

1 Gong (1996) analyses retranslations of Katherine Mansfield in China and reports a similar case for Chinese: she lists five different translations of "Bliss", two of them published in the 1920s–1930s and three of them in the 1980s. The early translations are ascribed to individual preferences of the translators and their wish to render the short story into Chinese at a time when Chinese was developing a particular register for literary texts.

2 Brazilian writer and translator Érico Veríssimo voices his concern about the challenges in rendering Mansfield into Portuguese in a short story, whose main character is a translator of Katherine Mansfield's stories (Veríssimo 1942); Ana Cristina Cesar's annotated translation of Bliss was part of her MA dissertation submitted to the University of Essex in the 1980s and is fully documented through preface and notes (Cesar 1999).

References

Baker, M., and G. Saldanha (eds). (2009). *Routledge Encyclopedia of Translation Studies*. London, New York: Routledge.

Berman, A. (1990). "La Retraduction Come Espace de la Traduction." *Palimpsestes* 4:1–7.

Cesar, A. C. (1999). *Crítica e Tradução*. São Paulo: Atica.

Desmidt, I. (2009). "(Re)translation Revisited." *Meta* 54 (4): 669–83. http://dx.doi.org/10.7202/038898ar.

Figueredo, G. (2011). "Introdução ao Perfil Metafuncional do Português Brasileiro". PhD diss., Federal University of Minas Gerais.

Gambier, Y. (1994). "La Retraduction, Retour et Detour." *Meta* 39 (3): 413–7. http://dx.doi.org/10.7202/002799ar.

Gong, S. (1996). "Katherine Mansfield in Chinese Translations." *Journal of Commonwealth Literature* 31 (2): 117–37. http://dx.doi.org/10.1177/002198949603100210.
Gries, S. Th., and S. Wulff. (2012). "Regression analysis in translation studies." In *Quantitative Methods in Corpus-Based Translation Studies: A Practical Guide to Descriptive Translation Research*, ed. Michael P Oakes and Meng Ji, 35–52. Amsterdam: John Benjamins. http://dx.doi.org/10.1075/scl.51.02gri.
Halliday, M.A.K. (1993). "A Quantitative Study of Polarity and Primary Tense in the English Finite Clause." In *Techniques of Description: Spoken and Written Discourse: a Festschrift for Malcolm Coulthard*, ed. John Sinclair, Michael Hoey, Gwyneth Fox, and Malcolm Coulthard. London: Routledge.
Halliday, M.A.K. (1978). *Language as social semiotic: the social interpretation of language and meaning*. London, Baltimore: Edward Arnold and University Park Press.
Halliday, M.A.K. (1991). "Towards probabilistic interpretations." In *Functional and Systemic Linguistics: Approaches and Uses*, ed. Eija Ventola. Berlin, 39–62: Mouton de Gruyter. http://dx.doi.org/10.1515/9783110883527.39.
Halliday, M.A.K. (1992). "Language as System and Language as Instance: the Corpus as a Theoretical Construct." In *Directions in Corpus Linguistics: Proceedings of Nobel Symposium 82, Stockholm, 4–8 August 1991*, ed. Jan Svartvik. Berlin: Mouton de Gruyter. http://dx.doi.org/10.1515/9783110867275.61.
Halliday, M.A.K. (1996). "On Grammar and Grammatics." In *Functional Descriptions: Theory in Practice. (CILT121)*, ed. Ruqaiya Hasan, Carmel Cloran, and David G. Butt, 1–38. Amsterdam, Philadelphia: John Benjamins. http://dx.doi.org/10.1075/cilt.121.03hal.
Halliday, M.A.K. (2001). "Towards a Theory of Good Translation." In *Exploring Translation and Multilingual Text Production: Beyond Content*, ed. Erich Steiner and Colin Yallop, 13–18. Berlin: Mouton de Gruyter. http://dx.doi.org/10.1515/9783110866193.13.
Halliday, M.A.K. (2002). "On Grammar." In *Collected Works*, ed. J.J. Webster. London, New York: Continuum.
Halliday, M.A.K. (1994). *An Introduction to Functional Grammar*. London: Arnold.
Halliday, M.A.K., and C.M.I.M. Matthiessen. (2004). *An Introduction to Functional Grammar*. London: Arnold.
Halliday, M.A.K., and Z. James. (1993). "A Quantitative Study of Polarity and Primary Tense in the English Finite Clause." In J. Sinclair, M. Hoey, G. Fox and M. Coulthard (eds), *Techniques of Description: Spoken and Written Discourse: a Festschrift for Malcolm Coulthard*, London: Routledge.
Ji, M., and M. P. Oakes. (2012). "A Corpus study of early English translations of Cao Xueqin's *Hongloumeng*." In M. P. Oakes and M. Ji (eds), *Quantitative Methods in Corpus-Based Translation Studies: A Practical Guide to Descriptive Translation Research*, Amsterdam: John Benjamins. http://dx.doi.org/10.1075/scl.51.07ji.
Ke, S.-W. (2012). "Clustering a translational corpus". In M. P. Oakes and M. Ji (eds), *Quantitative Methods in Corpus-Based Translation Studies: A Practical Guide to Descriptive Translation Research*, Amsterdam: John Benjamins. http://dx.doi.org/10.1075/scl.51.06ke.
Lefevere, A. (1992). *Translation, Rewriting and the Manipulation of Literary Fame*. London, New York: Routledge.
Mansfield, K. (1918). "Bliss." *English Review* 117:108–19.

Mansfield, K. (1940). "Felicidade." trans. Érico Veríssimo. Rio de Janeiro: Nova Fronteira.

Mansfield, K. (1945). "Felicidad." trans. Jose Maria Souviron. Santiago de Chile: Zig Zag.

Mansfield, K. (1959). "Felicidad." trans. Esther de Andreis. Barcelona: Libros Plaza.

Mansfield, K. (1976). "Dicha." trans. Juana Heredia. Buenos Aires: Sogol.

Mansfield, K. (1999, 1980). "Êxtase." trans. Ana Cristina Cesar. In *Crítica e Tradução*. São Paulo: Ática.

Mansfield, K. (1984). "Infinita felicidade." trans. Edla van Steen and Eduardo Brandão. In *Aula de canto*. São Paulo: Global.

Mansfield, K. (1991). "Felicidade." trans. Julieta Cupertino. In *Felicidade e outros contos*. Rio de Janeiro: Revan.

Mansfield, K. (1993). "Felicidade." trans. Maura Sardinha. In *As filhas do falecido coronel e outras historias*. Rio de Janeiro: Ediouro.

Mansfield, K. (1998). "Felicidad Perfecta." trans. Lucía Graves and Elena Lambea. Barcelona: Alianza Editorial.

Mansfield, K. (2000). "Éxtasis." trans. Juani Guerra. In *Relatos breves*. Madrid: Cátedra.

O'Driscoll, K. (2010). "Around the World in Eighty Changes: A diachronic study of the multiple causality of six complete translations (1873–2004), from French to English, of Jules Verne's novel *Le Tour du Monde en Quatre-Vingts Jours*." PhD diss., Dublin City University.

Oakes, M. P., and M. Ji (eds). (2012). *Quantitative Methods in Corpus-Based Translation Studies: A Practical Guide to Descriptive Translation Research*. Amsterdam: John Benjamins.

Oakes, M. P. (2012). "Describing a translational corpus." In M. P. Oakes and M. Ji (eds), *Quantitative Methods in Corpus-Based Translation Studies: A Practical Guide to Descriptive Translation Research*. Amsterdam: John Benjamins. http://dx.doi.org/10.1075/scl.51.05oak.

Pagano, A., and A. Lukin. (2010). "Exploring language in verbal art: A case study of Katherine Mansfield's Bliss." Paper presented at the *22nd European Systemic Functional Linguistics Conference and Workshop,* Univerza na Primorskem, Koper, 9–12 July.

Pagano, A. (2001). "'Something Called Books': Translations and Publishers' Collections in the Editorial Booms in Brazil and Argentina from 1930 to 1950." *CROP* 6:171–94.

Pym, A. (1998). *Method in Translation History*. Manchester: St. Jerome Publishing.

Rybicki, J., and M. Eder. (2011). "Deeper Delta across genres and languages: do we really need the most frequent words?" *Literary and Linguistic Computing* 26 (3): 315–21. http://dx.doi.org/10.1093/llc/fqr031.

Rybicki, J., and M. Heydel. (2013). "The stylistics and stylometry of collaborative translation: Woolf's 'Night and Day' in Polish." *Literary and Linguistic Computing* 28 (4): 708–17. http://dx.doi.org/10.1093/llc/fqt027.

Rybicki, J. (2012). "The great mystery of the (almost) invisible translator: stylometry in translation." In M. P. Oakes and M. Ji (eds), *Quantitative Methods in Corpus-Based Translation Studies: A Practical Guide to Descriptive Translation Research*, Amsterdam: John Benjamins. http://dx.doi.org/10.1075/scl.51.09ryb.

Tognini-Bonelli, E. (2010). "Theoretical overview of the evolution of corpus linguistics." In A. O'Keeffe and M. McCarthy (eds), *The Routledge Handbook of Corpus Linguistics*, New York, NY: Routledge.
Toolan, M. (1988). *Narrative*. New York: Routledge.
Toolan, M. (2001). *Narrative*. 2nd ed. New York: Routledge.
Vanderschelden, I. (2000). "Why Retranslate the French Classics? The Impact of Retranslation on Quality." In *On Translating French Literature and Film II*, ed. Myriam Salama-Carr. Amsterdam: Atlanta.
Venuti, L. (2003). "Retranslations: The Creation of Value." *Bucknell Review* 47.
Veríssimo, É. (1942). "Conversa com o fantasma de K. Mansfield." In E, Verissimo, ed. *As Mãos de Meu Filho*. Porto Alegre: Meridiano.
Wu, C. (2000). "Modelling Linguistic Resources." PhD diss., Macquarie University.

On semantic differences between translated and non-translated Dutch. Using bidirectional parallel corpus data for measuring and visualizing distances between lexemes in the semantic field of inceptiveness

Lore Vandevoorde, Gert De Sutter and Koen Plevoets

1. Introduction

In her 1993 seminal paper "Corpus Linguistics and Translation Studies," Mona Baker proposed a research programme for translation universals (also: TU's) which she defined as "features which typically occur in translated text rather than original utterances and which are not the result of interference from specific linguistic systems" (Baker, 1993: 243). Translated texts were thought to be more explicit (TU of explicitation) and simpler (TU of simplification) than original language, the overall language use in translated text more conservative (TU of conservatism). This opened the way for numerous corpus-based studies concerned with both the validation and refutation of the so-called universals which have been operationalized via different linguistic features (Malmkjaer 1997; Laviosa 1998, 2002; Mauranen 2000; Olohan and Baker 2000; Baker 2004; Bernardini and Ferraresi 2011, Delaere et al. 2012; De Sutter et al. 2012 – see Kruger 2012 for an overview).

Given the attested linguistic differences between translated and non-translated language, one could wonder whether differences on the semantic level exist too. Translational features on the *semantic level* have though been somewhat neglected (Laviosa, 2002: 28). The question, for instance, whether semantic relations between words in a specific semantic field are identical in translated and original language has rarely been raised[1] within translation studies. Unsurprisingly though, as strategies to detect simpler, more explicit or more conservative language (via the comparison of grammatical structures or vocabulary between translated and original texts) do not necessarily apply to semantic networks. How can we recognize a 'more conservative' semantic relation, how can we even see it (in contrast)? Admittedly, Cognitive Translation Studies have engaged with this question, but so far, the discussion has been pursued mainly on a theoretical level. In that respect, models of bilingual semantic representation have been proposed by researchers like Halverson (2003, 2010), combining psycholinguistic models of bilingual semantic representation and cognitive-linguistic concepts, like the salience of prototypes and network schemas. Halverson affirms that these models of bilingual semantic representation can help us to understand the workings of translational phenomena and she advocates the use of combined experimental and corpus-based methodologies to understand the patterns found in parallel corpora from a cognitive perspective. Nevertheless, the step towards descriptive testing has not yet been taken.

Hence, the aim of this paper is to make a first attempt towards measuring semantic differences between translated and non-translated language. More particularly, we present a quantitative bottom-up corpus-based method for the identification of lexical items in a semantic field. The proposed method will enable us to measure and to visualize semantic similarity between the elements in that field (i.c. the field of inceptiveness in Dutch), using bidirectional parallel corpus data (Dutch-French). This method builds on the successful implementation of parallel corpora within contrastive linguistics to discern semantic fields (Dyvik 1998; 2004; Aijmer and Simon-Vandenbergen 2004, 2006; Simon-Vandenbergen 2013), while simultaneously overcoming one of its drawbacks, viz. the accurate, statistics-based visualization of the observed fields.

The structure of this paper is as follows: In section 2, an overview is given of the way parallel corpora have been used recently by contrastive corpus linguists for the investigation of semantic issues. Then, we put forward a translational approach to the retrieval of semantic fields based on a technique of back-and-forth translation (section 3). Next, semantic similarity is measured via the statistical technique of correspondence analysis (section 4), which enables us to visualize the semantic fields of translated and original Belgian-Dutch inceptiveness. Finally, the last section summarizes the main findings of this study and looks ahead to future research steps.

2. Background

Whereas the empirical study of semantic differences in Corpus-based Translation Studies is still in its infancy, contrastive linguists have successfully developed and used methods based on translational equivalence[2] to define semantic properties of and relations among lexemes, providing thus an empirical basis for semantic claims (Noël, 2003). The underlying idea is that cross-linguistic lexicalization can determine the different senses of a word (Resnik and Yarowsky, 1997, 1999): "[...] if another language lexicalizes a word in two or more ways, there must be a conceptual motivation" (Ide et al., 2002: 61). A method that is well known in this regard is Dyvik's Semantic Mirrors approach.

Based on the assumption that semantically closely related words ought to have strongly overlapping sets of translations, Dyvik (1998, 2004) purports the use of parallel corpora for the identification of semantic relations. In his own research, he uses parallel corpora to derive large-scale semantically classified vocabularies for machine translation and other kinds of multilingual processing (1998: 51). His Semantic Mirroring Technique also gives way to a translational basis for semantic descriptions in a context that is wider than computational linguistics. He attributes several advantages to the use of parallel corpora, for translation is both a "large-scale" and a "normal kind of" linguistic activity that does not involve any kind of "meta-linguistic, philosophical or theoretical reflection" (Ibid.), a property rather difficult to obtain in (contrastive) linguistic studies. Dyvik's methodology has been acknowledged for its ability "to define lexical properties as ambiguity, vagueness and synonymy, as well as lexical fields, feature-specified hierarchies and overlap relations with these fields (e.g. prototypicality, hyponymy)" (Altenberg and Granger, 2002: 29).

Several researchers have made use of (a derived form of) the Semantic Mirrors, mostly for intralinguistic and contrastive purposes, and with respect to discourse markers (Mortier and Degand, 2009), pragmatic markers (Aijmer and Simon-Vandenbergen 2004), and adverbs (Simon-Vandenbergen 2013). Aijmer and Simon-Vandenbergen (2004), for instance, describe the semantic field of expectation in English by looking at the Dutch and Swedish translations of English lexemes. The sets of translations back into English (called the 'back-translations') of both the Dutch and the Swedish translations are then compared to each other cross-linguistically. From their study, it appears that similar back-translations around different pivot languages do indeed indicate similar meanings. Aijmer and Simon-Vandenbergen also point out some advantages of a method based on parallel corpora:

> Firstly, the translation data can be used for a more detailed description of the polysemy of a lexical item [...]. Secondly, the picture emerging from the approach shows which meanings are close to each other and which are distant or peripheral in the field. Thus the translations are in many ways more reliable than the paraphrases provided by earlier researchers and can confirm or reject meaning hypotheses based on a single language only. (Aijmer and Simon-Vandenbergen, 2004: 1786).

They conclude that mirroring allows for an expansion of the semantic field with lexemes that intuitively would not appear in the described semantic field. The (simplified) representations of the semantic fields yielded via mirroring provide information about the semantic fields in all the languages involved in the cross-linguistic comparison (Aijmer and Simon-Vandenbergen, 2004: 1797).

3. Methodology

In this paper, we apply Dyvik's Semantic Mirroring technique, which uses Ivir's (1983, 1987) procedure of back-translation to control for unwanted translational effects, such as translators' idiosyncrasies or particular communicative or textual strategies applied in translation (Altenberg and Granger, 2002: 17). One important difference with previous applications of the Semantic Mirroring is that we apply Dyvik's technique in such a way that (i) it creates semantic fields of inceptiveness in both translated and original Dutch[3] and (ii) it provides a statistically reliable way of visualizing semantic distances between the lexical items in the semantic fields. In this section, we first explicate the Semantic Mirroring Technique (section 3.1) as it was described by Dyvik. Then, we propose an extension of the technique in order to create both translated and original semantic fields (section 3.2). Finally, we apply the extended technique to the semantic field of Dutch inceptiveness (3.3).

3.1 Semantic mirrors

Dyvik starts from an initial polysemous *lexeme a in Language A* and extracts all its translations in Language B manually from the English-Norwegian Parallel Corpus (ENPC), a sentence-aligned corpus. He calls this set of translations the *first T-image of a in Language B.* Then, commensurably, the translations back in Language A (the back-translations) of the T-image (themselves translations from a) are looked up. This is called the *Inverse T-image of a in Language A.* It is worth noting that at this point, Dyvik's method differs considerably from classical translation-based WSD techniques, where translations are merely used to disambiguate between the senses of the initial lexeme (e.g., Ide 2002; Lefever 2012). Finally, the initial procedure is applied a second time: the translations in Language B of the Inverse T-image lexemes in Language A are looked up (this is called the *second T-image*), resulting in a structure that depicts the senses of both Language A and Language B lexemes. Schematically, the procedure looks as follows:

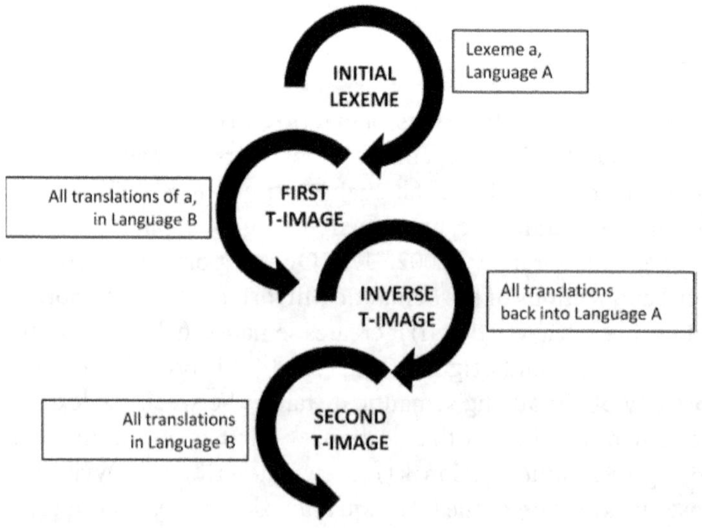

Applied to the example of the Dutch polysemous lexeme *papier* (lexeme a in Language A), we obtain a T-image in English (Language B) of *papier* with *paper, sheet, document, bond.*

The Inverse T-image back into Dutch (Language A) of these English (Language B) lexemes then looks as follows:

[paper] *papier, krant, toets, behangpapier, bankbiljet;*
[sheet] *laken, blad;*
[document] *document, akte;*
[bond] *obligatie.*

The Inverse T-image allows us to differentiate between Dutch papier$_1$ (the material), papier$_2$ (a blank sheet of paper) and papier$_3$ (a valuable piece of paper). Finally, the resulting Dutch lexemes of the Inverse T-image are used to create a second T-image in English, allowing a structuration of sense relations in both Language A and B. Hereunder follows the second T-image. The underlined lexemes are the ones recurring from the first T-image:

[papier] paper, sheet, document, bond
[krant] paper, *newspaper, daily;*
[toets] *test,* paper, *analysis, key;*
[behangpapier] *wall*paper;
[bankbiljet] *note, bill,* paper *currency*
[laken] sheet, *tablecloth;*
[blad] *leaf, tray,* sheet, paper;
[document] *document,* paper;
[akte] document, *contract, act, contract, deed;*
[obligatie] bond, *debenture.*

3.2 Extending the Semantic Mirroring Technique

3.2.1 A rationale for extension

We now implement two new elements in Dyvik's technique in order to extend its use for the creation of translated and original semantic fields. First, drawing on Dyvik's (2004: 311) assumption that "semantically closely related words ought to have strongly overlapping sets of translations," overlapping sets of translations should commensurably reveal semantic relations between translations, between translations and their source language items and between the source language items themselves. Dyvik uses translations as a means to reveal semantic relations, but does not implement the nature (translated or original) of the data that are used at the different stages of the Mirroring. However, within Semantic Mirrors, Language A is a source language in the first and the second T-image and a target language in the Inverse T-image. This implies the possibility to distinguish between translated and original Dutch semantic fields within the Mirroring Technique. Another difficulty is that the Mirroring Technique does in fact only reveal the relational structure between polysemous lexemes, but does not tell us anything about the degree of semantic similarity between the lexemes in the created field. The degree of similarity can be implemented by inserting (source and target language) frequencies into the rationale. This will enable us to measure and visualize semantic similarities between the lexical items in the semantic field of inceptiveness, once as a 'translated' semantic field and a second time as an 'original' semantic field. By doing so, we use the Semantic Mirroring Technique in such a way that is useful for Corpus-based Translation Scholars who are interested in semantic differences between translations and original texts. Moreover, we use the (quantitative) output of the Mirroring Technique and plug it in the statistical technique of correspondence analysis in order to adequately measure and visualize the semantic relationships between the lexical items in the semantic field.

3.2.2 Applying the extended Mirroring technique

The extended technique works as follows. First, all translations of a given (set of) lexeme(s) in a large parallel corpus are checked manually (T-image). Then, inversely, all translations of these translations back into the initial source language (Dutch) are looked up in the same parallel corpus. This is the Inverse T-image. These 'back-translations' enable us to access the structure of the semantic field via the first-order translations. Via an application of the statistical technique of correspondence analysis, this leads to the first visualization, which includes the lexemes of the *Inverse T-image* of an initial set of lexemes. All members of the *Inverse T-image* are in fact translations (of the lexemes of the first T-image). Their exact position in the semantic field and the distance to other lexemes in that field is based on their frequencies as translations of the first T-image and thus depicts their position in the semantic field in translated Dutch via a statistically founded visualization. We can consider the created semantic field as a translated semantic field, for both the variation and the frequencies of the lexemes are determined on the basis of translation.

In order to create a non-translated semantic field comparable to the translated semantic field, we take the set of lexemes of the previous Inverse T-image but we now consider these lexemes as *source-language items*. This means that (i) we take the Dutch lexemes of the previous Inverse T-image, (ii) we query them from the parallel corpus as source language items (this corresponds to Dyvik's second T-image), (iii) we look up their translations in the corpus and (iv) we visualize the Dutch lexemes (as source-language items) via the same statistical technique of correspondence analysis. In this second visualization, the position of the lexemes is based on their frequencies as source language items, and, in this way, it depicts the semantic field in original Dutch. Translational data have thus been used solely as a sense-discrimination technique. The plotted lexemes themselves are the same in both visualizations/plots, which makes them comparable. This technique enables us to regard the first visualization as a representation of the *translated* semantic field of inceptiveness and the second visualization as a representation of the *original* (non-translated) field of inceptiveness.

3.3 Applying the method to the Dutch semantic field of inceptiveness

The data for this study were extracted from the Dutch Parallel Corpus (DPC), a 10-million-word, sentence aligned, both parallel and comparable corpus. It is balanced with respect to five text types (external communication, journalistic texts, instructive texts, administrative text, fictional and non-fictional literature) and four translation directions (Dutch to French, French to Dutch, Dutch to English and English to Dutch). Each text type accounts for 2,000,000 words and within each text type, each translation direction contains 500,000 words (Macken et al., 2011: 376–378). Due to copyright difficulties (a persistent obstacle in large corpus building including fictional texts), the DPC is not balanced for fictional literary texts and so the results of our study do not apply for this text type. We chose to extract only the Belgian-Dutch data from the DPC. We did not take into consideration the data for Dutch (Netherlandic)-Dutch. The text providers of the DPC are, save a few, all Belgian (Netherlandic Dutch providers supplied mostly fictional literature, a genre that cannot be taken into consideration for this study due to the scarcity of the data), hence our choice to eliminate the Dutch-Dutch data.

In order to generate the semantic field of BEGINNEN and to initiate the technique of back-and-forth translation, we selected a concise set of near-synonyms of BEGINNEN "to begin," consisting of *aanvangen, een aanvang nemen, starten, van start gaan* and *aanvatten*. Our selection is based on careful lexicographic analysis, starting from the most prototypical expression of the concept of inceptiveness, namely BEGINNEN [TO BEGIN]. First, we examined eight dictionaries[4] for their synonyms of *beginnen* without taking into account any lexicographic meta-information about hypernymy or hyponymy[5] provided by the dictionaries (for different dictionaries have different policies about meta-data). Nineteen out of a total of 104 synonyms were attested in at least three of the eight consulted dictionaries. After having extracted all sentences in the DPC-corpus containing BEGINNEN (n = 1,435), we subjected all these sentences to an interchangeability test for these 19 lexicography-based synonyms. This resulted in a set of five prototypical synonyms.

The French translations of this set of onomasiological variants of BEGINNEN (n = 564) were manually checked,[6] returning a total of 74 different translations. We then selected those French lexemes that were attested as translations of at least two of the initial Dutch lexemes (minimal overlap criterion). Furthermore, we applied a frequency threshold of 5, signifying that the French types had to be attested at least five times in the corpus as translations of the initial set of Dutch lexemes. This yielded a T-image of 12 different French lexemes. The T-image lexemes were inversely queried from the corpus as source-language lexemes (n = 1,064). Their translations back into Dutch were manually checked, and, applying the same selection criteria (minimal overlap, frequency threshold of 5), this resulted in an inverse T-image of 22 Dutch lexemes. The resulting frequency tables of both the T-image (Dutch rows, French columns) and the inverse T-image (French rows, Dutch columns) were analysed with the technique of correspondence analysis (Greenacre, 2007; Lebart et al., 1998). Correspondence analysis arrives at a lower-dimensional representation of the row and column associations, thereby visualizing the semantic distances between the lexical items in the field. The position of these 22 lexemes is based on their frequencies as translations and thus depicts their position in the semantic field of inceptiveness in translated Dutch via a statistically founded visualization.

In order to visualize the original semantic field, the 22 Dutch lexemes were now inversely queried from the corpus as source-language lexemes (n = 5,322) and their French translations were checked (second T-image).

The visualization of the original semantic field uses the same selection of lexemes and the same statistical technique as the visualization of the translated semantic field, which makes them comparable, but differs in this way that it is based on source-language frequencies, which ensures their visualization as original Dutch. The use of translational data for the second visualization is limited to a sense-discrimination technique and has no further impact on their position in the semantic field.

4. Results: measuring and visualizing semantic similarity between lexical items

4.1 Correspondence analysis

Figure 1 shows the semantic field of translated Dutch BEGINNEN. We observe that most lexemes (and in fact all lexemes that were selected after the lexicographic analysis) are in the plot's origin, viz. *beginnen* [to begin], *aanvangen* [to start], *van start gaan* [to start], *starten* [to start], *aanvatten* [to commence]. This cluster can consequently be interpreted as the prototypical centre, consisting of lexemes with the basic meaning of the inceptive category, viz. "start of a general process." The lexemes of the second cluster have in common that none of them are verbs. This would imply that, for instance, *aanvankelijk* [first] and *begin* [beginning] are semantically closer to each other than *begin* [beginning] is to *beginnen* [to begin]. We also observe two outlying lexemes: *openen* [to open] and *vertrekken* [to leave] and a small outlying cluster with *invoeren* [to introduce] and *instellen* [to establish]. *Invoeren* and *instellen,* mostly refer to a "rule or legislation becoming effective," so they typically appear in formal, legislative texts, hence their outlying position. The inchoative meaning of *openen* is (i) a formal form of inchoativity, as in "to open a sitting or a meeting," and (ii) a metaphor (as in: "His new job *opened doors* for his future"), which could explain its outlying position. Finally, the outlying position of *vertrekken* [to leave] in the translated semantic field could be due to translational interference. The position of the Dutch lexemes in the translated field depends on the underlying position of the French lexemes, so their position can actually inform us on the (possible) translational effects. The closest neighbour lexemes of *vertrekken* in the plot are the cluster of non-verbs, for instance *aanvankelijk* [first, in the beginning] and *aanvang* [outset]. This leads to the hypothesis that *vertrekken* in its gerund form *vertrekkende (van)* [departing from] is semantically closer to *aanvankelijk* and *aanvang* than to the prototypical inceptive lexemes. This gerund form could be an example of translational *shining through* of French *à partir de* [leaving from, as from].

Now we take a look at Figure 2 (the semantic field of original Dutch BEGINNEN). The most obvious resemblances between the translated and the original semantic field are the two main clusters: in the origin of the original Dutch plot, we find the prototypical centre and we equally observe a separate cluster with the non-verbs. The lexemes in each of the clusters are almost identical to the ones of the translated plot (apart from *vertrekken*, which is now in the plot's origin). We do notice that, in the origin, lexemes are further apart from each other, which indicates that small meaning differences are somewhat flattened in translated language. Furthermore, we observe that *vertrekken* has become prototypical. Based on this observation, we could conclude that *vertrekken* is a prototypical expression of inceptiveness in original Dutch, but it is not used as such in translated Dutch, hence its outlying position. *Openen* remains its outlying position, which confirms the findings in the translated plot. Overall, we did not observe any major differences between the semantic fields of translated and original Dutch, although we did detect some smaller differences, assumedly pointing out differences between the original and the translated semantic field.

4.2 Correspondence analysis with anchoring

From the visualizations of the first correspondence analysis (see Figures 1 and 2), we observed that lexemes with the same word class seemed to systematically cluster together, an outcome one would not intuitively expect (we would not expect *aanvankelijk* [first] and *begin* [beginning] to be semantically closer to each other than *begin* [beginning] to *beginnen* [to begin]). If, in fact what we want to know is how the lexemes are related within the semantic field of inceptiveness, it might be desirable to first restrict the semantic space in which the lexemes will appear to the field of inceptiveness. For the second correspondence analysis (see Figures 3 and 4), we thus decided to first create a "space of inceptiveness" based on the first T-image. More specifically, before we actually plotted the 22 Dutch lexemes, we applied a correspondence analysis on the original six Dutch lexemes with their 12 French translations. This had the effect that the positions of the 12 French lexemes were 'anchored' with respect to the six prototypical

Dutch lexemes. In other words, this allowed us to create a 'stable' space of inceptiveness. On the basis of these 12 'anchored' positions, the 22 Dutch lexemes were subsequently visualised,[7] once as target-language items (translated Dutch, Figure 3) and once as source-language items (original Dutch, Figure 4).

When we look at these analyses (Figures 3 and 4), we find a different distribution. In both Figures 3 and 4, we find *beginnen* in the plot's origin. So far, this is the same observation as with the first correspondence analysis. But when we look at the separate clusters in each figure, we find that they are now clearly meaning-based and formed independently of the word class of each lexeme. This could be explained by the fact that the position of the lexemes in this second analysis is clearly restricted to the field of inceptiveness (by the previous creation of the 'stable inceptive space'), which avoids the position of the lexemes to be biased by their relation to other semantic fields than the one of inceptiveness.

In Figure 3 (translated semantic field) we find, next to the prototypical centre, a second cluster with lexemes like *oprichten* [to set up], *lanceren* [to launch], *opstarten* [to start up], all referring to the "beginning of a project, an initiative or a business." *Invoeren* [to establish] and *instellen* [to set up] are again outlying, which confirms our analysis based on classical statistical techniques. *Aanvangen* [to commence] and especially *ingaan* [to take effect] are outlying, which could be due to their formal character. Figure 4 shows us the original Dutch semantic field. Parallel to the classical analysis, we observe that the lexemes are lying further apart, which shows that the differences between the lexemes are more clearly expressed. This confirms our idea from the first analysis that translation flattens meaning differentiation. We again notice two clusters, the one in the origin is the prototypical one, the one to the right of the prototypical cluster consists of lexemes referring to the "beginning of a project, an initiative or a business." Note that in the original Dutch field, the lexemes seem to gradually descend from the protypical centre, towards the right, and towards a slightly outlying position. Following this line from centre to periphery, we clearly remark that the lexemes become more formal, with at the end of this line, *invoeren* [to establish] and *instellen* [to set up]. Note also the difference with the translated semantic field where those two lexemes are clearly outlying. This shows that the gradual meaning differentiation we observe in original language has somewhat disappeared in translated language. Also parallel to the translated semantic field, we observe *aanvangen* [to commence]. Both in translated and in original language, this lexeme seems to hold a kind of middle position, as shown by its similar position in both plots. Finally, we see that outlying *ingaan* [to take effect] is now rejoined by *vanaf* [as from]. In original Dutch, the inceptive aspect of *vanaf* is rather remote, whereas in translated language, *vanaf* is even prototypical. This could again be explained via translation: *vanaf* is often a good equivalent for many of the French inceptive lexemes like *débuter* [to start] or *départ* [departure] but is intuitively not inceptive.

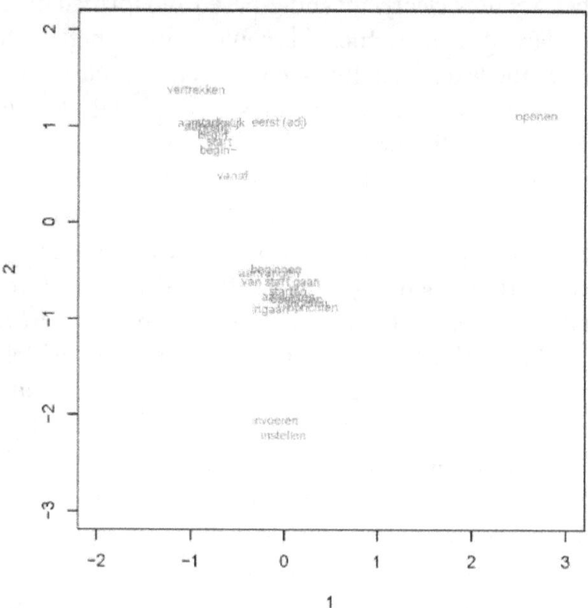

Figure 1: Semantic field of translated Dutch BEGINNEN

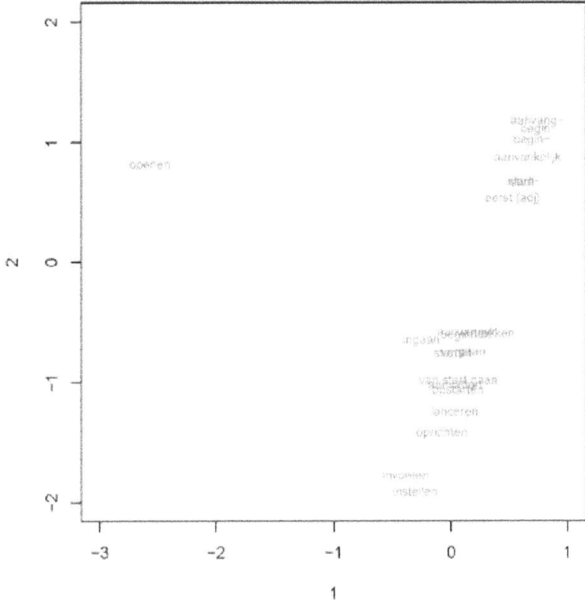

Figure 2: Semantic field of original Dutch BEGINNEN

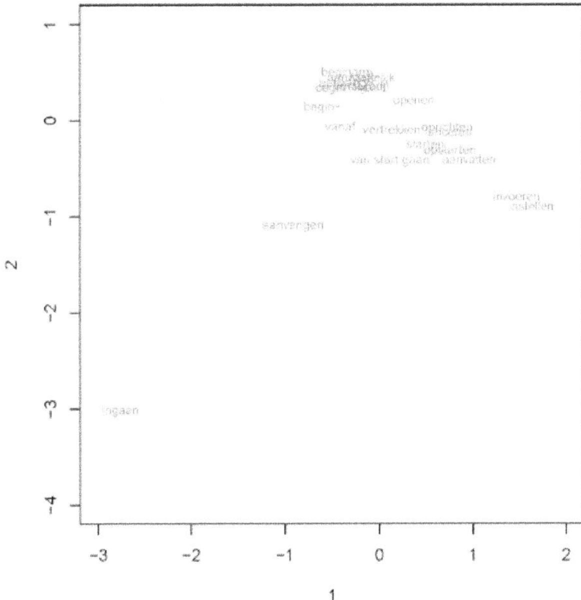

Figure 3: Semantic field of translated Dutch BEGINNEN — with anchoring

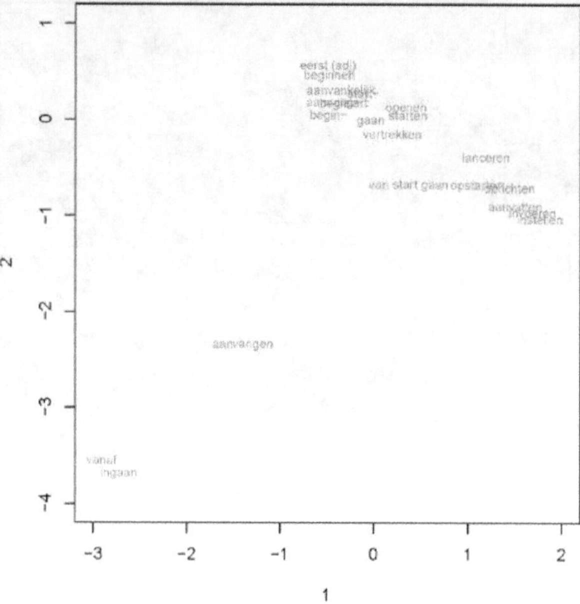

Figure 4: Semantic field of original Dutch BEGINNEN — with anchoring

5. Conclusion

In this article, we have made a first attempt to measure semantic differences between translated and non-translated language. We therefore have presented a quantitative bottom-up corpus-based method which enabled us to identify, to measure and to visualize semantic similarity between the elements in the field of Dutch inceptiveness. The method we applied is an extension to Helge Dyvik's Semantic Mirroring Technique, enabling the creation of both translated and non-translated semantic fields; it is translational and makes use of both a comparable and parallel corpus. We found that translational data are an interesting source for the bottom-up identification of a semantic field's structure and for the differentiation of prototypical meanings from peripheral ones. Moreover, the method enabled us to compare semantic fields in original and in translated language, while using the same data set. In a next step, we 'stabilised' the semantic field by 'anchoring' the positions of the 12 French lexemes. This approach revealed more meaning-differentiated semantic fields. The application of the back-and-forth technique to the semantic field of Dutch inceptiveness, did indeed show differences between the translated and the original field. The differences were especially laid bare by the anchored points technique. When we compared the two semantic fields, we observed a tendency towards a 'flatter' image in the translated field: the lexemes were plotted closer together, which indicated that the sense distinctions were less clearly present in the translated semantic field of inceptiveness. The created field is thus less fine-grained than when we use original language frequencies.

Our choice for the case of Dutch inceptiveness (BEGINNEN), might not have been the most appropriate one to test a method that is initially interested in conceptual meaning differentiation, for BEGINNEN is not really what one would call highly polysemous, making the sense distinctions less obvious, more subtle and thus harder to capture. Despite this somewhat unfortunate choice, the visualizations did show us detailed differences between and within the semantic fields and did enable a comparison between translated and original semantic fields. Meaning-differentiated semantic fields are thus very likely to corroborate the obtained results for BEGINNEN.

The proposed technique should be validated in several ways. A first validation can be done by implementing a different 'pivot-language', e.g. English (also available in the DPC). In this way, the semantic field of inceptiveness in both original and translated language can be created in the same way as proposed in this study, the only difference being the pivot language. A second step in the validation process can be made via the creation of semantic fields of inceptiveness in a different language (e.g. French), which enables us to make a cross-linguistic comparison of semantic fields and of the possible (language dependent or independent) influence of translation on semantic fields. This influence is not necessarily similar in different languages (for different languages have different attitudes towards translations) but we do expect to observe similar patterns. Finally, our translational method could be completed via aspects of distributional methods like the Behavioural Profile method (Divjak and Gries, 2006; Gries and Divjak, 2009). In computational linguistics, the assumption that words with a similar meaning tend to occur in similar contexts (Harris 1968) has led to the advent of distributional approaches like first and second order bag-of-words models (Manning and Schütze, 1999) and the behavioural profiles method (Divjak and Gries, 2006; Gries and Divjak, 2009). The combination of a context bound sense discrimination method with the translation based approach could provide us with a solid 'mixed' both distributional and translational instrument for the mapping of semantic networks.

Notes

1 This does not mean that the role of semantics itself in translation has not been addressed (e.g., Klaudy, 2010), but this kind of research is rarely corpus-based and barely ever involves with denotational issues.
2 Constrastive Linguistics have indeed used distributional methods for monolingual semantic differentiation (like the Behavioral Profile method developed by Divjak and Gries 2006; 2009). As the current study does not involve with distributional techniques, we will not elaborate further on this matter.
3 Note that we do not consider back-translations as translation-effect neutral. We do acknowledge that the technique rules out idiosyncratic translations and translations that are purely context-bound. Whether or not back-translations indeed rule out any translational effect, is exactly what emerges from our results.
4 de Clerck (1981); Reinsma (1993), Reinsma (1995), Boon and Geeraerts (2005), De Boer (2006), Van Dale (2010), Den Boon and Geeraerts (2011), Van Dale (2012).
5 Antonyms were excluded, though.
6 At every level of the back-and-forth translation technique, invalid alignments are eliminated from the data. Furthermore, if, in the translated sentence containing the lexeme under study, there is no translation equivalent (identifiable as such), the observation is not taken into account. In this way, we only take into account 'linguistically predictable translations' (Dyvik, 1998: 52).
7 The technical term in correpondence analysis is that the 22 Dutch lexemes are depicted as so-called "supplementary" or "illustrative" points.

References

Aijmer, K., and A.-M. Simon-Vandenbergen. (2004). "A model and a methodology for the study of pragmatic markers: the semantic field of expectation." *Journal of Pragmatics* 36 (10): 1781–1805. http://dx.doi.org/10.1016/j.pragma.2004.05.005.

Aijmer, K., and A.-M. Simon-Vandenbergen. (2006). *Pragmatic Markers in Contrast.* Amsterdam: Elsevier.

Altenberg, B., and S. Granger. (2002). "Recent trends in cross-linguistic lexical studies." In *Lexis in Contrast: Corpus-Based Approaches*, ed. B. Altenberg and S. Granger, 3–48. Amsterdam: John Benjamins. http://dx.doi.org/10.1075/scl.7.04alt.

Baker, M. (1993). "Corpus linguistics and translation studies. Implications and applications." In *Text and Technology. In Honour of John Sinclair*, ed. M. Baker, G. Francis, and E. Tognini-Bonelli, 233–245. Philadelphia, Amsterdam: John Benjamins. http://dx.doi.org/10.1075/z.64.15bak.

Baker, M. (2004). "A corpus-based view of similarity and difference in translation." *International Journal of Corpus Linguistics* 9 (2): 167–93. http://dx.doi.org/10.1075/ijcl.9.2.02bak.

Bernardini, S., and A. Ferraresi. (2011). "Practice, Description and Theory Come Together: Normalization or Interference in Italian Technical Translation?" *Meta* 56 (2): 226–46. http://dx.doi.org/10.7202/1006174ar.

Boon, T.d., and D. Geeraerts. (2005). "Van Dale: Groot Woordenboek der Nederlandse Taal: 3 Dl." In V. Dale (ed.) *Van Dale: Groot Woordenboek der Nederlandse Taal: 3 Dl*, 14th ed. Utrecht: Van Dale Lexicografie.

Dale, V. (ed.) (2010). *Van Dale thesaurus. Synoniemen en betekenisverwante woorden* (Eerste editie, eerste oplage ed.). Utrecht and Antwerpen: Van Dale Uitgevers.

Dale, V. (ed.) (2012). *Van Dale Onlinewoordenboek hedendaags Nederlands..* Utrecht: Van Dale Uitgevers.

De Boer, W.T.e. (ed.) (2006). *Koenen Woordenboek Nederlands.* Utrecht and Antwerpen: Van Dale Uitgevers.

de Clerck, W. (ed.) (1981). *Nijhoffs Zuid Nederlands woordenboek. 's*-Gravenshage and Antwerpen: Martinus Nijhoff.

De Sutter, G., I. Delaere, and K. Plevoets. (2012). "Lexical lectometry in corpus-based translation studies. Combining profile-based correspondence analysis and logistic regression modeling." In M. Oakes and J. Meng (eds), *Quantitative Methods in Corpus-based Translation Studies. A practical guide to descriptive translation research*, 325–346. Amsterdam, Philadelphia: John Benjamins Publishing Company. http://dx.doi.org/10.1075/scl.51.13sut.

Delaere, I., G. De Sutter, and K. Plevoets. (2012). "Is translated language more standardized than non-translated language? Using profile-based correspondence analysis for measuring linguistic distances between language varieties. *Target.*" *International Journal of Translation Studies* 24 (2): 203–24. http://dx.doi.org/10.1075/target.24.2.01del.

Den Boon, C.A., and D. Geeraerts eds. (2011). *Dikke Van Dale.* Utrecht: Van Dale Uitgevers.

Divjak, D., and S. Gries. (2006). "Ways of Trying in Russian. Clustering Behavioral Profiles." *Corpus Linguistics and Linguistic Theory* 2 (1): 23–60. http://dx.doi.org/10.1515/CLLT.2006.002.

Dyvik, H. (1998). "A translational basis for semantics." In S. Johansson and S. Oksefjell (eds), *Corpora and cross-linguistic research: theory, method, and case studies*, 51–86. Amsterdam: Rodopi.

Dyvik, H. (2004). "Translations as semantic mirrors from parallel corpus to wordnet." In *Advances in Corpus Linguistics*, ed. K. Aijmer and B. Altenberg, 311–326. Amsterdam, New York: Rodopi.

Greenacre, M. (2007). *Correspondence analysis in practice.* 2nd ed. Boca Raton: Chapman & Hall/CRC. http://dx.doi.org/10.1201/9781420011234.

Gries, S., and D. Divjak. (2009). "Behavioral Profiles. A Corpus-Based Approach to Cognitive Semantic Analysis." In V. Evans and S.S. Pourcel (eds), *New Directions in Cognitive Linguistics*, 57–75. Amsterdam, Philadelphia: John Benjamins. http://dx.doi.org/10.1075/hcp.24.07gri.

Halverson, S. (2003). "The Cognitive Basis of Translation Universals." *Target* 15 (2): 197–241. http://dx.doi.org/10.1075/target.15.2.02hal.

Halverson, S. (2010). "Cognitive translation studies: developments in theory and method." In G. Shreve and E. Angelone (eds), *Translation and cognition*, 349–369. Amsterdam: John Benjamins. http://dx.doi.org/10.1075/ata.xv.18hal.

Harris, Z.S. (1968). *Mathematical structures of language.* Wiley.

Ide, N., T. Erjavec, and D. Tufis. (2002). *Sense discrimination with parallel corpora.* Paper presented at the Proceedings of the SIGLEX/SENSEVAL workshop on Word sense disambiguation: recent successes and future directions, Philadelphia.

Ivir, V. (1983). "A Translation-based Model of Contrastive Analysis." *Jyväskylä Cross-Language Studies* 9:171–8.

Ivir, V. (1987). "Functionalism in Contrastive Analysis and Translation Studies." In *Functionalism in Linguistics*, ed. R. Dirven and V. Fried, 471–481. Amsterdam, Philadelphia: John Benjamins. http://dx.doi.org/10.1075/llsee.20.25ivi.

Klaudy, K. (2010). "Specification and Generalisation of Meaning in Translation." In B. Lewandowska-Tomasczyk and M. Thelen (Eds.), *Meaning in Translation* (Vol. 19, pp. 81–103). Frankfurt a.M: Peter Lang.

Kruger, H. (2012). "A corpus-based study of the mediation effect in translated and edited language." *Target* 24 (2): 355–88. http://dx.doi.org/10.1075/target.24.2.07kru.

Laviosa, S. (1998). "Core patterns of lexical use in a comparable corpus of English narrative prose." *Meta* 43 (4): 557–70. http://dx.doi.org/10.7202/003425ar.

Laviosa, S. (2002). *Corpus-based Translation Studies. Theory, Findings, Applications*. Amsterdam, New York: Rodopi.

Lebart, L., A. Salem, and L. Berry. (1998). *Exploring textual data*. Dordrecht: Kluwer Academic Publishers. http://dx.doi.org/10.1007/978-94-017-1525-6.

Lefever, E. (2012). *ParaSense: parallel corpora for word sense disambiguation*. Ghent: Ghent University.

Macken, L., O. De Clercq, and H. Paulussen. (2011). "Dutch Parallel Corpus: a Balanced Copyright-Cleared Parallel Corpus." *Meta* 56 (2): 374. http://dx.doi.org/10.7202/1006182ar.

Malmkjaer, K. (1997). "Punctuation in Hans Christian Andersen's stories and in their translations into English." In *Nonverbal Communication and Translation*, ed. F. Poyatos. Philadelphia: John Benjamins. http://dx.doi.org/10.1075/btl.17.13mal.

Manning, C.D., and H. Schütze. (1999). *Foundations of Statistical Natural Language Processing*. MIT Press.

Mauranen, A. (2000). "Strange strings in translated language. A study on corpora." In M. Olohan, (ed.), *Intercultural Faultlines: Research Models in Translation Studies I: Textual and Cognitive Aspects*, 119–141. Manchester: St Jerome.

Mortier, L., and L. Degand. (2009). "Adversative discourse markers in contrast: The need for a combined corpus approach." *International Journal of Corpus Linguistics* 14 (3): 338–66. http://dx.doi.org/10.1075/ijcl.14.3.03mor.

Noël, D. (2003). "Translations as evidence for semantics: an illustration." *Linguistics* 41 (4): 757–85. http://dx.doi.org/10.1515/ling.2003.024.

Olohan, M., and M. Baker. (2000). "Reporting that in Translated English: Evidence for Subconscious Processes of Explicitation?" *Across Languages and Cultures* 1 (2): 141–58. http://dx.doi.org/10.1556/Acr.1.2000.2.1.

Reinsma, R. (ed.) (1993). *Synoniemenwoordenboek*. Utrecht: Het Spectrum.

Reinsma, R. (ed.) (1995). *Prisma van de Synoniemen. Woorden met verwante betekenissen*. Utrecht: Het Spectrum.

Resnik, P., and D. Yarowsky. (1997). *A perspective on word sense disambiguation methods and their evaluation*. Paper presented at the ACL-SIGLEX Workshop Taggin Text with Lexical Semantics: Why, What and How? Washington D.C.

Resnik, P., and D. Yarowsky. (1999). "Distinguishing systems and distinguishing senses: New evaluation methods for word sense disambiguation." *Natural Language Engineering* 5 (2): 113–33. http://dx.doi.org/10.1017/S1351324999002211.

Simon-Vandenbergen, A.-M. (2013). "English adverbs of essence and their equivalents in Dutch and French." *Advances in Corpus-Based Contrastive Linguistics: Studies in Honour of Stig Johansson* 54:83–102. http://dx.doi.org/10.1075/scl.54.06sim.

Part IV

Multimedia Approach to Translation

Well as a discourse marker in learner interlingual subtitles

Anna Bączkowska

This paper discusses the problem of subtitling discourse markers, in particular the functions and possible renderings of *well* are presented. Several approaches to discourse markers and to *well* are sketched in the first part of the paper, both the more traditional views (coherence-based) and the most recent proposals (multifunctional). In the empirical part, the translations of *well* retrieved from a learner corpus of subtitles (students of English at the tertiary level with translation route) are examined in line with the multifunctional approach to *well*.

1. Discourse markers

Despite a bulk of literature devoted to discourse markers (DMs), they still seem to express a fuzzy, elusive and ambivalent concept that defies description and taxonomy. The very term discourse marker (employed by e.g.: Zwicky 1985, Schiffrin 1987, Lenk 1998, Carter and McCarthy 2006) is often used interchangeably with a number of other terms, such as: discourse particle (Schourup 1985, Labove and Fanshel 1987, Abraham 1991, Kroon 1995), discourse operator (Redeker 1991, Ariel 1994), pragmatic marker (Fraser 1996, Brinton 1996, Aijmer et al. 2006), gambit (Faerch and Kasper 1984), pragmatic particle (Östman 1981), D-item (i.e., discourse items, Stenström 1990), cue phrase (Knot and Sanders 1998) and discourse connective (Blakemore 1987). Discourse marker, however, seems to be the most common term and thus it will be used in the present paper to avoid terminological dissent.

The category of DMs includes a collection of heterogeneous items, prevalent in spoken discourse, that are "elements which bracket units of talk" (Schiffrin 1987: 31) and mark "relationships between units of discourse" (Blakemore 2004:221). They signal how units of discourse (rather than a sentence) are related to other fragments of discourse, either foregoing or following. Thus, DMs are contextual clues, topic transition devices and discourse-organizational elements that enable the hearer to infer the meaning while processing the upcoming signals in order to bridge discourse units. Discourse units may show whether another discourse unit continues a prior message, contradicts it, questions it, etc.

This early and generally accepted discourse organization oriented perspective is replaced by a more recent epistemic stance proposed by Schourup (2001), who sees DMs, and *well* in particular, as signals of consideration, a mental activity embarked on by the speaker during interaction. Aijmer (2013: 13) is more meticulous and sees two possible options within the epistemic stance encoded by *well*: the expression of uncertainty and politeness. Along with the epistemic stance, some scholars also emphasize the affective stance typically conveyed by DMs. Ochs (1996: 410) delineates affective stance as attitude, mood, disposition, feeling and emotional intensity. Both epistemic stance and affective stance are stressed by Fischer (2006: 445) for whom pragmatic markers are indicators of interactants' involvement in a situated discourse.

Considering the structural, attitudinal and affective perspectives, the functions of DMs most often quoted by scholars include: connecting discourse, revealing hesitation, prompting, signalling turn-taking and theme, hedging, disclosing attitude to interlocutor, regulating interlocutors' relationship, seeking approbation, filling silent pauses and marking turn boundaries (Jucker and Ziv 1998: 1).

A more specific typology by Bozzanella (2006: 456–457) distinguishes a number of functions categorized into three main groups: interactional, metatextual and cognitive. Interactional markers are either speaker- or hearer-related. Within this group, turn-taking/yielding, comprehension checking, attention-getting and phatic devices, fillers, hedges and boosters are the means the speaker employs, whereas interrupting, back-channelling, attention/comprehension confirming, requests for clarification, agreement/support, or disagreement and phatics are the devices at the hearer's disposal. Metatextual functions are related to discourse organization and they comprise structuring devices (e.g. frame, transition, digression, ending), focusing devices (local and global), and reformulation markers (paraphrase, correction and exemplification markers). Finally, cognitive DMs involve procedural markers (e.g. inference or other cognitive-related processes), epistemic markers (to do with subjectivity and commitment), and modulation markers (influencing illocutionary force and propositional content).

This typology partially converges with previous studies. For example, cognitive-epistemic markers overlap with Schourup's (2001) epistemic stance and Aijmer's (2002) hedges, which are treated as politeness devices, are seen by Bozzanella (2006) as a broader category representing interactional hedges (one of which may be politeness-related). Self-repairs classified by Aijmer under the rubric of coherence devices, on the other hand, are congruent with Bozzanella's class of metatextual reformulation markers (corrections). Aijmer's typology, apart from being less specific, merges metatextual discourse organization markers with interaction organization markers. By virtue of the fact that the textual, attitudinal, interactional and cognitive domains tend to overlap, as Jucker and Ziv (1998: 5) maintain, they cannot be treated as ultimate and absolute functional criteria in the description of DMs. On a more general note, the main function of DMs may be embraced by the notion of indexicality. This means that they have a context-bound reading, binding both linguistic elements and going beyond the discourse, and binding the speech act with the speaker and hearer, with their identities as well as epistemic and affective stance (Aijmer 2013: 13).

Regardless of the typology adopted, DMs have certain features and these were described in detail by Brinton (1996: 33–35). Their properties are divided into five groups: (a) phonological and lexical features, (b) syntactic, (c) semantic, (d) functional and (e) sociolinguistic and stylistic features. Thus, to cite the most common features, DMs tend to be phonologically reduced, they often form a separate tone group, they are typically sentence-initial and optional, have minute or no propositional meaning, are multifunctional, and are restricted mainly to spoken discourse where they occur with high frequency.

There are several theoretical approaches to the description of DMs. Coarsely speaking, there is the coherence-oriented integrative approach (Schiffrin 1987), the relevance-theoretic framework (Jucker 1993, Blakemore 2004), and the variational pragmatic approach (Aijmer 2013). The proposals shuttle from structural (Schiffrin) to functional (Aijmer) theoretical models, and from DMs seen as semantically void categories (Schiffrin) to pragmatically rich metalinguistic indicators (Bozzanella

2006, Aijmer 2013). In our study we are inclined to follow Aijmer's proposal of DMs meaning potential stance, thus DMs are treated as meaningful elements.

DMs may encode contradictory pragmatic meanings as well as different functions. To give an example, *surely* rarely indicates certainty; more often it conveys doubt and uncertainty (Aijmer 2002), while *you know* is used in cases when the speaker realizes that the hearer does not know what the speaker is about to say (Östman 1981). Here, the meaning is metacommunicative, in that it discloses the speaker's will to create common ground and to acknowledge solidarity, and thus it functions on a purely rhetorical plane. Because DMs are often underspecified, it is relatively easy to accept Aijmer et al.'s (2006) claim that DMs are vehicles of multifunctional meaning.

The multifunctional (or polyfunctional) approaches to DMs may have distinct sources. Fischer (2006: 13) distinguishes monosemic, homonymic and polysemic models of polyfunctionality and defends the last two as the most adequate ones for the description of DMs. It will be remembered that monosemy assumes that there exists an invariant core meaning, and occurrences of a given word are only contextual realizations (variants) of the core meaning. Homonymy also assumes a number of meanings yet they are perceived as distinct and unrelated. Cuenca (2008: 1381) notices that homonymy does not do justice to the analysis of DMs as some of them are fully context-dependent, i.e., they have no meaning on their own. If distinct meanings are acknowledged and they are believed to be related, polysemy is assumed. The polysemy approach to the description of *well* proposes no core (prototypical) meaning but permits a number of senses, which are interrelated. These links may stem from metaphorical or metonymic extensions, and may form radial networks or family resemblance models. In our view, even if a common meaning can emerge out of the instantiations of *well* realized in a number of contexts, it does not have an ontological status; it is used solely for descriptive purposes (cf. Lewandowska-Tomaszczyk 2007, Bączkowska 2011). It is the range of possible options of how *well* can be rendered in given contexts that is the object of this study. By adhering to the polysemy approach, we also endorse the polyfunctionality model to DMs.

In sum, DMs are items that resist truth-conditional treatment (Levinson 1983: 88), whose meaning may be ad hoc and speaker/hearer specific, and are negotiable by the speech act participants (Fischer 1999). DMs are sense-dynamic, to the extent that their interpretation by ratified participants may differ from their reading by co-present speech event participants (Ochs 1996: 413). Finally, DMs may have a number of meanings and functions, and the meanings may be related or unrelated. The rules that govern the explication of their relation depend on which theoretical model is adopted.

2. **Well** *as a discourse marker: approaches to* **well** *and its functions*

Well has been studied by a number of scholars representing different theoretical approaches and emphasizing sundry aspects of this marker. To Lakoff (1973), for example, *well* reveals insufficiency of response, while to Svartvik (1980) it signals a topic shift. Carlson (1984: 31) treats *well* as acceptance of an indifferent or defective situation (suboptimal) or acceptance of an exceptional situation. Svartvik (1980) and Carlson (1984) analyse *well* structurally, typically used for opening or closing discourse units; alternatively, it may be used to indicate a pause as well as a change of topic or orientation in a conversation. Owen (1981) attributed *well* a mitigation function in the context of confrontation. In Schiffrin's (1987) integrative model, it is a semantically empty word used in discourse slots where expectations of content are not met, in other words when there is lack of coherence in discourse. This coherence-based approach was challenged by Bolinger (1989) for whom *well* may, but does not always, encode failure in coherence and expectations but also may be an expression of disagreement. In addition, Bolinger sees a close relation between *well* as a discourse marker and its original adverbial use. A relevance-theoretic formulation proposed by Jucker (1993) states that *well* is a deviation from optimal relevance, wherein the hearer must reconstruct the background information to allow interpretation (inference) of the upcoming message that is not the most expected (relevant) utterance. A semantic-pragmatic account has been voiced by Schourup (2001) and Blakemore (2002), while a cognitive linguistic approach (radial network) to *well* has been offered by Cuenca (2008). Fraser (2006: 190) delimits *well* as a parallel pragmatic marker that is used for conversational management purposes, reserving the term "discourse marker" for elements "which signal a relation between the discourse segment which hosts them and the prior discourse segment." Aijmer and Simon-Vandenbergen (2006) approach *well* from a (multi) functional stance and perceive it as an item whose interpretations are dependent upon the speaker, context and the relationship between the speaker and the hearer. Thus, *well* may encode a wide spectrum of senses, including opposite meanings, as well as a number of functions. In a similar vein, Aijmer (2013) delineates *well* from a variational pragmatic approach and sees it as a pragmatic marker with meaning potential, whose sense is uncovered by the simple expedient of gleaning contextual clues, of which prosodic features are one of the most important, yet social varieties (e.g. speaker roles, social situation) are also powerful factors affecting its meaning. Thus the meaning is seen as underspecified in the text but enriched by the hearer with the help of current clues therein. The interaction with contextual resources as well as the hearer's inference skills remain the key determinants of what *well* conveys in a specific context. Aijmer (2013: 18) also contends that *well* may be assigned to several overlapping meanings simultaneously as well as novel ad hoc senses invented by the interactants.

Bolinger (1989) suggests that *well* should be analysed in context with interjections, e.g.: *Oh, well* (with falling intonation to express resignation) or in the vicinity of *hmm* (deliberation) as they tend to co-occur. Moreover, he sees a close correlation between *well* used as a DM and *well* used as adverb-adjective (non-marker). Schourup (2001: 1036) does not agree with Bolinger's semantic identity claim of *well* used as marker and non-marker. Instead, he proposes a pragmatic-semantic account of *well* claiming that Bolinger's examples are illustrative of *well* being epistemic. In line with the epistemic stance, *well* is not a conceptually empty expressive vocable; moreover, it is not a marker with "invariant semantic or functional core" but a meaningful word which reflects the mental activity of the speaker, an ongoing consideration and deliberation, and requires inference based on current information and assumptions (Schourup 2001: 1026–1058).

Like DMs in general, *well* may be assigned a number of functions. Within the epistemic meaning, Schourup distinguishes the following functions of *well*: expressing divergence, prompting, continuing (continuative) and pointing (gestural function). To these roles, Aijmer (2013: 15) adds expression of reluctance, disappointment or resignation on the one hand, and, on the positive note, coherence, involvement and politeness (Aijmer 2013: 30). She also proposes the following classification of sub-senses of *well* used in informal conversation within the three functions: coherence involves word sense and self-repair, projecting a new turn and transition in line with an agenda; involvement is associated with agreement, disagreement, evaluation and feedback to a preceding question; finally, politeness is connected with hedging. Bolinger proposed a plethora of functions of *well*, e.g. exclamation of surprise, disapproval, commenting on misbehaviour, prompt, acceptance, etc. To these functions, defensive vs. diffident functions of *well* may be added, as proposed by Blakemore (2002: 131). On the other hand, the three functional levels distinguished by Andersen (2001) – textual, subjective and interactional – have been replaced by Cuenca (2008) by two – structural (i.e., textual) and modal (which integrates subjective and interactional). When *well* is used with modal meaning, a range of attitudes may be encoded, from agreement to contraposition (Cuenca 2008: 1380), namely: partial agreement, doubt, partial disagreement, contraposition. Cuenca also stresses that when used in the intermediate position it can be also used with the intention of reformulation, a change of topic or a need to search for the adequate form of expression, in which she agrees with Schourup.

The position of *well*, like other DMs, may be utterance-initial (or discourse-initial), utterance-internal or utterance-final, with the last two options being much less frequent. It primarily occurs in declarative sentences and is typically parenthetical, i.e., syntactically independent, yet it often co-occurs with interjections, such as *oh well*; *well, you know* (Bolinger 1989, Schourup 2001, Aijmer 2013). *Well* itself cannot be classified as the interjection as it does not convey strong emotions (it is non-exclamatory). It is also more likely to be used in a clause-internal position as, being often deliberative, it does not interrupt an utterance as much as interjections do.

Taken together, *well* is primarily considerative (Schourup 2001), a deliberation marker (Biber et al. 1999: 1986), i.e., it signposts a mental process ongoing as a conversation pans out, it signals weighing and collecting thoughts, as well as groping for the right word and self-repair (Jucker 1993, Bozzanella 2006, Aijmer 2013). Given its affective function, it may take an emotional cast but does not have to, yet it remains attitudinal as it reveals the speaker's stance on information at issue. When it latches onto other words, in particular on interjections (e.g. *oh*) and verbal pauses (e.g. *you know*), the expressions of hesitation, epistemic uncertainty or deliberation are even more stressed. Equally important, *well* may be also used for a purely rhetorical function, encoding conversational strategic moves. Aijmer et al. (2006: 109), for example, notice that *I think* may be used to stress authority. Further, *well* may be a marker used to negotiate common ground and to express politeness (Johansson 2006: 135, Aijmer and Simon-Vandenbergen 2006). It has indexical function as it binds the ongoing communication with the prior text or the upcoming information as well as with the participants involved in the speech event (discourse binding function). It may have little propositional meaning and, as such, it does not change the propositional content of the whole utterance but it may signal additional information which reveals the interactants' attitude and relations, thus having implicative force (indexicality), and it may implicitly comment on the ongoing speech event (reflexivity).

3. Discourse markers in (audiovisual) translation

There are many studies into the nature of *well* as a discourse marker but the investigations that deal with the translation of *well* are scarce, let alone the treatment of *well* in audiovisual translation[1]. A corpus-based research conducted by Aijmer and Simon-Vandenbergen (2006), one of the few studies, relies on the assumption that *well* seems to have a number of functionally related meanings which allow the formation of a semantic field. In order to establish the semantic fields of *well* in Dutch and German, they proposed a cross-linguistic, comparative method. The investigation in line with the comparative method allows them to conclude that by analysing the non-core, contextually dependent functional equivalents of *well* in the target language, one can enrich the meanings assigned to *well* in the source language, as they "might be less accessible in a monolingual approach" (Aijmer et al. 2006: 113). Finding correspondences that go beyond the prototypical (core) meanings and which span the whole semantic field is particularly important in the case of discourse particles, as their intertranslatability is not expected to achieve high values. As a result, it is more important to establish correspondences between the semantic fields of DMs rather than between single (and most typical) items.

Among few accounts on DMs in audiovisual translation, Chaume (2004a) reports on the use of several discourse markers – *now, you know, oh, (you) see, look* – in both dubbed and subtitled versions of *Pulp Fiction* in Spanish. He does not analyse the rendering of *well,* but his observations regarding DMs as such are both interesting and important for our study. He notices that these discourse markers are rarely rendered, in particular the value is very low for subtitles. He concludes that since DMs are coherence devices and since a viewer is exposed to images which enrich the understanding of the film content rendered verbally, their absence does not seriously impoverish the message conveyed by the source text because the audience can repair any possible misunderstandings or ambiguities thanks to their "linguistic and textual competence." On the whole, this is a pithy remark with the proviso, though, that the contexts which contain DMs are sufficiently transparent to delegate the audience to visual signals on-screen and their linguistic/textual competence. It seems reasonable to expect that it may not always be the case. Moreover, Chaume defines DMs following the structural approach proposed by Schiffrin (1987) and thus the study focuses primarily on the role of DMs as cohesive and connective devices. More importantly, however, Chaume notices that the conventional translations of some DMs, for example of *now* and its Spanish equivalent *ahora* or the English *oh* vs. Spanish *oh*, differ in their core meaning and thus they may fail to render their meaning as a DM. For example, the Spanish *oh* is suggestive of either surprise or disappointment, while the English *oh* is used as an intensifier or is an information management marker used in repairs. It seems obvious then that their renditions might substantially depart from their core semantic meanings in order to retain their context-dependent reading. This observation supports the claim voiced by Aijmer and Simon-Vandenbergen (2006) that it is the meaning potential and the semantic field (or a network of meanings) that is important while searching for translation equivalents rather than single one-to-one correspondences based on prototypical meanings.

Cuenca (2008: 1379) reports that in English-Catalan corpus of film translations the omission of DMs value is 25% in the dubbed version of *Four Weddings and a Funeral*, in the corpus analysed by González and Sol (2004) the value reaches 35.5%, and it is 46% in Matamala's (2004) corpus of English-Catalan film translations. In the material analysed in this paper, the students omitted *well* in translation on average in c. 60%, while the professional subtitles omitted *well* practically in all cases. The results obtained by nonprofessional subtitlers are therefore closer to those obtained by professional dubbing translators reported by Cuenca.

In subtitles, which represent a form of written discourse that floats between the spoken and written text, DMs are recommended to be omitted as a rule, except in a few cases when retaining orality, i.e., features of colloquial language, is the intention of the subtitler. Placing subtitles on a cline between the spoken language and the written discourse, they occupy a mid-way position as they combine selected features of talk spotted with hesitations, reformulations, pauses, interjections, etc., with more ordered and formal language. This shift from the spoken to the written mode of expression, where the written mode also contains vestiges of the spoken mode, is known in audiovisual translation as diamesic shift (Gottlieb 2008: 210). Subtitling is said to be diagonal as it crosses over from the spoken language in the source language to the written text in the target language.

Since the so-called "all-encompassing" words, such as *you know, I think, actually*, typical of spoken discourse, are in principle avoided in subtitling due to time and space constraints (Díaz Cintas and Remael 2007: 151), one may wonder whether it is at all reasonable to analyse different cases of students' translations of *well*. It seems tempting to just set a rule for the subtitler training sessions not to translate *well* at all. As attractive as this suggestion may seem, and as true as it might be in some cases, in line with the polyfunctional approach to DMs (Bozzanella 2006, Aijmer 2013), this marker may convey the whole range of readings and may be a carrier of non-prototypical information, such as attitude towards the topic or interlocutor or imposing authority and power, and thus it may implicitly affect the whole utterance. As already mentioned, being underspecified, *well* gains a fine-grained meaning and function from contextual clues, thus it is necessary that its interpretation be open to new possible options flowing from a given context. *Well* may have little propositional meaning, but as a carrier of metacognitive meaning it has an impact on the interpretation of the utterance which accommodates it. Therefore, the function/meaning of *well* is not to be ignored by a subtitler, and the lexical choices (or grammatical structures) proposed by a subtitler should conflate the function/meaning of *well* and the utterance which hosts it. It is our suggestion to re-consider the legitimacy of either rendering *well* (occasionally) or integrating its function with the whole sentence in which they occur. The latter may be enacted by careful choices of lexical items and grammatical structures that may on the surface depart from the (proto)typical semantic meanings of the markers in the source text, but on the pragmatic-functional level they may convey the message encoded by the original utterance.

4. Corpus data

The data retrieved for the present study have been extracted from a corpus of subtitles written by students of modern languages (Learner Corpus of Subtitles, henceforth LeCoS) as part of their course of translation studies conducted at Kazimierz Wielki University, Bydgoszcz, Poland. The aim of the LeCoS project is to diagnose subtitling skills of the students, to teach them subtitling strategies using students' own subtitles, and to propose some recommendations concerning a future syllabus for the subtitling module. The corpus has been compiled over the last four years and it is now about 1,000,000 tokens in size. Every year a different group of students prepares subtitles for romantic comedies, thus the data are divided into subcorpora representing a given group of students and the film selected for their tutorials. The data analysed in the present paper come from a subcorpus 250,000 words in size (labelled Corpus C). It consists of 20 versions of each subtitle written for *Notting Hill*[2] by 40 students (31 females and 9 males), c. 23 years of age. The trainees are all native speakers of Polish and they are at the language level oscillating between B2 and C1 of the Common European Framework of Reference for Language. The amount of time at the instructor's disposal was limited to one semester spanning 30 hours of classes, so only half of the film was subtitled by the students (about 15 hours of tutorials), from subtitle number 1 to 610. The other half of the module (a. 15 hours) was devoted to (1) the analysis of students' own translations and their correction in line with previously presented subtitling strategies and (2) to the explicit teaching of select subtitling strategies.

5. Data analysis

The approach to data analysis adopted in the present study may be described as hermeneutic. This means that it is interpretative and combines a top-down with bottom-up analysis, which evolved in tandem as the study progressed. Some tentative assumptions concerning, for example, functions of *well* had been assumed, yet as more data were retrieved, the theoretical framework was verified.

Thirty-one subtitles containing *well* have been found in the original soundtrack in Corpus C. Out of these, 25 examples illustrate the sentence-initial position (I) of *well*, five present a mid-sentential (M) position and in one case *well* is used in sentence-final position (F). The sentence-final position sample contains *well* in the function of mitigation of a surprise. The medial cases convey evaluation and hesitation. Sentence-initial examples signal a number of categories, such as: prompt (P), hedging and mitigation (He/M), dis/agreement (D/A), contraposition (Ctr), diffidence (Diff), divergence from expectations (Div), hesitation (H), evaluation (E) and surprise (S). Table 1 shows the distribution of functions of *well* at different discourse organization levels across 31 scenes.

Table 1. Distribution of functions of *well* across scenes and discourse organisation levels in the original soundtrack.

Scene	1	2	3	4	5	6	7	8	9	10	11	12	13	14	15	16
	M	I	I	I	M	I	I	I	I	I	I	F	I	I	I	I
	E	P	He	A	H	HeM	Ctr	P	Diff	D	S	HeM	HeM	E	D	Diff

Scene	17	18	19	20	21	22	23	24	25	26	27	28	29	30	31
	I	I	I	I	I	I	M	I	I	M	M	I	I	I	I
	P	P	S	A	H	HeM	E	HeM	A	H	H	D	Div	D	H

The main categories distinguished for the purpose of the present study comprise: involvement, mitigation, prompt, evaluation, and surprise. In line with Aijmer (2013), involvement may indicate agreement or disagreement; two additional subcategories are included in involvement, namely contraposition (following Cuenca 2008) and divergence from expectations (following Schourup 2001), as they are closely related to the notion of dis/agreement. Most examples found in our corpus represent the category of politeness and/or using softeners (13 occurrences) as well as involvement (9 occurrences). In the whole corpus, the majority of contexts with *well* illustrate hedging/mitigating behaviour (6), hesitation (5 samples) and disagreement (4 samples).

Table 2. Categories and types of functions in the original soundtrack

INVOLVEMENT-9				POLITENESS/ SOFTENERS-13			PROMPT	SURPRISE	EVALUATION
A	D	Ctr	Div	H	Diff	HeM	P	S	E
3	4	1	1	5	2	6	4	2	3

The 31 scenes identified in the original soundtrack represent largely dialogic text and they were categorized in terms of the pragmatic meaning of *well*. Next, the translations of all scenes provided by 20 groups of students were analysed; as a result, 620 subtitled scenes have been examined. The renditions of *well* were classified according to the same pre-established types of functions conveyed by *well*. Surprisingly, instances of *well* were omitted in learners' subtitles at the level of around 62%, while in the professional subtitles almost all instances of *well* were ignored (94%).

The translation of *well* encompasses a wide array of options in the data analysed, in total 41 renditions, and these include (in decreasing order of occurrences): *cóż* (English *well*, as well as: *no cóż, cóż ...*), *więc* (*so*; as well as *więc ..., no więc, tak więc, więc tak*), vocables (*hmm, uhmm, yyy, heh*), three dots, *OK* (as well as *Okej*), *tak* (*yes*, as well as *no tak, tak ...*), *wiesz* (*you know*, as well as *no wiesz, no nie wiem*), *właściwie* (*actually*), *dobrze* (adj. *well*, or *no dobrze*), *ale* (*but*), *h/ej, jasne* (*sure*); and a number of single instances of other translations, such as *noo, oczywiście* (*of course*), *spoko* (slang for *easy*), *chociaż* (*although*), *zgoda* (*deal*, lit. *agreement*), *chyba nie* (*probably not*), *niestety* (*unfortunatelly*), *super, w każdym razie* (*anyway*), *tak że* (*so*), *może* (*maybe*), *dzięki wielkie* (*thanks a lot*), *chwileczkę* (*just a minute*), *no nie* (*oh no*). Strangely enough, the deletable vocables are unnecessarily rendered in most cases. The equivalents proposed by students are not surprising. *Well* is most often rendered as *więc* and *cóż*, which is explicable on the grounds that the two translations are perceived as prototypical, i.e., most often associated with the English equivalent; they are also explained by dictionaries as the conventional translations of *well*. Other equivalents offered by students are context-specific and stem from the pragmatic meaning of the whole utterance; hence they are not provided in lexicographic data but appeared in the corpus at issue.

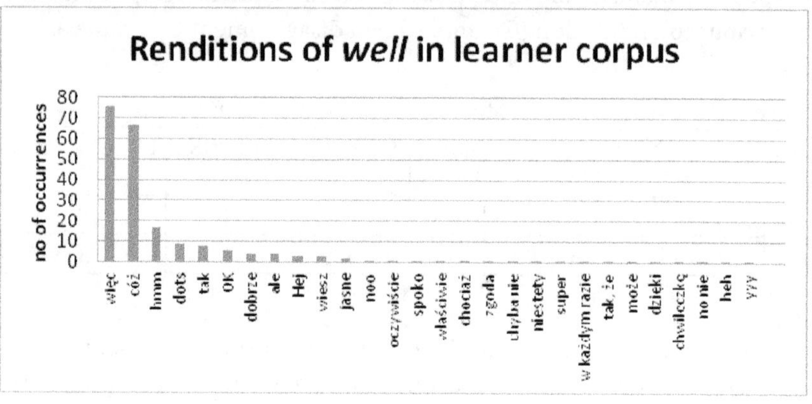

Figure 1

In what follows, we shall present selected fragments of students' subtitles which illustrate (1) omission of *well*, (2) changing *well* into suspension dots, and (3) subtitling *well* and (a) either retaining its original function or (b) shifting it to other functions. Table 3 visualizes shifts of functions, function retention, and omission of *well* across categories and across all 20 groups of students.

Table 3. Functional shifts, function retention and omission of *well* in the LeCoS data.

Func-tions	Types of shifts and number of occurrences						% of shifts	% of no shift within function	Omission within function
E	5H	1A	1S				11,6%	16,7%	71,6%
P	2H	2Diff	2A	5Cont			13,8%	21,3%	65%
HeM	3H	5D	12Cont	1Div	2A	1S	19,2%	29,2%	51,6%
A	5H	1Div	1D	2Ctr	2Diff		18,3%	18,3%	63%
H	3A	7Cont					10%	34%	58%
Ctr	4Cont	2H	1A				36,8%	15,8%	52,6%
Diff	2A	2Cont					10%	7,5%	82,5%
D	8H	4A	3CA3	1Cont			20%	23,8%	56,3%
S	6Cont	3HeM	2A	1Div			30%	5%	65%
Div	3H						15%	15%	70%
Total							Shifts-18,5%	Retention-18,7%	Omission-63,6%

Even cursory examination of the data tabulated in Table 3 allows us to notice that the tendency to retain the original functions by trainees is almost the same as to shift them. This suggests that the students most probably did not analyse the meaning of *well* in terms of its pragmatic functions. Had they tried to adhere to the functional meaning of *well*, the value for retention would exceed the value for shifts. The other conspicuous information emerging from the data is the fact that omission was applied much less frequently than in the case of the professional version, where it oscillates around 100%. The lower value for omission, however, is not necessarily a token of a bad translation as it is retention of the category that appears to be of prior importance for achieving pragmatic equivalence. Finally, of the three techniques analysed in the present paper (omission, retention and shifting), it was nevertheless omission that was most often employed by students.

Considering the coarse-grained categories of functions, when Politeness was not omitted it was more often congruent with the original category. On the other hand, when Involvement was not omitted, it was more often shifted to other functional categories, typically to Continuatives. Evaluation, Prompt and Surprise are the functions most frequently omitted in the trainees' subtitles (with values oscillating between 65% and 71%).

The function which was most often shifted by trainees is Contraposition (a.37%), largely to Continuative (50%). Students who avoided shifts of functions were not eager to retain them (a.16%), rather they resorted to omission (a.53%). The second function most often shifted is Surprise (30%), and, again, in half of the cases it was changed into Continuatives. If students decided against shifting the category, Surprise was rarely retained (5%), rather it was more likely to be omitted altogether (65%).

The retention of the original functions in students' subtitles is most conspicuous in the case of the category of Politeness, specifically Hesitation (34%) and Hedging/Mitigation (a. 29%). As mentioned above (cf. Table 2), Politeness is also the category which is most frequently represented by *well* in the original text (in the fragment under inspection), so it may be concluded that the students' rendition of *well* by and large reflects the aura of politeness present in the original soundtrack.

Omission in the whole corpus of students' subtitles oscillates around 64%. This value is lower than in the case of professional subtitlers, where almost no instances of *well* were rendered (only in four contexts *well* was replaced by suspension dots). The strategy of omission was mostly applied by trainees to: Diffidence (c. 83%), Evaluation (a. 72%), Divergence from expectations (70%), Prompt (a. 65%), Surprise (65%), Hesitation (58%), Disagreement (a. 56%), and Hedging/Mitigation (a. 52%). While diffidence, hesitation and hedging/mitigation are usually retrievable from visual-aural signals (body language, voice pitch and strength, intonation patterns), and thus they are more likely to be omitted in subtitles, the expression of evaluation, disagreement, divergence from expectations or surprise as well as prompting the interlocutor are typically expressed mainly verbally, and thus they are more likely to be retained in subtitles. On the positive side, whenever hesitation, hedging or mitigation were not omitted, their renderings usually mirrored the original function, so they were most often functionally equivalent.

There are four utterances in the professional subtitles (henceforth PS) where vestiges of the original *well* are signalled by three dots. In the sample below, William Thacker, the main character, is involved in internal monologue about a famous American film star who has just arrived in London to shoot her new film. The professional subtitle signals that the character is looking for the right word to describe the fame and glory of the woman.

Scene 1

	Of course I've seen her films ... /and always thought she was, **well**, fabulous.
PS:	Oglądałem jej filmy/i uważałem, że jest ... boska. (I watched her films /and I thought that she was (in Present Tense) ... divine.

Apart from group 10, the non-professional renditions either omit *well* or propose *cóż* as an equivalent of *well*, which remains colloquial and is not typical of written discourse. In group 10, the medial position of three dots follows the footsteps of the professional version.

G10: I zawsze myślałem, że ona była ... cudowna. (And I have always thought that she is (in Past Tense) ... wonderful).

Another group (G13) also proposed three dots but at the end of the utterance, which changes the attitude of the speaker: while deliberation dots in an utterance-medial position before the adjective focus one's attention on the main female character, as the speaker is groping for the right word to describe the woman, when put at the end of the utterance they focus one's attention on the speaker's process of thinking, and thus they highlight the speaker rather than the object of the speaker's description.

G13: I zawsze uważałem, ze jest nieziemska ... (And I've always thought that she is heavenly ...)

Another group places three dots in medial position, which introduces hesitation, followed by stylistically low *cóż*. By so doing, the deliberative function is expressed twice. This subtitle shares most with the professional rendition.

G27: I zawsze myslałam, że była ... cóż, cudowna (And I have always thought that she was ... well, wonderful)

The fact that the students resorted to dots as equivalents of *well* shows that they notice the function of *well* signalling hesitation. This is a good symptom of their awareness of the mood expressed by the utterance. On the whole, however, the three dots are not often used by students in their translations.

Suspension points, as a rule, are used in subtitling to indicate a pause (Chaume 2004b: 17, 198–201). The professional subtitler uses dots to signal deliberation on the one hand, and on the other, to introduce unexpected information and to strengthen comic effect.

Scene 10

- Do you have any books by Dickens?
- No, I'm afraid we're a travel bookshop. We only sell travel books.
- Oh, right. How about the new John Grisham thriller?
- **Well, no**, 'cause that's, uh – that's a novel too, isn't it?

PS: Nie, bo to ... /także powieść, prawda? (No, because it ... / is also a novel, isn't it?)

The suspension pause is placed just before the punch line, which ridicules the previous speaker. This attenuates the speaker's criticism of what he has just heard. Along with *well*, the function of politeness and mitigation is also encoded by a very short vocable *uh*. The overall impression of this utterance is providing a polite reply yet it is coated with a slight irritation. This meaning may be teased out from the professional translation.

Group 21 has proposed a rendition which expresses politeness and mitigation, thus the function of disagreement is downgraded. Even so, the comic effect has been also retained. The utterance-initial vocable is followed by an expression of hesitation (*no nie wiem*) (colloquial phrase "I don't know"), which is additionally intensified by *chyba* ("perhaps," "probably") in the next line of the subtitle.

G21: Hmm no nie wiem ... /To chyba też nowela prawda? (Hmm well I don't know ... /It is probably a novella too, isn't it?)

Group 24 has resorted to irony expressed through a question. It also contains the comic effect as the viewer is aware that the speaker knows the book by Dickens is a novel and thus cannot be found in a travel bookshop. The use of an indirect speech act renders both disagreement and mitigation well as criticism expressed through the interrogative is milder than when expressed by a declarative yet it is definitely sensed in this utterance. Disagreement thus is not as blatant as in the professional subtitle but stronger than in G21.

G24: A to przypadkiem też nie jest powieść? (Isn't it by any chance a novel too?)

Students who decided to translate *well* proposed renderings which did not always reflect the DM category present in the original soundtrack. Among the cases when *well* was shifted most often are Contraposition, Surprise and Disagreement. Regrettably, the shifts changed the meaning of the whole utterance. Cases in which the function of *well* were retained comprise three categories – Hesitation, Hedging/Mitigation and Disagreement.

In Scene 12, William Thacker arrives to Anna Scott's apartment to meet her but he is unaware that he will find a number of journalists there ready to interview her. Anna's manager, who shows him in, assumes that William is also a journalist and asks him which journal he represents. Surprised by this question, William looks away for a moment to think about what to say when he notices a magazine (*Horse and Hound*) lying on a coffee table nearby. He mentions the title in his reply. In the sample below *well* is attached to a question encoding, as it seems, surprise uttered by the manager. The function of *well* as such, however, is not solely a surprise, rather it has an attenuating function, which reduces the woman's spontaneous reaction that may be perceived as tactless. It could potentially encode only surprise, were it stressed by a higher pitch of voice at the onset of the falling intonation pattern. In this context, the intonation is falling, the pitch of voice is low, and the word is not stressed. The meaning of *well* may be read here as "it is surprising but it's okay."

Scene 12

306

And you're from, uh, "Horse and Hound."

307

Is that so? **Well**.

PS: Naprawdę? (Really?)

G11: **Więc**? (So?)

The professional subtitler focused only on the feeling of surprise encoded by the utterance preceding *well*, while nonprofessional rendering offered a drastic change of the function from surprise to prompt. The mitigating role of *well* in the utterance-final position is ignored in both cases.

In the samples below, we may observe several subtitles that illustrate the problem of rendering *well* by either changing the grammatical structure or lexical items of the whole utterance instead of a literal translation of *well.* In scene 7, the professional subtitler bypassed the DM and rendered only the main content, which sounds stylistically and semantically appropriate in Polish.

Scene 7

	Well, on second thought,//um, maybe it's not that bad after all.
PS:	Jeśli się zastanowić, wcale nie jest zła. (If you think of it, it is not that bad at all.)

The main category in this sample is hesitation. The speaker says something like "I am going to express my opinion which is contrary to my prior opinion." The professional rendition conveys the notion of hesitation by resorting to a conditional sentence. In this way, the function of hesitation is integrated with the whole utterance and the DM *well* could be omitted without any loss. G10 used the word *właściwie* ("actually") in the place of *well,* followed by a phrase *po namyśle* ("on second thought"). Even though *właściwie* is a typical example of "all-encompassing words" mentioned above, leaving it out would affect the function of hesitation. On the other hand, deleting *on second thought* in the translation would keep this function. The situation is similar in the rendering offered by G11.

G10:	**Właściwie** po namyśle/może wcale nie jest taka zła. (Actually, on second thought/maybe it's not that bad.)
G11:	**Chociaż** z drugiej strony, może to nie jest aż takie złe. (Though, on the other hand, maybe it is not that bad.)

Groups 13 and 14 adhered to the equivalent of *well* only, yet the mood encoded by the category in question is also retained.

G13:	**W sumie**, to ona nie jest aż taka zła. (In essence, it is not that bad.)
G14:	**Być może** nie jest taka zła, za jaką ją uważałem. (Maybe it is not as bad as I thought before.)

The above renderings demonstrate that *well* may be subtitled through its integration with the utterance rather than its stand-alone literal translation, and its function and meaning may be mirrored either through a change of grammatical structure of the utterance or via changing lexical choices.

The next sample illustrates a shift of category from Hesitation to Agreement. The original text presents an opposing viewpoint on the quality of a book a customer is going to buy. At first, the salesman (the main character) discourages the customer (the main female character) from buying a guidebook, but once the woman decides to buy it despite the man's discouragement, William wants to withdraw from his previous opinion and praises the woman's choice, trying thus to share common ground with her. In this context, *well* may be interpreted as "I have changed my mind, maybe I was wrong, and I feel awkward about it."

Scene 7

	Well, on second thought,/um, maybe it's not that bad after all.
G22:	**Zgoda**, po namyśle,/może nie jest taka zła. (All right, on second thought/maybe it is not that bad.)

The rendition offered by G22 is suggestive of a situation where the word *zgoda* (meaning "I agree") signals agreement. It implies that following an exchange of opinions finally the speaker agrees with the interlocutor. However, in this scene the woman is hardly speaking and approaches the man in silence. The man's part, on the other hand, resembles a monologue. He is trying to catch the woman's attention as she is a famous American film star who visits his modest bookshop, so he keeps talking (about guidebooks on Turkey). The word *zgoda* introduces a sense of an ongoing exchange of opinions, which is not the case. In the original soundtrack, the use of *well* is to attenuate the awkward situation stemming from a sudden change of opinion and a surprising recommendation of a book that has just been criticized. Likewise, the vocable *um* and the lexical choice *after all*, which is semantically empty, mitigates incoherence of his opinion. All these elements are clear attempts by the man to save his face. This mitigation has been rendered by the professional translator and the students in distinct ways:

PS:	Jeśli się zastanowić, wcale nie jest zła. (If you think of it it is not that bad at all.)

G27: Jakby się dłużej nad tym zastanowić um, może nie jest najgorsza. (If you think about it longer um, maybe it is not the worst (book).)

G12: Chociaż z drugiej strony, może to nie jest aż takie złe. (Although, on the other hand, maybe it is not that bad at all.)

The professional version resorts to a structural change and introduces first conditional. Likewise, group 27 uses first conditional, which has a mitigating function. Other groups decided on lexical choices – *właściwie, chociaż, w sumie, być może* ("actually," "although," "in essence," "maybe") – all of which perform mitigating functions carried in the original version by *well*. The attenuation is introduced to justify the woman's choice.

Scene 9 exemplifies diffidence of the main character, who rather lacks self-confidence and seems intimidated by the fact that a beautiful woman and a film star is in his flat. The weightiness of this visit is emphasized by the modest man when just before saying good-bye he admits that it was heavenly for him to meet her. When they say good-bye the situation becomes awkward. William, the main character, is very hesitant throughout the conversation. The woman thanks him for inviting her and William replies:

Scene 9

Yeah./**Well**, my pleasure.

G20: Nie ma za co. (You're welcome.)

Diffidence seems to be lost in this rendering, rather self-assurance and indifference emerge. These words contradict the visual signals available on-screen: the man does not know what to do with his hands, there are pauses in the conversation, and vocables betray his hesitation and the feeling of awkwardness. The professional subtitler copes with the situation by adding three dots to mark uncertainty and diffidence of the man, combined with his confusion and embarrassment.

PS: Tak ... Cała przyjemność po mojej stronie. (Yes ... The pleasure is mine.)

Hesitation is changed into certainty (agreement) in the citation below (G16). The scene shows the main character walking along Portobello Road in London on his way to his travel bookshop. The shop he owns does not generate too much income, hence the owner is hesitant while saying that he sells travel books, as he does not actually sell many of them. Group 16 glossed *well* as *oczywiście* ("of course"), which deprived the subtitle of hesitation. This may result from the fact that the viewer learns about the financial problems of the business only in the subsequent subtitle and the students did not allow for this upcoming information while writing their rendition (even though they had seen the whole scene prior to the task of subtitling). This example shows that it is important to approach writing subtitles above the sentence level as the function of an utterance may span longer stretches of speech.

Scene 5

	This is work, by the way, /my little travel bookshop,
49	(- Morning, Martin./- Morning, Monsignor.)
50	which, um, **well**, sells travel books.
G16:	48 To jest praca, i przy okazji,/Mój mały sklep z książkami podróżniczymi, (This is work, and by the way,/ my little travel bookshop)
50	w której, **oczywiście**, sprzedaję książki podróżnicze. (in which, of course, I sell travel books.)

Cases recognized by students as belonging to the category of Continuatives marred the subtitles most conspicuously – signalling that an utterance is a continuation of the previous utterance seemed to be least expected by a potential viewer who is already aware of how the given conversation pans out. At the interactional level they play the role of a filler (an "all-encompassing word") and at the textual level they function as transition or digression. These functions are not crucial factors in terms of propositional content and thus can be deleted without a great loss for a viewer. In Scene 6, the bookshop owner notices a dishonest customer stealing a book by putting it into his trousers. Instead of accusing the customer of theft, to minimize the threat to his face, the owner approaches him and says in a calm and polite way that the book should be either bought or (taken out of the man's trousers and) put on the shelf, otherwise he will call the police. The owner explains to the customer that there are cameras in the bookshop and thus he saw the man stealing the book. As a result, the customer is considering withdrawing from the act of stealing by saying:

Scene 6

Customer: Okay. What if ... I did//have a book down my trousers?
Owner: **Well**, ideally,/when I went back to the desk,//you'd remove the Cadogan Guide/to Bali from your trousers ... //and either wipe it/and put it back or buy it.

The initial *well* proceeding *ideally* conveys something like "in this case." It signals a sequence of possible events in a polite form; in this way *well* functions here as a face-threat mitigator. In the trainees' subtitles, politeness is changed into continuative by G16, and thus mitigation was replaced by focusing on a sequence of events. This function does not seem to add any propositional value to the understanding of the scene and thus keeping it in the subtitle is less than helpful. It unnecessarily introduces a sense of a consequence, which may be easily omitted in a subtitle as an example of an all-encompassing word.

G16:
Customer: Okay. A co jesli mam książkę w moich spodniach ?
Owner: **Wtedy**, wrócę do kasy,//Ty wyciągniesz ze swoich spodni przewodnik po Bali ... //i wyczyścisz go i odłożysz albo kupisz. (Then, I'll go back to my desk// you take out the guide to Bali ... / and wipe it and put it back or buy it.)

Students' translations did not always entail categorical shifts. In the example below, the original agreement (along with evaluation and hesitation) is present in some Polish renditions. The main character's roommate is trying on several T-shirts while preparing for a date and asking William for his opinion. G18 proposed an interesting solution of using a metaphor *strzelić w dziesiątkę* ("scored the bull's eye") to emphasize the pithiness of the choice. G15 used a simple form expressing agreement straightforwardly and left out *well.* The professional subtitle is also explicit in expressing agreement, yet at the same time hesitation is retained by means of three dots in the place of the backchannel item *uhm.* Group 12, too, resorted to omission of *well* and using three dots to stress hesitation originally encoded by *uhm*; however, this was achieved at the cost of keeping agreement in the background (it is expressed only implicitly).

Scene 4

	Well, yeah. Yeah, that's – /that's, um, perfect.
G18:	Hmmm ... To jest strzał w dziesiątkę! (lit. This is a shot in the centre (of a chart); i.e. you scored the bull's eye)
G15:	Tak, idealna.
PS:	Tak. Ten jest ... /idealny. (Yes. This is ... /ideal.)
G12:	Ta jest ... idealna. (This is ... ideal.)

Another example illustrates the rendition of *well* into *ale* (*but*) to express impatience being illustrative of a prompt. The scene shows William Thacker (WT) walking in a street of London and bumping into Anne Scott (AS) while looking at something else on the other side of the street that caught his attention. As a result, he spilt his take-away coffee and juice he had just bought on the woman's T-shirt. He immediately offered going to his place, which was just across the street, so that she could wash and change her clothes. The woman is angry but, in the absence of other reasonable options, after some hesitation finally decides to accept the invitation.

Scene 8

WT:	I'm really sorry./I – I live just over the street. //I have, um, water and soap./You can get cleaned up.
AS:	No, thank you./I just need to get my car back.
WT:	I also have a phone./I'm confident that in five minutes ... //we could have you spic-and-span/and back on the street again.//In the non-prostitute sense,/obviously.
AS:	All right. **Well** – What do you mean,/"just over the street" ?
G10:	No dobra. **Ale** – Co masz na myśli mówiąc,/"przy tej ulicy" ? (OK. But–what do you mean by saying „over the street"?)

Interestingly, the original *well* is translated as *ale* ("but"), which drifts away substantially from the conventional (lexicographic) equivalent *cóż* or *więc* conveying hesitation or consequence. *Ale* is a rather unusual option for the word *well* as such, but it may fit perfectly well in this context, when the meaning of *well* is examined on turn level. The sense of anger and irritation permeates the whole scene, and given the visual and aural signals, *well* is emotionally invested and functions in this context as a prompt; it means something like "Given the circumstances,

I might consider your offer but I need more details." The same function may be easily ascribed to *ale* in this scene, which urges the man to give more details and introduces a sense of opposition. One of the groups (G26) offered a very similar translation but *well* was rendered as *więc*, which introduces an aura of consequence and agreement. Given the visual-aural signals *więc* is less congruent with the scene than *ale*.

An interesting case is presented in the next example. The scene shows several people (family and friends) sitting at a table and having a competition for telling the saddest story about oneself. The winner gets the last brownie. One of the hosts, having finished his story, concludes that he deserves the last brownie as the sad story about his life misfortunes was best. The host's husband protests and encourages the main character (William) to tell a story about himself, suggesting in this way that his life is full of failures. The utterance begins with *well*, which at first glance expresses hesitation; when analysed with *I don't know*, which follows it, however, together they function as a hedger, wherein the words mitigate the disagreement expressed by the whole turn. In the subsequent words, the host is pointing verbally at another person ("Look at William") thus implicitly expressing disagreement with the previous speaker.

Scene 28

538 But surely that's worth a brownie.
539 **Well**, I don't know./Look at William.

The overall meaning of the scene is thus disagreement, even though at the sentence level it encodes mitigation, and at the word level hesitation can be sensed. This example shows that meaning cannot be analysed at the local level but should allow for a wider context, at least at the speech-act level. The professional subtitler proposed the following rendition:

PS: No nie wiem. A William? (I don't know, really. And William?)

In this translation *well* has been rendered by *no* (colloquial translation of "well") and merged with the next words to make one phrase *No nie wiem* ("Well, I don't know," "I don't really know"). This option conveys doubt and it attenuates disagreement, which is further stressed by drawing attention to William, who is another (better) candidate for the winner.

As a result, the whole scene in the PS version retains disagreement, the overpowering category, as well as hedging/mitigation through which disagreement is signalled. A number of trainees employed a similar strategy (G12, G23, G24, G26). Group 18 followed the same strategy but expressed disagreement more strongly (*Nie byłbym taki pewien*, "I wouldn't be so sure") and thereby weakened hesitation.

G18:	538 Ale z pewnością to jest warte ostatniego kawałka ciasta. (But surely this is worth the last brownie.)
539	Nie byłbym taki pewien. Spójrz na Williama. (I wouldn't be so sure. Look at William.)

Bearing in mind that the whole scene conveys first and foremost disagreement, it is tempting to recommend the structure proposed by G18. Given the time and space constraints a subtitler must reckon with (the maximum six second exposure and maximum 72 characters per two-liner), both versions can do justice in this case. The professional version contains 35 characters displayed during slightly more than five seconds, and the longer version consists of 43 characters.

Concluding remarks

This paper has demonstrated that students tend to over-rely upon the original soundtrack and imitate the nature of the spoken discourse to an unnecessary extent, which results in creating texts full of vocables or mars them with an excessive number of short lexical discourse markers like *well*. The other observation concerns the fact that the suggested renditions of *well* are not always at the appropriate stylistic level. Importantly, *well* per se does not have to be subtitled literally but because its meaning often affects the mood and attitude expressed by the utterance in which it occurs, and thereby the interpretation of the whole utterance may change, *well* should be considered and rendered by integrating the mood/attitude it conveys into a host utterance. This integration may be achieved through the use of certain grammatical structures or by lexical choices which reflect both the content of an utterance and the emotional and attitudinal stance encoded by *well*. Another suggestion for future subtitler training stemming from these conclusions may be that *well* should be rendered with lesser frequency as it is an element typical of the spoken discourse specific item and thus writing its equivalents should take place only in special cases, such as when achieving special rhetoric purposes, marking the epistemic stance of the speaker or when expressing politeness. Finally, it is important to analyse discourse above the word or sentence level and focus on the speech-act level, or even beyond speech-acts, as the pragmatic meaning of *well* seen in isolation may differ substantially from one spanning the whole utterance or turn.

Theoretically, the investigation supports Aijmer's claims concerning the distribution of *well* and the network model of meaning. In our data, the majority of contexts contained *well* in declarative sentences in the utterance-initial position and in the function of involvement or politeness. The study also supports the claim of *well* being a polyfunctional item, which forms a network of interrelated meanings without the necessity to decide on one prototypical meaning. The network model of meaning endorsed in the present account has been supported by our data as a number of readings have been identified, some of which may seem distinct yet may be grouped in larger categories (such as involvement). This fact notwithstanding, while the two most often used equivalents of *well* surface in our data (*cóż* and *więc*), it is difficult to find one core (prototypical) meaning of all the senses occurring in the students' subtitles at issue. Rather than seeking the single proper meaning, it seems advisable to delineate a pool of meaning potential and to establish correspondences between two languages on the level of the semantic fields or networks of meanings. Considering the fact that *well* is underspecified and gains its meaning from contextual clues, finding functional correspondences between meanings remaining within one semantic field or network of meanings fares better to the description of the meaning potential of *well* in the compared languages, and thus to its translations.

Notes

1 The translation of *well* in literary translation into Italian was examined by Bozzanella (2006).

2 *Notting Hill* was released in 1999 and directed by Roger Michell. The main characters are Anna Scott (Julia Roberts) and William Thacker (Hugh Grant).

3 CA stands for the category of Calling Attention.

References

Abraham, W. (ed.). (1991). *Discourse Particles: descriptive and theoretical investigations on the logical, syntactic and pragmatic properties of discourse particles in German*. Amsterdam: John Benjamins. http://dx.doi.org/10.1075/pbns.12.

Aijmer, K. (2002). *English Discourse Particles: Evidence from a corpus*. Amsterdam: John Benjamins. http://dx.doi.org/10.1075/scl.10.

Aijmer, K., A. Foolen, and A.-M. Simon-Vandenbergern. (2006). "Pragmatic markers in translation: a methodological approach." In *Approaches to Discourse Particles*, ed. K. Fischer, 101–114. Amsterdam: John Benjamins.

Aijmer, K. (2013). *Understanding Pragmatic Markers*. Edinburgh: Edinburgh University Press.

Aijmer, K., and A.-M. Simon-Vandenbergen. (2006). "The discourse particle well and its equivalents in Swedish and Dutch." *Linguistics* 41 (6): 1123–1161.

Andersen, G. (2001). *English Discourse Particles: evidence from a corpus*. Amsterdam: John Benjamins.

Ariel, M. 1994. *Pragmatic operators. The Encyclopedia of Language and Linguistics.*, 3250–3253. Oxford: Pergamon Press.

Bączkowska, A. (2011). *Space, Time and Language: a cognitive analysis of English prepositions*. Bydgoszcz: Kazimierz Wielki University.

Biber, D., S. Johansson, G. Leech, S. Conrad, and E. Finegan. (1999). *Longman Grammar of Spoken and Written English*. London: Pearson Education.

Blakemore, D. (1987). *Semantic Constraints on Relevance*. Oxford: Blackwell.

Blakemore, D. (2002). *Relevance and Linguistic Meaning: the semantics and pragmatics of discourse markers*. Cambridge: CUP. http://dx.doi.org/10.1017/CBO9780511486456.

Blakemore, D. (2004). "Discourse markers." In *Handbook of Pragmatics*, ed. L.P. Horn and G. Ward, 221–240. Oxford: Blackwell.

Bolinger, D. (1989). *Intonation and its Uses: melody and grammar in discourse*. Stanford: Stanford University Press.

Bozzanella, C. (2006). "Discourse markers in Italian: towards a compositional meaning." In K. Firscher, (ed.), *Approaches to Discourse Markers*, 449–464. Amsterdam: John Benjamins.

Brinton, L.J. (1996). *Pragmatic Markers in English: grammaticalization and discourse functions*. Berlin: Mouton de Gruyter. http://dx.doi.org/10.1515/9783110907582.

Carlson, L. (1984). *'Well' in Dialogue Games: a discourse analysis of the interjection 'well' in idealized conversation*. Amsterdam: Benjamins. http://dx.doi.org/10.1075/pb.v.5.

Carter, R.A., and M.J. McCarthy. (2006). *The Cambridge Grammar of English*. Cambridge: CUP.

Chaume, F. (2004a). "Discourse markers in audiovisual translating." *Meta* 49 (4): 843–55. http://dx.doi.org/10.7202/009785ar.

Chaume, F. (2004b). *Cine y Traducción*. Madrid: Cátedra.

Cuenca, M.J. (2008). "Pragmatic markers in contrast: the case of *well*." *Journal of Pragmatics* 40 (8): 1373–91. http://dx.doi.org/10.1016/j.pragma.2008.02.013.

Díaz Cintas, J., and A. Remael. (2007.) *Audiovisual Translation: subtitling*. Manchester: St. Jerome.

Faerch, C., and G. Kasper. (1984). "Two ways of defining communication strategies." *Language Learning* 34 (1): 45–63. http://dx.doi.org/10.1111/j.1467-1770.1984.tb00995.x.

Fischer, K. (1999). "Die Ikonizität der Pause. Zwischen kognitiver Last und kommunikativer Funktion." In: I. Wachsmuth, B. Jung (eds.), KogWis99: Proceedings der 4. Fachtagung der Gesellschaft für Kognitionswissenschaft, Bielefeld, 28. September - 1. Oktober 1999. nfix, Sankt Augustin. pp. 250–255.

Fischer, K. (2006). "Towards an understanding of the spectrum of approaches to discourse particles: introduction to the volume." In K. Fischer, (ed.), *Approaches to Discourse Particles*, 1–18. Amsterdam: John Benjamins.

Fraser, B. (1996). "Pragmatic markers." *Pragmatics* 6:167–90.

Fraser, B. (2006). "Towards a theory of discourse markers." In K. Fischer (ed.), *Approaches to Discourse Markers*, 189–204. Oxford: Elsevier.

González, M., and U. Sol. (2004). *Pragmatic Markers in Oral Narrative: the case of English and Catalan*. Amsterdam: John Benjamins. http://dx.doi.org/10.1075/pbns.122.

Gottlieb, H. (2008). "Multidimensional translation." In A. Schjoldager, H. Gottlieb and I. Klitgård (eds), *Understanding Translation*, 39–66. Aarhus: Academica.

Johansson, M. (2006). "Constructing objects of discourse in the broadcast political interview." *Journal of Pragmatics* 38 (2): 216–29. http://dx.doi.org/10.1016/j.pragma.2005.06.016.

Jucker, A.H. (1993). "The discourse marker *well*: a relevance-theoretical account." *Journal of Pragmatics* 19 (5): 435–52. http://dx.doi.org/10.1016/0378-2166(93)90004-9.

Jucker, A.H., and Y. Ziv. (1998). "Discourse Markers: introduction." In A.H. Jucker and Y. Ziv (eds), *Discourse Markers*, 1–12. Amsterdam: John Benjamins. http://dx.doi.org/10.1075/pbns.57.03juc.

Knot, A., and T. Sanders. (1998). "The classification of coherence relations and their linguistic markers: An exploration of two languages." *Journal of Pragmatics* 30 (2): 135–75. http://dx.doi.org/10.1016/S0378-2166(98)00023-X.

Kroon, C. (1995). *Discourse Particles in Latin. A Study of nam, enim, autem, vero, and at*. Amsterdam: Giebven.

Labove, W. and D. Fanshel. (1987). *Therapeutic Discourse*. New York: Academic Press.

Lakoff, R. (1973). "Questionable answers and answerable questions." In ed. B.B. Kachru, R.B. Lees, Y. Malkiel, A. Pietrangeli and S. Saporta, *Issues in Linguistics: Papers in Honour of Henry and Renée Kahane*, 453–467. Champaign: University of Illinois Press.

Lenk, U. (1998). "Discourse markers and global coherence in conversation." *Journal of Pragmatics* 30 (2): 245–57. http://dx.doi.org/10.1016/S0378-2166(98)00027-7.

Levinson, S.C. (1983). *Pragmatics*. Cambridge: Cambridge University Press.

Lewandowska-Tomaszczyk, B. (2007). "Polysemy, prototypes and radial categories." In D. Geeraerts and H. Cuyckens (eds), *The Oxford Handbook of Cognitive Linguistics*, 139–169. Oxford: OUP.

Matamala, A. (2004). *Les interjeccions en un corpus audiovisual. Descripció i representació lexicogràfica*. PhD dissertation. Universitat Pompeu Fabra.

Ochs, E. (1996). "Linguistic resources for socializing humanity." In J.J. Gumperz and S.C. Levinson (eds), *Rethinking Linguistic Relativity*, 407–437. Cambridge: Cambridge University Press.
Östman, J.-O. (1981). *"You Know": a discourse-functional study*. Amsterdam: John Benjamins.
Owen, M. (1981). "Conversational units and the use of 'well." In P. Werth (ed.), *Conversation and Discourse. Structure and Interpretation*, 155–178. London: Croom-Helm.
Redeker, G. (1991). "Review of Schiffrin, 1987." *Linguistics* 29:1139–72.
Schiffrin, D. (1987). *Discourse Markers*. Cambridge: Cambridge University Press. http://dx.doi.org/10.1017/CBO9780511611841.
Schourup, L. (1985). *Common Discourse Particles in English Conversation*. New York: Garland.
Schourup, L. (2001). "Rethinking *well*." *Journal of Pragmatics* 33 (7): 1025–60. http://dx.doi.org/10.1016/S0378-2166(00)00053-9.
Stenström, A.-B. (1990). "Lexical items peculiar to spoken discourse." In J. Svartvik (ed.), *The London-Lund Corpus of Spoken English: description and research*, 137–176. Lund: Lund University Press.
Svartvik, J. (1980). "*Well* in conversation." In S. Greenbaum, G. Leech and J. Svartvik (eds), *Studies in English Linguistics for Randolph Quirk*, 167–177. London: Longman.
Zwicky, A. (1985). "Clitics and particles." *Language* 61 (2): 283–305. http://dx.doi.org/10.2307/414146.

Translating introductions and wishes in audio-visual dialogue. Evidence from a corpus

Veronica Bonsignori
Silvia Bruti[1]

Abstract

In previous studies (Bonsignori, Bruti, Masi 2011, 2012), we have focused on greetings, leave-takings and good wishes as "complex" expressions that convey a vast array of socio-pragmatic meanings. The importance of such expressions and the consequences of their complexities in translation in general and in dubbing in particular have also emerged, especially as they correspond to cultural practices and habits.

This paper investigates the role of two rather neglected conversational routines, namely introductions and good wishes, in audiovisual dialogue by establishing how much narrative space they are granted, which specific linguistic features they have, how frequent conventional expressions are used in both original dialogues and translation, and, finally, the emerging patterns of translation in dubbing.

1. Introduction

As hinted at before, the aim is to discuss the role of introductions and good wishes in audiovisual texts and in their translation. Given the centrality of TV products, the study focuses on the use of such routines in two recent Anglo-American TV series which have both been dubbed into Italian and broadcast on various national and private channels.

The data are retrieved from a small self-compiled parallel corpus which comprises the transcription of the original dialogues of two seasons (one for each series) of *Brothers & Sisters* and *Gilmore Girls*,[2] and their dubbed versions into Italian. Both series are mostly "conversational", as they are centred on the conversational exchanges between characters in their everyday life, a fact that potentially grants more space to the use of the two types of conversational routines under investigation.

The reference framework of this work and the previous ones from which it has developed is a multidisciplinary approach, more specifically, one that integrates corpus-based approaches to translation and an analysis of audiovisual dialogue with the aim of identifying general trends in terms of language use and translational practices, as in the works by Pavesi (2005), Romero Fresco (2006; 2009), Freddi and Pavesi (2009), and Baños-Piñero and Chaume (2009).

2. The nature of conversational routines

The label of conversational routines was first used by Florian Coulmas in 1981 to encompass a whole series of speech acts that convey a vast array of socio-pragmatic meanings and that are rather repetitive in form. They include greetings, leave-takings, compliments, thanks, apologies and the like. As Bardovi-Harlig (2013) points out, these expressions are referred to with a plurality of terms, among which routine, formula, or formulaic expressions (many of which used in the seminal volume edited by Coulmas in 1981). Despite their somewhat predictable nature, these expressions turn out to be quite complex in translation as they presuppose practices and habits that change across cultures. As Laver (1981: 304) puts it, "routines of greeting and parting, far from being relatively meaningless and mechanical social behaviour" are particularly important strategies for the negotiation and control of social identity and social relationships between participants in a conversation.

Within this group, requests and apologies have perhaps been granted more attention. Quite recently also greetings have been focused upon, in that they betray different attitudes associated to different politeness requirements in lingua-cultures. As Coulmas (1979: 239) makes clear, the pragmatic conditions of their appropriate use can be accounted for "in terms of cognitive systems of beliefs, wants, wishes, preferences, norms, and values" (1979: 239–266).

Yet, the nature of conversational routines appears to be irregular and uneven. Requests,[3] for example, only occur *ex ante* and set a transaction in motion, whereas apologies, which also belong to transactions, are not initiative like requests, but occur most typically *ex post*, i.e., as a sanctioning move at the end of a speech event. These speech acts are quite different from greetings, good wishes and introductions, whose purpose can be described as the exchange of expressions and pleasantries between two people or a group interacting for the purpose of fulfilling social duties or for the purpose of creating or consolidating rapport. In most cases, greetings are used as a prelude to making a proper conversation or introducing the topic of a talk. Their specular counterpart, i.e., leave-takings, appear instead in closing sequences when people part and they neatly round off a conversation. Coulmas (1981: 11) ascribes frequency and distribution of routines to two main factors, the organization of the speech community and the structural order of its language. He exemplifies the first parameter by making reference to Japanese culture, in which, quite evidently, routines abound because they respond to Japanese etiquette and politeness requirements. The second factor has to do with the fact that many routines can be used to smooth up interaction, as they may signal important transitional points in conversation, such as turn-taking management. Other parameters that account for the frequency and the nature of conversational routines are the degree of formality among speakers and the familiarity of the situation of utterance, and the genre of the text under consideration. The first factor is quite intuitive: the more speakers are familiar with one another, the less social rituals and politeness norms are needed. That also explains why unmitigated directives are perfectly acceptable when two requirements are met: either the situation is extremely urgent and makes it possible to dispense with politeness norms, or the speakers are on friendly terms. The genre of the text also has a direct bearing on the use of social rituals: if in spontaneous conversation much time is granted to phatic talk, i.e., talk that is conducive to solidarity but does not achieve other discursive aims, in other genres social chit-chat might be far less employed. This is, for example, the case of cinematic language: both films and television employ language that is planned to sound natural but is in fact carefully scripted and rehearsed (cf., among many, Taylor 1999, Baños-Piñero, Chaume 2009, Chaume 2012). Furthermore, a film or an episode of a TV series are – to a different extent but in similar ways

– severely limited in time and thus need to squeeze the narrative into the time boundaries imposed by the format. So there is usually little time for phatic talk and sequences that do not favour plot progression, unless they are instrumental to the current situation. To make an example from the data we will analyse later, sometimes the first meeting between two people is not shown onscreen, to save precious showing time, but the introduction is "reabsorbed" in the departure formula that these people use, e.g. saying something like 'It has been a pleasure meeting you'.

3. Introductions and good wishes

Both introductions and wishes are conversational routines, but they have been rarely focused upon as more marginal rituals in interaction. They both belong to phatic talk, although their nature is quite different. Introducing people is a necessary step to establish contact prior to interacting, so it is unavoidable to be able to communicate for a purpose, to go beyond the stage of mere talk-for-talk's-sake. Good wishes (Verschueren 1981: 135) are similar to compliments, in that they are, as Kerbrat-Orecchioni says (1987), kinds of "verbal gifts". They often employ unoriginal and formulaic expressions, which normally accompany social rituals such as celebrations, festivities and the like, and may be inserted in closing sequences. Even though wishes make use of ritual talk, they are a good way to show one's social interest in people and their welfare.

In our previous works on conversational routines in film language (Bonsignori, Bruti, Masi 2011, 2012), we mainly focused on opening and closing sequences, analysing thoroughly all those more or less formulaic expressions that were used to greet and take the leave, including introductions and good wishes, to which only marginal attention was devoted.

For the present study, a description of the macro-functions and linguistic categories that will be investigated in the next paragraph is in order. First of all, as reported in Bonsignori, Bruti, Masi (2012), among the relevant macro-functions, Introductions [I] as well as Openings [O] tend to occur at the beginning of conversational exchanges, while Closings [C] tend to correlate with final turns and, finally, Wishes [W] are much more flexible as to sequential positioning. Second of all, concerning the linguistic categories that fulfil the macro-functions just mentioned, in the present work we are going to concentrate on introductory formulae [*i*], e.g. *nice to meet you, how do you do, my name is…*, *it's me* (in phone calls); and good wishes [*w*], e.g. *good luck, have fun, cheers* (in toasts). However, since it is possible to find various linguistic expressions in the same turn, here follows a list of all the remaining categories:

g = greetings proper, e.g. *hello, hi, hey, good morning,* etc.
v = vocatives, e.g. *darling, Mr President, is that Joan?* (in phone calls);
ℓ1 = leave-takings with formulaic expressions, e.g. good forms, *bye bye, see you, farewell,* etc.
ℓ2 = leave-takings with slightly less formulaic expressions. These usually involve additions and/or variations, as well as more restricted applicability to situations of use (cf. *see you* or *see you later* vs. the more specific *see you at my wedding*); this category also covers expressions with motion verbs, which are rather fixed in their format, but manifest the intention of leaving rather than expressing a salutation, e.g. *I must go, I'm off*;
p = more or less formulaic expressions of phatic communion (sometimes also called small talk), e.g. *How are you?, Good to see you!,* along with less formulaic speech acts, e.g. thanking, apologizing, and promising, which typically open or close the exchange and which may have, for example, the function of defusing the potential hostility of silence at the beginning of an exchange or that of mitigating and consolidating at the end (see Bonsignori, Bruti, Masi 2011);
x = a hybrid category accommodating speech acts of various natures; even though they may represent either the very first turn of speech or the last one in a conversational exchange, they do not appear to fulfil any of the phatic functions associated with expressions that typically occur in the Opening or Closing phases of interaction. Examples from this category might be an Opening with a directive, an order issued by a boss towards his/her employee, or a Closing with an expressive act, such as a compliment or thanks.
α = used for classifying expressive gestures in relevant positions (e.g. bowing, blowing a kiss, shaking hands).

As for the medium of communication, it is specified whether the exchange is: a telephone call (T) (including intercom and radio programmes), a letter or written message (L), an internet chat (C), an SMS (sms), an email (E), or a video call (V) (cf. Bonsignori, Bruti, Masi 2012: 359–60).

However, in the present work, we will be focusing on exchanges of TV dialogue where introductions and good wishes are present, either as part of the same macro-function (indicated as I and W) or occurring as part of others, in both original and dubbed dialogues (indicated in this case as *i* and *w*).

4. The language of TV Series

TV series have gained enormous popularity over the last decades, to the point that they have given rise to a community of TV watchers that know everything about their favourite programmes. As Italian TV critic Aldo Grasso has recently stated (2011), TV series have replaced the so-called classic novel in the "sentimental education" of adolescents and youngsters. He claims that there is no pronounced difference between the classical novel and this new narrative text, the main divergences residing in the different medium and language that are used. The result is a hybrid product, both in content and style. As for content, TV series may be thematic, but more often they can hardly be defined as belonging to only one genre, so much so that the term that is often used to classify some of them is "dramedy". Even medical or legal series (e.g. *House, M.D., Scrubs*, or *Law & Order, The Good Wife*) are mainly dramatic, but accommodate humorous elements (Bednarek 2010: 13–14).

The two main factors responsible for the differences between TV series and films are their broadcasting time and modality. Episodes last for approximately 40 minutes, so dialogues have to be constructed with this time limit in mind as well as with twists and turns in the plot to keep the audience's attention alive.

Series have two different types of plots, a horizontal one, which extends over several episodes or the whole season; and a vertical one, which, on the contrary, is limited to a single episode. In this case the story begins and ends within the boundaries of the episode. Occasional viewers, who are not necessarily familiar with minute details of the vertical plot, might take advantage of recaps of past events or episodes in the lives of some of the characters. To this end, TV series very often employ flashbacks and flashforwards which explain episodes in the lives of the characters.

Specific features of TV series also include more technical choices that affect editing and camera use: as Creeber (2004: 115) points out, close ups are very often used to convey confidential conversation, whereas quickly edited scenes serve the purpose of meshing different storylines together.

The dialogues of TV series are a subtype of "scripted/constructed dialogue" (Bednarek 2010: 63), similarly to film and dramatic dialogue, but with some specific features of their own, having to do with the above-described requirements and with genre constraints. The comparability of fictional (either film or television) dialogue with spontaneous conversation has been the object of debate, with more space granted, until very recently, to film products. Results basically depend on the different stance towards the study of audiovisual products: for example, specialized studies like Quaglio (2009a, 2009b) and Forchini (2012), both relying on Biber's (1988) multidimensional corpus methodology, highlight rather similar uses and patterning between fictional and spontaneous conversation, for example in dealing with the so-called "interpersonal dimension" (Biber 1988). Analyses of some specific features of fictional dialogue, e.g. vague language in Quaglio (2009b), show however that differences with spontaneous conversation might affect frequency but certainly go beyond it, as they intersect the need for comprehensibility of the show and its search for attractiveness.

Studies that rely on corpus methodology but that also advocate taking into account the conventions of audiovisual dialogues and of the specific genre the audiovisual product belongs to, like Baños-Piñero and Chaume (2009) and Baños-Piñero (2013), arrive at somewhat different conclusions. Scriptwriters purposely select features of spontaneous conversation that are recognized as such by the public, but struggle between the two opposite poles of creativity and standardization, and tend to conform to the rules of synchronism in dubbed products, to the norms imposed by dubbing studios (e.g. as for standardization, self-censorship, patronage), and to the strong link that exists between image and word (Chaume 2012, Baños-Piñero 2013).

As hinted at above, the majority of the studies on this topic analyze the language of films, so there is still much work to do on the language of TV series and their translation, following in the footsteps of illuminating works such as Quaglio (2009a), Romero-Fresco (2006; 2009), Bednarek (2010), Baños-Piñero (2013).

5. The corpus

The data were retrieved from a small self-compiled parallel corpus which comprises transcriptions of the original dialogues of two recent Anglo-American TV series, namely *Brothers & Sisters* and *Gilmore Girls*, and their dubbed versions into Italian. Both series are mostly "conversational", as they are centred on the conversational exchanges between characters in their everyday life, a fact that potentially grants more space to the two types of conversational routines under investigation.

Gilmore Girls is an American dramedy that debuted on the WB television network in 2000 and ended in its seventh season in 2007.

The show revolves around the lives of a single mother, Lorelai Gilmore (interpreted by Golden Globe nominee Lauren Graham) and her daughter Rory (played by Teen Choice Award winner Alexis Bledel) in the fictional town of Stars Hollow, Connecticut. The series is well-known for its fast-paced dialogue[4] filled with pop-culture references and has earned several award nominations, among which, notably, one Emmy Award in 2004. *Brothers & Sisters* is an American family drama that premiered on ABC in 2006 and ended in its fifth season in 2011. The show centres on the Walker family and their life in Pasadena, California, especially focusing on the relationships among five siblings (interpreted by Calista Flockhart and Rachel Griffith, among others) and their mother (played by Emmy Award winner Sally Field), their love lives and business fortunes. For this reason, the situations that are shown on-screen are everyday and familiar, like the language being used.

For the purposes of the present study, episodes from 1 to 11 of Season 3 of *GG* (2002–2003) and of Season 1 of *BS* (2006–2007) have been transcribed in their original and dubbed version.

6. Analysis

As stated in the introductory paragraph to introductions and wishes, the present section is devoted to the analysis of the sequences in which introductions and wishes are present, both as macro-functions and as linguistic categories. The aim of this paper is in fact to shed light on the role of these two rather neglected conversational routines in audiovisual dialogue by ascertaining how much narrative space they are given, which specific linguistic features they have, how frequent stock phrases are used in both original dialogues and translation, and, finally, the emerging patterns of translation in dubbing.

6.1. Introductions

Generally, introductions are well-represented in the 11 episodes of both season 1 of *BS* and season 3 of *GG*, with a minimum of one to a maximum of nine sequences per episode – e.g. episode 3 of *GG* is characterized by the highest number of introduction sequences – and occurring in all episodes of the two TV series, even though the overall number is higher in *GG* than in *BS* – i.e., 39 vs. 31 sequences. In fact, the number of introductions contained in *GG* is nearly double than that in *BS* – i.e., 74 vs. 44, respectively – and therefore also the types of expressions employed are more varied. Generally speaking, the phrases used in this kind of speech act, especially when they are used as macro-function [I], are multiple and vary according to the situational context, which may be more or less formal, thus requiring a certain variation in register, to whether a third party introduces two strangers or the interlocutor introduces himself/herself, and finally, to the stage of the introduction process, that is the actual introduction or the following "introductory" greeting[6]. Compare the examples below:

(1) [***GG*** **S03e10**]

LORELAI to Michel:	Oh, Michel, great!
to Gran:	Gran, **I'd like you to meet Michel Gerard, our concierge.** > I-*i*-*i*
to Michel:	Michel, **this is my grandmother, Lorelai.** > I-*i*-*i*
MICHEL to Gran:	((bowing)) **Very pleased to meet you.** > I-*i*-*α*

(2) [***BS*** **S01e05**]

AMBER to Kittty:	Miss Walker? **I'm Amber. I'm your new intern.** If you need absolutely anything, just ask. > I-*i*-*i*
KITTY:	**Hi, Amber.** Um, you know, you can uh – call me Kitty. > I-*g*-*ν*

(3) [***GG*** **S03e10**]

RORY to Clara	**That's** Jess. > I-*i*
to Jess:	**This is** Clara. > I-*i*

In example (1) from *GG*, Lorelai is having lunch with her posh aristocratic grandmother at the restaurant of her own inn and is happy to introduce her to some members of her staff, among whom, Michel, the French concierge. As can be noticed, when she addresses to her granny she uses a rather formal phrase to introduce Michel, while when she addresses to him, she prefers the simpler, neutral and most commonly used phrase 'this is x[7]'. Such difference in register expresses the kind of relationship between Lorelai and the two interlocutors: friendship with Michel, with whom she spends much of her time, sharing the same workplace, and formal detachment towards her grandmother, whom she sees every now and then and who is very concerned with etiquette and high class privileges. The social gap between the two people being introduced is also mirrored in the extremely polite and obsequious introduction greeting Michel addresses to Lorelai's grandmother accompanying it with a bow. Comparing example (1) with (3), still from *GG*, we can notice a downgrade in register, since the introduction sequence in (3) is among peers, more specifically among youngsters, therefore the use of more informal phrases such as 'this is x' and 'that's y' is perfectly suited to the situational context. Finally, example (2) from *BS* shows a case in which the interlocutor formally introduces herself to her new boss, Kitty, by simply using the phrase 'I'm x', followed by a more detailed description of her subordinate role. In her reply, Kitty prefers to use a more informal tone and therefore asks Amber to call her simply Kitty instead of Ms Walker, a request that is in line with the kind of greeting she uses in the introduction sequence, that is the very informal greeting proper 'hi'.

The choice of certain introduction phrases may also depend on the medium used. This is the case of the phrase 'N + speaking', which is in fact always uttered on the phone. Other phrases can also become suitable expressions in such contexts, and in all these cases they tend to occur in Opening sequences [O]. See the following examples:

(4) [*GG* S03e01]

LORELAI:	((answering the phone at the inn)) Independence Inn, Lorelai **speaking**. > (T) O-*i*-*i*

(5) [*BS* S01e09]

SARAH to Joe:	((on the phone)) Hey, Joe. **It's** me. I'm gonna be a little longer than I thought. > (T) O-*g*-*v*-*i*

(6) [*BS* S01e11]

HOLLY:	((answering the phone at work)) Holly Harper. > (T) O-*i*

All the introduction phrases used in the episodes of the two TV series analyzed are listed in Table 1, which shows an equal number of tokens in *BS* and *GG*, but a different number of types, which are much more varied in the latter series.

Table 1. types of introduction phrases in *BS* vs. *GG*.

Introduction phrases	***BS***	***GG***
This is x	8 (1T)	14 (3T)
x	16 (7T)	7
That's x	1	1
I want you to meet x	1	1
I'd like you to meet x	-	1
Here's x	-	1
You've got x	-	1
You must be x	2	-
Say hello to x	-	1
Descriptions	-	3
I'm x	11	5
It's x	4 (3T)	3 (2T)
My name's x	-	1(T)
x + x + speaking	-	5(T)
Tot.	43	44

As can be noticed in Table 1, apart from various formulaic expressions, introductions can also be made using "descriptions," as in the examples below:

(7) [***GG* S03e04**]
DEBBIE to audience: (...) We have two local luminaries here to talk to us today. **You probably all recognize Luke Danes from his fabulous diner.** > I-*I*
But we're really excited to begin with **a former Stars Hollow High mom, Lorelai Gilmore**. > I-*i*

As regards introductory greetings and, broadly speaking, the phrases used in replies, occurring either in Introduction or Opening sequences [I; O], the formulaic phrase 'nice to meet you' is the only one occurring in both TV series. However, *GG* displays a higher number and also a wider range of expressions that are variants of such phrase and which are totally absent in *BS* (cf. Table 2). Moreover, as can be seen in (8) and (9), other very common linguistic expressions that can be used in these contexts are greetings proper, such as 'hi,' 'hello' and 'hey,' which may accompany an introduction phrase proper or stand alone (cf. example 9):

(8) [*BS* S01e01]

JACK to Warren:	Oh, no, no, no, no. Hold up. **I want you to meet Kitty Walker.** > I-*i*
to Kitty:	Kitty, Warren Slater. Warren's our blue chair guy. > I-*i*-*i*
WARREN to Kitty:	**Nice to meet you.** > I-*i*
JACK to Warren:	Hi, **nice to meet you.** > I-*g*-*i*

(9) [*BS* S01e04]

SCOTTY to Randy:	Randy, **this is the lawyer I mentioned. Uh, Kevin Walker.** > I-*i*
to Kevin:	**Randy Stuart.** > I-*i*
KEVIN to Randy:	*Hi.* > I-*g*
JACK to Warren:	*Hi.* I've heard a lot about you. > I-*g*

(10) [*GG* S03e03]

JENNIFER to Lorelai and Rory: **It's nice to meet you**. > I-*i*
LORELAI: **Likewise**. > I-*i*

In example (10), a variation of 'nice to meet you' is used, to which the interlocutor replies with a very informal phrase, namely 'likewise,' which, together with similar expressions such as 'same here' and 'you too,' appears to be quite frequently used in Introduction sequences.

Table 2. Types of introductory greetings and reply phrases in *BS* vs. *GG*.

Introductory greetings and reply phrases	***BS***	***GG***
Nice to meet you	4	7
It's nice to meet you	-	1
It's very nice to meet you	-	1
Very nice to meet you	-	1
Very pleased to meet you	-	1
It's a pleasure	-	1
Likewise	-	1
Same here	-	1
You too	-	1
Greetings proper (*hi, hello, hey*)	19	23
Tot.	23	38

Finally, introduction phrases can also be found in Closing sequences [C], and apparently they are quite formulaic in nature. One of the most frequent type is 'nice to meet you' and all its variants, as shown in examples (11) and (12). However, it is worth noticing that in the last example the reply phrase 'same here' is also used by Rory to take leave. Sometimes references to an introduction that has not been shown onscreen are located in Closings, as this is a very economical way of condensing essential diegetic information.

(11) [*BS* S01e01]
WARREN: **Pleasure to meet you.** > C-*i*
KITTY: **Nice to meet you.** > C-*i*

(12) [*GG* S03e08]
PROF. HARRIS: **It was very nice meeting you.** > C-*i*
RORY: **Same here.** > C-*i*

Table 3 shows the types of introduction phrases used in Closing sequences in the two TV series: both types and tokens are much more frequent in *GG*, which also provides a wider set of expressions than *BS*.

Table 3. Types of introduction phrases in Closing sequences in *BS* vs. *GG*.

Introduction phrases in Closings	***BS***	***GG***
Nice to meet you	2	2
It was very nice meeting you	1	3
It was a pleasure to meet you	-	1
Pleasure to meet you	1	-
I'm glad to have met you	-	1
Nice knowing you	-	1
Same here	-	3
Tot.	4	11

6.1.1. Introductions in dubbing

In the present section we aim to compare the translating solutions of the various more or less formulaic phrases used in Introduction sequences in the two TV series under investigation in the Italian dub. Generally, as mentioned in the previous section, when strangers are introduced, the most typical phrases are 'this is x', 'that's x' and the simple use of the name of the person being introduced: there are not relevant differences in the dub of *BS* and *GG*, since in the first two cases the usual corresponding expressions in Italian are employed, that is *lui/lei è x* and *questo/a è x*, as in examples (13) and (14), while the same structure is maintained in the third case, as in example (15) below, where the only difference is the addition of a vocative in the target text:

(13) [*BS* S01e01]

CHARACTER	ORIGINAL	TYPE	DUBBING	TYPE
JUSTIN to Kevin	Kevin, this is Fawn.	I-*i*	Kevin, lei è Fawn.	I-*i*
to Fawn	Fawn, this is Kevin.	I-*i*	Fawn, lui è Kevin.	I-*i*

(14) [*BS* S01e08]

CHARACTER	ORIGINAL	TYPE	DUBBING	TYPE
JUSTIN to Tyler	**Uh – that's Fawn.** Um – she was just having a bad day.	I-*i*	**Questa è – Fawn.** Ieri – ha avuto una brutta giornata.	I-*i*

(15) [*GG* S03e05]

CHARACTER	ORIGINAL	TYPE	DUBBING	TYPE
EMILY to Lorelai	Ignore her, Natalie is just being Natalie.	I-*i*	Ignorala, ormai non cambia più.	I-*i*
to Natalie	**My daughter, Lorelai.**	I-*i*	*Natalie*, **mia figlia Lorelai.**	I-*v*-*i*

Moreover, when longer expressions are used, e.g. 'I want you to meet x' and 'I'd like you to meet x', the same Italian counterpart is employed in dubbing, namely *Ti/Le presento x.*

Differently, when someone introduces himself/herself directly to someone else or on the phone, using phrases like 'I'm x', 'It's x' or simply using his/her name, the dubbed version of *BS* is characterized by a wider set of translating options per type than *GG*. For instance, taking 'I'm x' as an example, together with the common phrases *Io sono/Sono x* and *(Io) Mi chiamo x*, in *BS* the name of the person or the name preceded by the first personal pronoun singular *Io* can also be found, as in the following example:

(16) [*BS* S01e07]

CHARACTER	ORIGINAL	TYPE	DUBBING	TYPE
WARREN	Well, uh, looks like you guys had the same idea we did. ***I'm Warren,*** **by the way.**	I-*i*	Ehm, è chiaro che avete avuto la nostra stessa idea. **A proposito, *sono Warren.***	I-*i*
DAVID	***I'm David,*** **Nora's contractor.**	I-*i*	***Io David,*** **lavoro per Nora.**	I-*i*

Concerning Introductions on the phone, which are usually included in Opening sequences, various translating options are employed, especially in *GG*, to render the same phrase, namely '*x* + *x* + speaking'. In fact, such phrase, used by Lorelai to answer the phone at work, occurs six times in the 11 episodes analysed and it is translated in two different ways in the Italian dub, as shown in (17) and (18) below:

(17) [*GG* S03e01]

CHARACTER	ORIGINAL	TYPE	DUBBING	TYPE
LORELAI (answering the phone)	**Independence Inn, Lorelai *speaking.***	(T) O-*i*-*i*	**Independence Inn, *sono* Lorelai.**	(T) O-*i*-*i*

(18) [*GG* S03e10]

CHARACTER	ORIGINAL	TYPE	DUBBING	TYPE
LORELAI (answering the phone)	**Independence Inn, Lorelai *speaking.***	(T) O-*i*-*i*	**Independence Inn, *parla* Lorelai.**	(T) O-*i*-*i*

There are three occurrences for each translating option in the target text, but the one with the verb 'be' sounds much more natural than the alternative with the verb 'speak', which closely follows the structure of the original.

As far as introductory greetings and responses are concerned, the wider repertoire of expressions used in *GG* is retained in its dubbed version as well, as can be observed in Table 4.

Table 4. Types of introductory greetings and reply phrases in the dub of *BS* vs. *GG*.

Introductory greetings and reply phrases	***BS***	***GG***
Nice to meet you	(1) Molto piacere (1) Piacere mio (1) Piacere di conoscerti (1) Anche a me	(3) Molto piacere (1) Piacere mio (1) Piacere di conoscerti (1) Lieta di conoscerti (1) Piacere
It's nice to meet you	-	(1) Lieta di conoscervi
It's very nice to meet you	-	(1) È un vero piacere conoscerla
Very nice to meet you	-	(1) È un vero piacere conoscerti
Very pleased to meet you	-	(1) Molto lieto di conoscerla
It's a pleasure	-	(1) Piacere
Likewise	-	(1) Piacere nostro
Same here	-	(1) Il piacere è mio
You too	-	(1) Piacere mio
Tot.	4	15

Table 4 does not comprise greetings proper as introductory greetings, because they deserve special attention. In fact, they can be translated either as greetings proper within an Introduction sequence or using a typical introduction phrase in the Italian dub, as in example (19):

(19) [*GG* S03e03]

CHARACTER	ORIGINAL	TYPE	DUBBING	TYPE
DARREN to Lorelai and Rory	Lorelai, Rory, ***say hello to* Marie, my wife.**	I-*v*-*i*	Lorelai, Rory, ***lei è* mia moglie, Marie.**	I-*v*-*i*
MARIE to Lorelai and Rory	*Hello*, so good to have you here.	I-*g*-*p*	**Molto lieta!** Sono così felice di avervi con noi!	I-*i*-*p*
LORELAI	*Hi.*	I-*g*	*Salve.*	I-*g*

As can be noticed, in the original version (19) showcases a rather unusual phrase being used by a third party to introduce strangers, which is transposed in a more formulaic way in the Italian dub. Then, both Marie on the one hand and Lorelai and Rory on the other use introductory greetings that are translated differently in the dubbed version: 'hello' is turned into the introduction phrase *Molto lieta*, while 'hi' is rendered with the greeting proper *salve*, so that the same linguistic category as in the source text is preserved. However, it is worth pointing out that the second translating option type is widely more used, with only three instances of the first, which are probably employed when necessary to make the whole sequence sound more natural by explicitly using typical expressions that pertain to the Introduction script.

Finally, a few words on the translation of introduction phrases in Closing sequences are in order. The highest number of types and tokens in *GG* is mirrored in its Italian dubbed version, which is characterized by an even wider set of expressions, which may also involve a change in the linguistic category. For instance, in (20) the phrase 'nice to meet you' is translated with the corresponding Italian counterpart in the target text, while in (21) it is substituted by a phatic phrase – roughly corresponding to 'excuse me' – to take leave:

(20) [*GG* S03e05]

CHARACTER	ORIGINAL	TYPE	DUBBING	TYPE
NATALIE	***Nice to meet you.***	C-*i*	**Piacere di averti conosciuto.**	C-*i*
LORELAI	**Same here.**	C-*i*	**Piacere mio.**	C-*i*

(21) [*GG* S03e10]

CHARACTER	ORIGINAL	TYPE	DUBBING	TYPE
SOOKIE to all	Okay, well, **nice to meet you**. I have to get back. We have quite a tight schedule to follow.	C-*i*-*ℓ2*-*x*	Ok, bene, ***ora chiedo scusa,*** ma devo andare. Abbiamo dei ritmi serrati.	C-*p*-*ℓ2*-*x*

6.2. Wishes

On the whole wishes are very few, with practically no gap in the number of occurrences between the two series (32 in *GG* and 36 in *BS*), whereas the difference in frequency for Introductions is remarkable, with *GG* scoring almost the double of *BS*.

Quite expectedly, wishes are used in some episodes and not in others, as they are strongly plot-dependent. It is true, however, that in both series there are frequent familiar gatherings or celebrations where wishes are exchanged.

In *BS*, wishes tend to appear in dedicated sequences, as "pure" Wishes, i.e., with no other ancillary function attached. In fact, 24 out of 36 wishes belong to this type, 10 appear instead in Closings and 2 in Openings.

(22) [***BS* S01e05**]
JONATHAN to all: Well, I'd like to make a toast. To Nora, who has kindly offered to endure the encroachment of me and my business in her lovely home. Thank you. > W-*w*

As can be noticed, the wish in (22) occurs within a family reunion, and Jonathan, the addressee's daughter's fiancé, uses it together with other face-enhancing or face-flattering acts (Kerbrat-Orecchioni 1987: 31), i.e., thanks and compliments, with the purpose of ingratiating her.

The same cannot be said for *GG*, in which wishes are mostly located in Openings (12 instances) and Closings (15 instances), with only five occurrences featuring as independent acts.

(23) [***GG* S03e09**]
BABETTE to Lorelai and Rory: Oh, hey there dollfaces. Happy Thanksgiving! > O-*g*-*v*-*w*

(24) [***GG* S03e03**]
CAROL to Rory: Good luck with Harvard. > C-*w*

In (23) Babette greets both Lorelai and Rory with some nice complimenting words and wishing them a happy Thanksgiving day, while in (24) Carol takes leave from Rory, who is about to start her new life in Harvard. In both cases, wishes integrate into the texture of greetings and leave-takings, adding complimentary words aimed at making the interlocutor feel at the centre of the speaker's concern and being taken care of. In these cases, wishes qualify as phatic talk, given their prefabricated nature and conventionality of use: it is in fact part of unwritten conversational rules that this kind of rapid wishes can substitute greeting and leave-taking formulae in conversational exchanges. When Wishes proper are used, the function is also phatic, but the presence of a contextualized scenario makes the act situation-bound and thus more significant for advancing the plot.

The occurrences of Wishes proper in *GG* are evenly distributed among the most typical types: 2 instances of 'congratulations', 1 'good luck' and 3 'Happy Thanksgiving'. In BS as well the set of types is also quite limited: in episode one there are 8 occurrences, of which 6 are toasts (only one being 'cheers'), and 2 'happy birthday'; in episode four there are 2 'cheers'; in episode five again 3 toasts, of which 1 'cheers' and 2 'to Nora'; in episode six 3 toasts (2 'cheers' and 1 'to Tommy'), and in episode nine 6 toasts (4 'cheers' and 3 'to the + N' formula) and 2 'Happy Thanksgiving'. In both series, as hinted at before, Wishes are concentrated in a few episodes, where they are used to describe celebrations. The majority are very routinized universal formulae, with the only exception of 'Happy Thanksgiving', which is typically American. The relatively high frequency of scenes depicting the celebration of Thanksgiving in these series – but in American series in general – makes it a typical feature and influences the perception of this cultural element also in the countries where the audiovisual product is distributed as a dubbed version. The Italian TV audience is by now familiar with the ritual of Thanksgiving thanks to the many American series and films that have been broadcast over the years.

As happens for Introductions (see e.g. 19), some character occasionally employs original phrasing to perform social rites.

(25) [*BS* S01e10]

ORIGINAL	DUBBING	
HOLLY to all	Enjoy your bankruptcy.> C-*w*	Vi auguro buona bancarotta.> C-*w*

In (25) the wish occurs in a closing sequence, in which Holly Harper leaves the scene in a rage. In fact Sarah, Tommy and Saul tried to deceive her upon finding out that William Walker had left her 10 million dollars. The wish counts as a farewell but exploits the rhetorical power of irony: on the surface level the formula looks like a wish because the word 'enjoy' is used, but what Holly really feels is the reverse: she wishes them to revel in their pride as she will stand apart watching them sink with their company, Ojai Foods.

6.2.1. Wishes in dubbing

There are almost no discrepancies between the original and the Italian dub as far as wishes are concerned. The only cases worth mentioning occur both in *GG*.

In (26) it is evident that the pattern used in the two versions is different: the original is a more explicit kind of leave-taking, because of the expression 'I'm going home', which is instead eliminated in the dubbing.

(26) [*GG* S03e07]

ORIGINAL	**DUBBING**	
SOOKIE to Lorelai	Well, I'm going home to figure out what I want. **Good luck.** Call me tomorrow.> C-*ℓ2-w-x*	Bene, a casa deciderò cosa voglio. **Buona fortuna!** Chiamami domani, eh?> C-*w-x*

In (27), on the contrary, the wish is only used in the Italian dub, whereas the utterance by Lorelai in the original is a generic greeting expression.

(27) [*GG* S03e09]

ORIGINAL	**DUBBING**	
LORELAI to Korean guest	Yung Kwan, *good to see you.*> O-*v-p*	Ah, **buon Ringraziamento**, giovane Kwan!> O-*w-v*

6.3. Some quantitative trends

The data for introductions and wishes were not abundant and the analysis was carried out manually, although we ran the concordancer of the free software AntConc 3.3.5w to check some of the most expected patterns, i.e., '... to meet you' for Introductions and 'happy ...' for Wishes. The first one yielded 20 results, 14 in *GG* and six in *BS*.

Table 5. Concordances for *...to meet you.*

1	Warren Salter. Warren's our blue chair guy. nice *to meet you.* Hi, nice to meet you. – Red hot? Wow!	B&S_S1_1.txt
2	's our blue chair guy. Nice *to meet you.* Hi, nice to meet you. – Red hot? Wow! So, I get blue – Oh	B&S_S1_1.txt
3	re together already? C'mon, it's insane! Pleasure *to meet you.* Nice to meet you. What are you doing	B&S_S1_1.txt
4	y? C'mon, it's insane! Pleasure *to meet you.* Nice to meet you. What are you doing in Saul's office?	B&S_S1_1.txt
5	es," or Sarah, Kevin's sister. Yeah. Scotty. Nice *to meet you.* For a second I thought maybe you were	B&S_S1_3.txt
6	together. So, um, we, come on. Let's go. Nice *to meet you,* Randy. We'll wait in the car. Night	B&S_S1_4.txt
7	Lorelai, this is Joe. Joe, Lorelai. Hi. Nice *to meet you.* This is Alex, my partner. Business pa	GG_S03e11.txt
8	iness partner. Oh, clarification duly noted. Nice *to meet you.* Joe and I worked together one summer	GG_S03e11.txt
9	lo, I'm Lorelai Gilmore. Darren Springsteen, nice *to meet you.* And this must be the reason we're a	GG_S03e03.txt
10	er, this is Lorelai and Rory. Hi there. It's nice *to meet you.* Likewise. Hi. Jack's premed at Prince	GG_S03e03.txt
11	lo and a book, that's my daughter Rory. Very nice *to meet you,* Lorelai. Nice to meet you too, Dwight	GG_S03e05.txt
12	ughter Rory. Very nice *to meet you,* Lorelai. Nice to meet you too, Dwight. Welcome to the neighbourho	GG_S03e05.txt
13	is just being Natalie. My daughter, Lorelai. Nice *to meet you.* Your mother's got such spunk. You mus	GG_S03e05.txt
14	h, now, stop it. You're humble. Don't be. Nice *to meet you.* Same here. Edna's group wants to give	GG_S03e05.txt
15	tanley Appleman. Mmhm. Okay, well, it's very nice *to meet you.* Stanley's said the nicest things abou	GG_S03e07.txt
16	w Haven. I need a cab company. It was a pleasure *to meet you.* I'll read that book you recommended.	GG_S03e08.txt
17	. This is Rory Gilmore and Mrs. Gilmore. Hi, nice *to meet you.* Oh, same here. I think I've seen you	GG_S03e09.txt
18	at the auction. Good to see you again. Yes. Nice *to meet you.* Yes, you, too. Same here. And this is	GG_S03e09.txt
19	is my grandmother, Lorelai. ((bow)) Very pleased *to meet you.* Do you have a pen? The – Uh, why, of	GG_S03e10.txt
20	to be there. Yes, apparently so. Okay, well, nice *to meet you.* I have to get back. We have quite a t	GG_S03e10.txt

From Table 5 it appears that querying the corpus for keywords only yields some of the occurrences, and that even using wildcards we would probably miss some interesting cases.

When we ran the search for the supposed keyword 'happy ...' (cf. Table 6), we came across a higher number of occurrences, but not all of them are Wishes: quite the contrary only 23 out of 66 are Wishes (concordances 4, 12, 13, 14, 15, 17, and from 50 to 66).

Table 6. Concordances for *happy...*

1	Hey, sweetie, let me – let me take this. Are you *happy now*? Excuse me? You heard me. Sarah, stop i	B&S-S1_7.txt
2	's not really our place ... No. No. No. If Kitty's *happy*. Hey, Hey. No, look, Not at all. I – I can't	B&S_S1_1.txt
3	Boo! Hey, Kit. I ordered you a martini. You look *happy*. I guess I do. I don't know, I don't know, I	B&S_S1_1.txt
4	opped loving. Not for one moment of her 38 years. *Happy* Birthday, Baby! Cheers. Thank you.It	B&S_S1_1.txt
5	I get a little something on the side, everyone's *happy*. You really saying you're surprised? No, I'm	B&S_S1_3.txt
6	had stopped cutting my hair. Mom and Dad look so *happy*. Yo, Julia is a babe. Mommy, save me! Slow d	B&S_S1_4.txt
7	o, I got – I got – I don't think your sister is *happy*. Well, give her time. I don't mean it that w	B&S_S1_6.txt
8	of my brother? Don't you want your brother to be *happy*? The sad thing is, Nora, Neither one of us r	B&S_S1_6.txt
9	e left as soon as we were finished. She ... wasn't *happy*. Excuse me. Hello? No, it's his stepmom. Who	B&S_S1_8.txt
10	n intact. Don't worry about that, man. Dan's just *happy* to see a woman out of uniform, you know? Lif	B&S_S1_9.txt
11	ours. Okay, Tommy, 500 miles, two cars later, you *happy* now? Yeah, come on, Tommy, let's go. We've g	B&S_S1_9.txt
12	se.Sure. What should I tell the senator? Hello? *Happy* Thanksgiving, and good interview. I thought	B&S_S1_9.txt
13	nk about it. Oh, yeah. Yeah, I'll think about it. *Happy* Thanksgiving, Senator. You, too. That's inc	B&S_S1_9.txt
14	m – I'm so grateful to all of you. Cheers. Cheers. *Happy* Thanksgiving, everyone! Happy Thanksgiving!	B&S_S1_9.txt
15	ou. Cheers. Cheers. Happy Thanksgiving, everyone! *Happy* Thanksgiving! Cheers. Go ahead. It's the rig	B&S_S1_9.txt

16	nowflake. What did you expect? That Mom would be *happy* to retrain one generation of Walkers. Unlike	B&S_S1_10.txt
17	's what I'm gonna do. I love you. You're so gay. *Happy* Holidays. If you've come here to bully me o	B&S_S1_10.txt
18	d no depth, that it wasn't real. It wasn't a big, *happy* family like you had, but it was real, Nora.	B&S_S1_10.txt
19	king him hate me. Hey, he hates us both now. You *happy*? No. I need a drink. You think there's any	B&S_S1_11.txt
20	e's a nice guy with good taste. I'm his Daisy. Be *happy* later. Right. I'm going in. Independence Inn	GG_S03e11.txt
21	and I want it to feel like our house. I'm totally *happy* with the way this house feels. How can you b	GG_S03e01.txt
22	put it back the way it was. No, I want you to be *happy*! I was happy, I told you I was happy, you ju	GG_S03e01.txt
23	the way it was. No, I want you to be happy! I was *happy*, I told you I was happy, you just didn't wan	GG_S03e01.txt
24	nt you to be happy! I was happy, I told you I was *happy*, you just didn't wanna believe I was happy!	GG_S03e01.txt
25	I was happy, you just didn't wanna believe I was *happy*! We'll just check on them a little later.	GG_S03e01.txt
26	s too important – Mom. And I just want you to be *happy*. Mom! All I did was think about what you sai	GG_S03e01.txt
27	s you. You are not serious. I just want you to be *happy*. "Hello, Headmaster Charleston, this is my s	GG_S03e02.txt
28	n, I welcome you. Assemblies like this are always *happy* ones for me. Initiating in a new group of sc	GG_S03e02.txt
29	id? Yes, I do. Well, good thing we're in time for *happy* hour. Wine, Lorelai? Uh, yeah, if there's an	GG_S03e02.txt
30	om. She's okay with anything I do. As long as I'm *happy*, she's good. You're sure? I'm very sure. The	GG_S03e03.txt
31	, and that his brother Bruce Springsteen would be *happy* to come and play at our next party or event.	GG_S03e03.txt
32	i to her and to Bill, and by the way, yes, I'd be *happy* to talk to the class. Terrific! Oh, the gang	GG_S03e04.txt
33	er all, she's your mother and she wants you to be *happy* ... On some level, I think. Maybe not. What a	GG_S03e04.txt
34	you by extension because, well, if one person is *happy*, then the other person is happy, and so I ha	GG_S03e04.txt
35	if one person is happy, then the other person is *happy*, and so I had an idea that, of how I could b	GG_S03e04.txt

36	okay. Something wrong? Uh, no. No, I just ... No. *Happy*? Thrilled. Now a tie with that would be just	GG_S03e04.txt
37	so good of you both to do this, really. Oh, we're *happy* to be here, right? Yup, zippity doo dah. Oh,	GG_S03e04.txt
38	for when I wow you with my brilliance. I'm really *happy* to be here with you all today. I recognize a	GG_S03e04.txt
39	at you bad back. That's right. Oh, that makes you *happy*? I'd do backflips but I am way too cool. Tha	GG_S03e04.txt
40	? LUKE: Yeah, I'm fine, I'm great. It's a big fat *happy* sunshine day for me. LORELAI: Business looks	GG_S03e05.txt
41	. So it's a girl? Yeah. Christopher would've been *happy* with either, but I really wanted a ballerina	GG_S03e06.txt
42	that. I'm glad you're here. Good. Chris would be *happy* you're here, too. Oh, great. I have to tell	GG_S03e06.txt
43	pose. I would respect her more. I just hope Dad's *happy*. Happy? With Sherry and G.G., the five o'clo	GG_S03e06.txt
44	would respect her more. I just hope Dad's *happy*. Happy? With Sherry and G.G., the five o'clock ball	GG_S03e06.txt
45	ow he thought about me all the time. Okay, there, *happy*? Wow, he likes you. I left an impression. Yo	GG_S03e07.txt
46	t for everybody. I know, but – Although I'm quite *happy* going an entire day without having to deal w	GG_S03e07.txt
47	s thing. Rory's made her choice, I want her to be *happy*. I'm just hoping for the best at this point.	GG_S03e08.txt
48	st amazing boyfriend in the world. You made me so *happy*. You made me laugh. You made my mother like	GG_S03e08.txt
49	le. Most people are very forgettable. And they're *happy*. They had their cats. And their raccoons. An	GG_S03e09.txt
50	n't mean we did. Good. That's good to hear. Well, *Happy* Thanksgiving. Yeah, Happy Thanksgiving. Oh	GG_S03e09.txt
51	t's good to hear. Well, *Happy* Thanksgiving. Yeah, Happy Thanksgiving. Oh, pretty! Yeah, good selec	GG_S03e09.txt
52	at some more. And eat and eat. Ah, the Gilmores. *Happy* Thanksgiving. Happy Thanksgiving. Happy Than	GG_S03e09.txt
53	t and eat. Ah, the Gilmores. Happy Thanksgiving. *Happy* Thanksgiving. Happy Thanksgiving. Come in. S	GG_S03e09.txt
54	Gilmores. Happy Thanksgiving. *Happy* Thanksgiving. Happy Thanksgiving. Come in. She's in a good mood	GG_S03e09.txt
55	u around town. Yeah, that might be a possibility. *Happy* Thanksgiving. Same to you. Hymn 17 please. Y	GG_S03e09.txt

56	e was anticipating my napkin manoeuvre. Hi, hon! *Happy* Thanksgiving. Ah, thank you. Thank God, civi	GG_S03e09.txt
57	coming. Hey, everybody. Oh, hey there dollfaces. *Happy* Thanksgiving. Yeah, Happy Thanksgiving. Hey.	GG_S03e09.txt
58	h, hey there dollfaces. Happy Thanksgiving. Yeah, *Happy* Thanksgiving. Hey. What's this? Flowers. Wha	GG_S03e09.txt
59	hen, just try to relax. Thanks. Hey. Hey. Hi. Hi, *Happy* Thanksgiving. So, aren't you joining us? Uh,	GG_S03e09.txt
60	ar. Oh, start your stopwatch. Hello. Hi, Grandma. *Happy* Thanksgiving. Thank you, Rory. Happy Thank	GG_S03e09.txt
61	, Grandma. Happy Thanksgiving. Thank you, Rory. *Happy* Thanksgiving, Lorelai. Happy Thanksgiving.	GG_S03e09.txt
62	. Thank you, Rory. Happy Thanksgiving, Lorelai. *Happy* Thanksgiving. One hour, 59 minutes	GG_S03e09.txt
63	ng, everyone's here. We're all here. Oh, good. *Happy* Thanksgiving, Rory. Happy Thanksgiving, Gran	GG_S03e09.txt
64	re all here. Oh, good. Happy Thanksgiving, Rory. *Happy* Thanksgiving, Grandpa. Lorelai. Dad. These a	GG_S03e09.txt
65	thing for your time. That's very nice, thank you. *Happy* Thanksgiving. Goodbye. Keep clearing. I'm	GG_S03e09.txt
66	nymore, and I like that feeling. I like it a lot. *Happy* Thanksgiving, Jess. So, how did the four di	GG_S03e09.txt

This led us to use automatic querying only for some tasks, as it would not permit us to find the totality of examples. As proven by Rose in an extensive study on compliments in film language (2001) and ascertained in the analysis of compliments and insults in the Pavia Corpus of Film Dialogue (Bruti 2009: 150), expressive speech acts in films are often not as formulaic as could be expected. As a consequence, querying the corpus for certain typical structures, e.g. lexical units frequently used in Introductions and Wishes, would result in missing out a whole series of examples where more creative expressions have been used.[8]

So we decided to carry out the analysis manually and to use the concordancer to generate wordlists, for *BS*, *GG* and both series together.

Table 7. Wordlists for *BS*, *GG* and both series together (only the 20 most frequent items).

GG	BS	Both
#Word types: 6633 **#Word tokens: 90972**	**#Word types: 4942** **#Word tokens: 65516**	**#Word types: 8898** **#Word tokens: 156488**
1 3919 i	1 3100 i	1 7019 i
2 3464 you	2 2887 you	2 6351 you
3 2463 the	3 1595 the	3 4058 the
4 1981 to	4 1535 to	4 3516 to
5 1923 a	5 1427 s	5 3337 s
6 1910 s	6 1290 it	6 3200 a
7 1775 it	7 1277 a	7 3065 it
8 1677 and	8 1059 and	8 2736 and
9 1435 that	9 991 t	9 2417 that
10 1091 t	10 982 that	10 2082 t
11 982 of	11 732 of	11 1714 of
12 854 what	12 680 what	12 1534 what
13 834 in	13 650 is	13 1460 is
14 810 is	14 612 me	14 1441 in
15 768 we	15 607 in	15 1375 we
16 759 me	16 607 we	16 1371 me
17 717 this	17 579 m	17 1293 this
18 686 m	18 576 this	18 1265 m
19 656 not	19 539 no	19 1129 for
20 650 for	20 529 know	20 1127 not

As can be seen, the wordlist for the two series (and for the two series together in the last column of Table 7) confirms that *GG* is more wordy than *BS*, given that the same number of episodes have been taken into account.

Another element which emerges is that, not surprisingly, content words do not appear among the 20 most frequent items. The first content word to appear (verbs and adjectives excluded) is 'mom' in *BS* and 'Rory' in *GG*, which again is hardly surprising, being Nora and Rory two central characters in these series.

The first six nouns for frequency of occurrence in *BS* are 'mom' (61 in rank), 'Kitty' (65), 'Justin' (85), 'god' (93), 'time' (94), 'family' (100), and 'Rory' (62), 'time' (75), 'mom' (83), 'Lorelai' (86), 'way' (101), 'thing' (118) in *GG*. This is instead more interesting, as, apart from the nouns of the main characters, pivotal words tend to appear: 'god', 'time' and 'family' in *BS*, 'time', 'mom' and 'thing' in *GG*. 'God' probably belongs in exclamation sequences, so its grammatical status is uncertain and should be more carefully checked through concordances. Probably, like similar words which were originally nouns, like 'man', 'god' has turned into an exclamation and then into something whose meaning is quite blurred but serves the purpose of releasing emotions, i.e., an interjection (see Bruti, Perego 2005: 39 for a discussion of 'man'). The word 'time' gives an idea of the frantic rhythm of the lives of some character, in particular Kitty, a very successful career woman, but also Nora, mother of five and involved with all her grown-up children. The same holds for *GG*, where the word 'time' is even more frequent. 'Family' and 'mom', respectively in *BS* and *GG*, are again some key elements in the narrative strands, but the interesting element is 'thing' in *GG*. 'Thing', together with other terms such as 'stuff', 'man', belongs to what has been termed 'vague language', that is expressions that are not very exact or precise and which are used either because the speaker is not sure of all the details of something, or to speak informally in a friendly way. This is quite meaningful in a scripted text, which means that the script has been carefully planned to sound spontaneous by using those redundant items that are employed in daily chit-chat.

A quick look at phatic language in the word lists suggests what follows: in both series there are phatic elements in the first two hundred words, as can be seen from Table 8. The asterisked items might be either strictly phatic or referential; for instance, 'right' might be an evaluative adjective or an affirmative response, a discourse marker, a filler, etc.

Table 8. Order of frequency of phatic language in *BS* and *GG*.

	BS	GG
hey	82	70
hi	143	122
oh	31	23
ok	74	42
right*	45	55
yeah	42	57
yes	99	61
well*	43	26

7. Conclusion

The two series under investigation are quite similar in genre and in the sociolinguistic configurations they display, at least in the season we analyzed, but *GG* displays a higher rhythm and density of speech. This difference does not appear from the figures concerning Wishes, which are more or less the same in number, but is instead evident from Introductions. These routines are significantly more frequent in *GG*, with a wider repertoire and, consequently, a higher number of translating options in dubbing. An interesting feature that has emerged is that sometimes introductory phrases appear in Closing sequences (and to a lesser extent in Openings), rounding off an event and saving precious showing time. The same can be observed for Wishes as well, of which half occur in dedicated sequences and half are located in either Openings or Closings.

On the whole, we have observed that these ritual formulae are well-represented in both TV series and most often they are translated into Italian. Sometimes, but the frequency is far from being statistically significant, some novel wordings are used, to make the ritual exchange more interesting through the use of irony.

The next steps in the research will be enlarging the corpus, so as to include more series and more data, which will confirm these initial trends, and also implement some more refined automatic searches through concordancing software.

Notes

1 This research was carried out by both authors together. Veronica Bonsignori wrote the following sections: 3., 5., 6., 6.1., 6.1.1., and 7. Silvia Bruti wrote the following sections: 1., 2., 4., 6.2., 6.2.1., and 6.3. *Some quantitative trends.*

2 From now on also referred to as *BS* and *GG*, respectively.

3 Aijmer, who devotes a monograph to conversational routines (1996), describes in detail thanking, apologies, requests and offers. She also considers some discourse markers being used as conversational routines.

4 Linguist Deborah Tannen published an article in *The Washington Post* (Jan. 5, 2003) on fast-paced conversation, taking *GG* as an example and trying to motivate this feature with the fact that "the fast-forward speech of 'Gilmore Girls' helps characters sound like hip teenagers". However, since apparently it also characterizes TV series that are aimed at an adult audience, she also reports Hollywood producers' preference for fast-paced speech as a way of sounding smart (http://faculty.georgetown.edu/tannend/catchthat.html).

6 'Introductory greetings' are the greetings that appear in introductions.

7 "*x*" stands for the name (e.g. Lorelai Gilmore) or any element (e.g. the lawyer) that qualifies and identifies the speaker or interlocutor in the introduction sequence.
8 It should also be added that a qualitative analysis of film language can not be divorced from the viewing of the corresponding film extracts. As advocated by Chaume (2004), it is only by considering the contribution of all the communicative channels that it is possible to evaluate the impact of politeness phenomena in the original and its dubbed version. So other channels, i.e. gestures, eye movements, proxemics, should be taken into account.

References

Aijmer, K. (1996). *Conversational Routines in English. Convention and Creativity.* Harlow: Longman.

Bardovi-Harlig, K. (2012). "Formulas, Routines, and Conventional Expressions in Pragmatics Research." *Annual Review of Applied Linguistics* 32:206–27. http://dx.doi.org/10.1017/S0267190512000086.

Bardovi-Harlig, K. (2013). "Pragmatic Routines." In C.A. Chapelle (ed.) *The Encyclopedia of Applied Linguistics*, 1–7. London: Wiley Blackwell.

Baños-Piñero, R., and F. Chaume. (2009). "Prefabricated Orality: A Challenge in Audiovisual Translation." In M. Giorgio Marrano, G. Nadiani and C. Rundle (eds), *InTRAlinea special issue: The Translation of Dialects in Multimedia.* Retrieved on 22 July 2013 from http://www.intralinea.org/specials/article/1714

Baños-Piñero, R. (2013). "'That is so cool': Investigating the Translation of Adverbial Intensifiers in English-Spanish Dubbing through a Parallel Corpus of Sitcoms." In R. Baños-Piñero, S. Bruti and S. Zanotti (eds), *Corpus Linguistics and AVT: In Search of an Integrated Approach*, Monographic number of *Perspectives.* 21(4): 526–542.

Bednarek, M. (2010). *The Language of Fictional Television: Drama and Identity.* London/New York: Continuum.

Biber, D. (1988). *Variation across Speech and Writing.* Cambridge: Cambridge University Press. http://dx.doi.org/10.1017/CBO9780511621024.

Bonsignori, V., S. Bruti, and S. Masi. (2011). "Formulae across Languages: English Greetings, Leave-takings and Good Wishes in Italian Dubbing." In J.-M. Lavaur, A. Matamala, and A. Serban (eds), *Audiovisual Translation in Close-up: Practical and Theoretical Approaches*, 23–44. Bern: Peter Lang.

Bonsignori, V., S. Bruti, and S. Masi. (2012). "Exploring Greetings and Leave-takings in Original and Dubbed Language." In A. Remael, P. Orero, and M. Carroll (eds), *Audiovisual Translation and Media Accessibility at the Crossroads – Media for All 3*, 357–379. Amsterdam, New York: Rodopi.

Bruti, S., and E. Perego. (2005). "Translating the Expressive Function in Subtitles: The Case of Vocatives." In J. Sanderson (ed.) *Research on Translation for Subtitling in Spain and Italy*, 27–48 Alicante: Publicaciones de la Universidad de Alicante.

Bruti, S. (2009). "Translating Compliments and Insults in the Pavia Corpus of Film Dialogue: Two Sides of the Same Coin?" In M. Freddi and M. Pavesi (eds), *Analysing Audiovisual Dialogue. Linguistic and Translational Insights*, 143–163. Bologna: Clueb.

Chaume, F. (2004). *Cine y traducción*. Madrid: Cátedra.

Chaume, F. (2012). *Audiovisual Translation: Dubbing*. Manchester: St. Jerome.

Coulmas, F. (1979). "On the Sociolinguistic Relevance of Routine Formula." *Journal of Pragmatics* 3 (3-4): 239–66. http://dx.doi.org/10.1016/0378-2166(79)90033-X.

Coulmas, F., (ed.) (1981). *Conversational Routine: Explorations in Standardized Communication Situations and Prepatterned Speech*. The Hague: Mouton.

Creeber, G. (2004). *Serial Television. Big Drama on the Small Screen*. London: Bfi Publishing.

Forchini, P. (2012). *Movie Language Revisited. Evidence from Multi-Dimensional Analysis and Corpora*. Bern: Peter Lang.

Freddi, M. and Pavesi, M. (eds). (2009). *Analysing Audiovisual Dialogue. Linguistic and Translational Insights*. 143–163 Bologna: Clueb.

Grasso, A. (2011). Accendi la TV. Il romanzo è un telefilm americano. Retrieved on 22 July 2013 from http://lettura.corriere.it/accendi-la-tv-il-romanzo-e-un-telefilm-americano/

Kerbrat-Orecchioni, C. (1987). "La description des échanges en analyse conversationelle: L'example du compliment." *DRLAV- Revue de Linguistique* 36(37): 1–53.

Laver, J. (1981). "Linguistic Routines and Politeness in Greeting and Parting." In F. Coulmas (ed.), *Conversational Routine: Explorations in Standardized Communication Situations and Prepatterned Speech*, 289–304. The Hague: Mouton.

Pavesi, M. (2005). *La traduzione filmica. Aspetti del parlato doppiato dall'inglese all'italiano*. Roma: Carocci.

Quaglio, P. (2009a). *Television Dialogue: The Sitcom Friends vs. Natural Conversation*. Amsterdam, Philadelphia: John Benjamins. http://dx.doi.org/10.1075/scl.36.

Quaglio, P. (2009b). "Vague Language in the Situation Comedy *Friends* vs. Natural Conversation." In M. Freddi and M. Pavesi (eds), *Analysing Audiovisual Dialogue. Linguistic and Translational Insights*, 75–91. Bologna: CLUEB.

Romero-Fresco, P. (2006). "The Spanish Dubbese: A Case of (un)idiomatic *Friends*." *Journal of Specialised Translation* 6: 134–51.

Romero-Fresco, P. (2009). "The Fictional and Translational Dimensions of the Language Used in Dubbing." In M. Freddi and M. Pavesi (eds), *Analysing Audiovisual Dialogue. Linguistic and Translational Insights*, 41–56. Bologna: CLUEB.

Rose, K.R. 2001. "Compliments and Compliment Responses in Film: Implications for Pragmatics Research and Language Teaching." *IRAL* 39 (4): 309–26. http://dx.doi.org/10.1515/iral.2001.007.

Tannen, D. (2003) Did you catch that? Why they're talking as fast as they can. In *The Washington Post*, 5 January, 2003. < http://faculty.georgetown.edu/tannend/catchthat.html>.

Taylor, C. (1999). "'Look who's talking'. An Analysis for Film Dialogue as a Variety of Spoken Discourse." In L. Lombardo, L. Haarman, J. Morley, C. Taylor (eds), *Massed Medias. Linguistic Tools for Interpreting Media Discourse*, 247–278. Milano: Led.

Verschueren, J. 1981. "The Semantics of Forgotten Routines." In F. Coulmas (ed.) *Conversational Routine: Explorations in Standardized Communication Situations and Prepatterned Speech*, 133–154. The Hague: Mouton.

Constrained meaning construction and attention re-allocation

Mikołaj Deckert
University of Łódź

1. Introduction

The chapter looks into interlingual subtitling through the concept of attention as understood in Cognitive Linguistics. More specifically, I will talk about attention as it has been addressed using the descriptive construct of "salience" (or "prominence"), a construal parameter proposed under Langacker's (1987, 2008) Cognitive Grammar. English-to-Polish subtitling data will be investigated to identify a set of translation shifts that result in different degrees of salience "re-calibration" between the source and target texts. As cases of attention re-allocation will be discussed on the example of an audiovisual translation mode, one has to consider a range of factors that limit the translator's decision-making, some of which are absent from monosemiotic interlingual transfer. This contribution draws on earlier work in cognitive semantics and subtitling in that it is intended to elaborate on one of the categories of translational construal manipulation outlined in Deckert (2013), and to discuss the plausible types of motivation behind prominence manipulation.

First, a brief discussion of this contribution's major theoretical premises will be provided, followed by on overview of subtitling as a mode of audiovisual translation vitally conditioned by a number of constraints. After the key descriptive notion – salience/prominence – has been defined in the next section, the chapter's main part will be devoted to exploring cases of attention re-allocation contrastively in English-Polish data, comprising both text as well as the accompanying audio and visual material.

2. Construals

The starting point for this work is that language form is itself meaningful. Linguistic expressions are taken to function as prompts that initiate the process of meaning construction drawing on vast repositories of knowledge and experience of language users. An essential explanatory construct here is that of "construal" understood as the conceptualizer's way of organizing a scene to be then expressed linguistically. Construal can be characterized through a set of parameters like granularity (the level of detail in which a scene is characterized), perspective (essentially, the relation between the conceptualizer and what is conceptualized) and prominence (salience). In this paper the focus will be on the last of these.

It should be mentioned that the tradition of inquiries into attentional phenomena is rich, if different terms have been proposed to discuss them, reflecting various perspectives. Notable works include those by Lambrecht (1994), or Tomlin's (1995, 1997) investigations involving the interlingual aspect. In functionalist linguistics the topic was notably tackled by Givón (1990) whilst a detailed cognitive-semantic account of the linguistic attention system has been proposed by Talmy (2007, in preparation).

The rudimentary tenet adopted for the present inquiry is that "language has an extensive system that assigns different degrees of salience to the parts of an expression or of its reference or of the context" (Talmy 2007: 264). Linguistic evidence produced by the addresser is processed by the addressee who allocates varied amounts of attention to different portions of conceptual representations as reflected in that evidence.

3. Audiovisual Translation Research: subtitling

Despite its long-lasting practice, audiovisual translation (AVT) was not a serious subject of scholarly examination until relatively recently. Actually, it is only in 1990s that a surge in academic interest in AVT can be observed. Currently, not only is it uncontroversial to say that this line of research is enjoying autonomy but also, as Díaz-Cintas and Anderman (2009: 8) remark, AVT "is now one of the most vibrant and vigorous fields within Translation Studies."

As for the initial inferiority of AVT studies, it was likely related to AVT's adaptive nature which in turn is correlated with the constrained nature of this type of transfer. Indeed, constraints are a major issue in the discipline – whether in subtitling, dubbing, voice-over, or any of the numerous other types now incorporated into the field.

In subtitling these are typically spatio-temporal. A caption can contain a limited, yet ranging across subtitling companies, number of characters per line (cf. Karamitroglou 1998, Bogucki 2004). The caption's exposition time has to meet fixed minimum/maximum time requirements (cf. e.g. Luyken et al. 1991) and its time-in and time-out need to be precisely aligned with the spoken input, allowing for the so-called lead-in – when the subtitle appears a fraction of a second before the utterance can be heard to create the impression of simultaneity – and a lag-out – when the subtitle is still on the screen after the acoustic signal is gone. As for timing, the subtitler is expected to heed shot changes and leave a minimum gap between subsequent subtitles making it easier for the eye to follow, especially if subtitles should be similar in shape. In the case of two-liners additional concerns are segmentation, line alignment and shape (cf. Karamitroglou 1998). Yet another parameter that plays a crucial role in subtitling (and to a varied extent in other modes of audiovisual translation) are semiotic channels. But while it provides extra-textual input, thus carrying a portion of the informative load and in a way unburdening the subtitler, it also rules out certain dynamically-geared (Nida 1964) or domesticating (Venuti 1995) solutions. That is to say, replacing potentially unfamiliar ST concepts with ones that are expectedly more congruent with the target audience's assumptions will be problematic because the original term can – to a different extent – be discerned aurally, but even more problematic can be cases where the element is present visually.

However, when discussing translation as a process of making choices one can understand constraints in a more general manner, going beyond the technical limitations, and thus universally inherent in all translation activity. In that sense "constraints" can be taken to stand for any set of criteria that the translator keeps in mind while designing the target text. These criteria will range from the type of text (cf. Reiss 1976), audience expectations (cf. Bell [1984] 1997, Toury 1995), function (Reiss and Vermeer 1984, Vermeer 1978, Nord 1991) to the relative incompatibility of the audiences' assumptions, or incommensurability of linguistic systems involved (Lakoff 1987, Lewandowska-Tomaszczyk 1987, 2010).

4. Salience in Cognitive Grammar

Salience can be understood as two-faceted, comprising trajector-landmark alignment and profiling. As for the former, trajector is the salient participant, the one on which attention is primarily focused with respect to the secondary focus, the landmark. Participants of a scene are not preset to function as either trajectors or landmarks. Still, while elements can be construed alternately as either of those, there are certain properties that make them more viable candidates for certain functions. For instance, trajectors tend to be smaller and more mobile than landmarks. Therefore a sentence like "The ball (TR) is next to the tree (LM)" sounds more plausible than its truth-conditional equivalent "The tree (TR) is next to the ball (LM)." As for profiling, an expression is argued to have a conceptual base defined as "the immediate scope in active domains – that is, the portion put 'onstage' and foregrounded as the general locus of viewing attention" (Langacker 2008: 66). Then, there is an expression's profile, a more particular formation, "the specific **focus** of attention within its immediate scope" (Langacker 2008: 66). Common profile-base sets would be a finger as a profile within the base of a hand, or substructures like a hub, spokes and a rim profiled within the superordinate structure of a wheel.

With the above in mind, what is of interest in this contribution is what has been termed "cognitive salience," as differentiated from "ontological salience." The former can be defined as a concept's activation in the current working memory, which may result from a "conscious selection mechanism" (Schmid 2007: 119) or by "spreading activation" whereby having been activated, one concept is conducive to the activation of another concept (Collins and Quillian 1969, Anderson 1983, Deane 1992). Ontological salience is more permanent and has to do with the claim that "by virtue of their very nature, some entities are better qualified to attract our attention than others and are thus more salient in this sense" (Schmid 2007: 120).

5. Analysis

The samples presented below demonstrate how attention can be re-directed in the process of English-to-Polish subtitling. To make it easier for the reader to relate the discussion to the film's story, the samples are presented in chronological order with respect to the film's progression and therefore also largely with respect to the actual events. The particular constructions that are of interest are introduced as embedded in broader samples, with time-aligned screenshots and additional notes meant to compensate for some of the properties of the filmic medium that are hard to represent (cf. Baldry and Thibault 2006). The ST in the tables is segmented artificially and approximately for mere expository purposes, with the readers that do not speak Polish in mind.

The material comes from Yoav Potash's 2011 documentary film "Crime after Crime" recounting the story of Deborah Peagler who serves a sentence of 25 years-to life in connection with being involved in the murder of her husband, Oliver Wilson. The filmmakers follow Deborah's story as her pro-bono lawyers – Nadia Costa and Joshua Safran – attempt to help her win freedom by re-opening her case. The attorneys draw on a 2002 California law which makes it possible to admit new evidence as Deborah had been abused by her partner.

In this work samples from a single production are presented for ease of exposition, as in many cases relevant elements of the film's plot must be elaborated on to explain the import of translational decisions. As for the data, it should be pointed out that contrary to what is the case in feature films, in documentaries the discourse is not "prefabricated" (cf. Chaume 2001). The linguistic evidence, hence, can be expected to display a higher degree of authenticity for it is mostly produced not by professional actors but by individuals who are very often emotionally involved in the topic, which contributes to the spontaneity of speech production. Besides, the documentary's informative function is fulfilled in the analysed data, among other things, through extensive use of language, giving the researcher a rich data set even if a single documentary film is examined.

Sample 1

If she was being abused or battered – Jeżeli on ją wykorzystywał albo bił [if he abused or beat her]

Sample 1			
source text	target text	image	comments
If she was being abused or battered it was a secret	Jeżeli on ją wykorzystywał albo bił, to wszystko odbywało się po kryjomu.		A photo of Oliver Wilson and Deborah Peagler
because at that point in time I was being abused	W tym samym czasie sama byłam wykorzystywana		Oliver Wilson's sister Zabrina speaking
and it was a secret.	i ukrywałam to.		A photo of Zabrina

In the original it is Debbie, as the victim of abuse, who is the trajector, and the actual agent – Oliver Wilson – remains unnamed. In the subtitles, Debbie is construed as the landmark and it is her husband who functions as the most prominent participant. The change is especially important because it is the first mention of the problem of abuse in the film's main body. The original gradually progresses from the picture of undisturbed peace in Debbie's relationship with Oliver to signalling the problem, not mentioning Oliver explicitly from the beginning.

Sample 2

I tried pimping – wkręciłem się w prostytucję [I got into prostitution]

Sample 2			
source text	target text	image	comments
He was always trying to be like me.	Zawsze chciał być taki jak ja.		A photo of Oliver Wilson's brother Melvin
I tried pimping.	Z czasem wkręciłem się w prostytucję.		
And I found out that I wasn't made out for pimping because… pimping…	I wtedy zrozumiałem, że to nie dla mnie.		Melvin Wilson speaking
You can pimp your mama, you can pimp your sister, you can pimp your daughter –	Wolno ci to robić z mamą, siostrą, córką		
you can't have no sympathy towards anybody.	i nie możesz im nawet współczuć.		

The above statement from Oliver's older brother is intertwined with Debbie's recounting how it was only at some point when she realized her husband's money was not all earned at a supermarket where he worked. Before Debbie elaborates on that, her account is foreshadowed by Melvin's from which it becomes quite clear that Oliver's additional source of income was "pimping." When coupled with Debbie's earlier story where she states that Oliver took her somewhere, it becomes evident he was about to get her involved in the business, whether or not she wanted it.

The Polish translation of Melvin's utterance in the form of "wkręciłem się w prostytucję" is broader than the original, as it leaves his actual role underspecified. In terms of attention allocation, a larger structure is profiled in the stead of its substructure being the profile originally, since "pimping" noticeably foregrounds one of the roles in the base of prostitution. Therefore, the English version is easier to follow because the viewer can instantly realize that Melvin, and by the same token Oliver, were not themselves prostitutes but rather acted as intermediaries, and Debbie was forced into the role of a prostitute as we later learn from the film.

Sample 3

Oliver's drug abuse really took off in a big way – Oliver na dobre uzależnił się od narkotyków [Oliver got addicted to drugs for good]

Sample 3			
source text	target text	image	comments
So after Oliver's drug abuse really took off in a big way	Po tym jak Oliver na dobre uzależnił się od narkotyków,		A caption: "1982 Deborah leaves Oliver"
Debbie and Oliver got an eviction notice.	Deborah i Oliver dostali wypowiedzenie mieszkania.		Joshua Safran speaking

Originally it is the drug abuse that gets structured as the most salient element. This separates the addiction from the person of the addict, which could suggest he has little control over it. Whether this serves to legitimise and justify Oliver Wilson's behaviour by implying that he is not to be held responsible, or quite the opposite, i.e., to suggest he was a weak and susceptible person, the mechanism is not secured in the target text where it is Oliver himself who operates as the trajector.

Sample 4

we'll take care of it, we'll take care of it – Obiecali się nim zająć. [they promised to take care of him]

Sample 4			
source text	target text	image	comments
And I was like, can you guys make him leave me alone, can you just make him leave me alone?	Spytałam, „Możecie się nim zająć? Tak, żeby dał mi spokój?"		
And he was like, yeah let us [unclear] we'll take care of it, we'll take care of it.	Obiecali się nim zająć.		Deborah Peagler speaking
OK.	Zgodziłam się na to.		

In the source text reiteration "it" is profiled, i.e., attention is directed to the problematic situation in which Oliver Wilson features as just one of the elements. In the Polish text a different pronoun is employed by which Oliver is precisely referred to. Such a construction prompts a more narrow interpretation in the sense that it points to some action being taken that deals directly with Oliver Wilson rather than a potentially indirect action that is to make him amend his conduct. Prominence configurations are critical in this passage as they are a constitutive element of the defendant's statement with respect to her alleged crime. What Debbie agreed on in relation to the actions that led to her husband's death is decisive in assessing her crime. The linguistic formulations she uses may be a way of incriminating herself and therefore every tiniest detail matters and vitally contributes to the film's holistically-viewed message, which should be borne in mind in cross-linguistic relay.

An analogous issue seems to pose a translation challenge farther in the passage.

> OK – Zgodziłam się na to. [I agreed to this]

This short fragment is potentially the most significant piece in the entire film because – despite, or perchance due to, its brevity – it is strongly indicative of Debbie's degree of involvement in the murder. "OK" is undoubtedly less precise than the more articulate Polish expression. The original can be interpreted in a host of ways and the translation limits that interpretational scope by foregrounding one reading, importantly – in accord with what was the case in the previous example – one which directly states that Debbie consciously or even actively gave her consent.

Sample 5

Debbie left – Deborah odeszła [Deborah walked away]

Sample 5			
source text	target text	image	comments
They were from the point of view of where the the camera is shooting from right now	Nadeszli z tego kierunku, gdzie teraz znajduje się kamera.		Bobby Buechler speaking
And they scaled this fence and they came down and they crawled down here	Przeskoczyli przez ogrodzenie, doczołgali si ę do tego miejsca		
and they attacked Oliver.	i zaatakowali Olivera.		
The moment that happened, Debbie left.	Gdy do tego doszło, Deborah odeszła,		
And Sibley and Lively continued to strangle Oliver.	a Sibley i Lively dalej dusili ofiarę	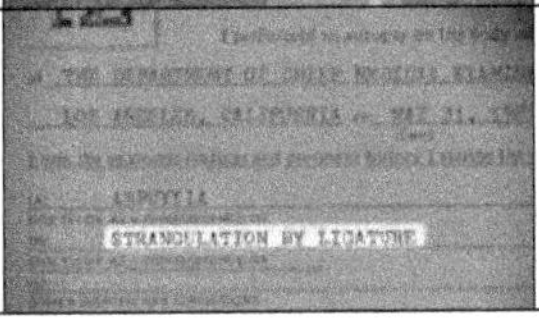	An autopsy report with the cause of death highlighted

Some salience shifts result in a target text variant that is counter-intuitive or possibly implausible. One such case can be found in the description of Oliver Wilson's death above. The target text profiles a substructure within what was originally left unprofiled. The action of "leaving" keeps the exact manner of moving unclear. The translator opts for the verb "odchodzić" [to walk away] which seems implausible due to the circumstances. As Debbie witnesses a strangulation scene, she would likely react more dynamically – for instance by "running away" – even given the fact that she might have been involved in planning the assault in which case her reaction could be less emotional. Arguably, to retain the original salience arrangement the subtitler would need to opt for a more formal verb like "oddalić się" which leaves unspecified properties such as the speed of the action. Thus, a viable explanation of the subtitler's decision is that it was dictated by the conventionalization constraint whereby some renderings were ruled out by registerial criteria. A National Corpus of Polish (NKJP) search shows that "oddali* się" occurs mostly in literary narration. The verbal construction is not typically found in spoken data. There are mere two occurrences of "oddali* się," neither of them pertaining to physical movement but rather used metaphorically.

> Sibley and Lively continued to strangle Oliver – Sibley i Lively dalej dusili ofiarę [Sibley and Lively continued to strangle the victim]

Despite the gravity of the account, the object of the assault is referred to exclusively as "Oliver." The Polish text goes for an analogous solution once, but then changes it to a narrower concept, which imposes an evaluative interpretation – "ofiara" [victim]. The relevance of this shift is mainly that by using the (first) name, the speaker refrains from assigning roles and if Oliver Wilson is labelled "victim," then naturally Debbie assumes the role of (an indirect) attacker and is herself denied the role of a victim. It should be mentioned that the utterance comes from a private investigator allied with Debbie and her attorneys – yet, the information is provided in the caption that introduces him and he himself does not attempt to pass himself off as indifferent to the issue. The problem of who the victim is in the case of battered women who are imprisoned for being involved in their partners' murder is explicitly brought up in the film less than 4 minutes later.

Sample 6

she did bring Oliver here – przyprowadziła Olivera w umówione miejsce [she led Oliver to the arranged place]

Sample 6			
source text	target text	image	comments
There was some discrepancy from their statement of the police of who did what.	W ich zeznaniach występują rozbieżności, jeśli chodzi o kwestię, kto co zrobił.		
I don't know, obviously, and no one will know exactly what happened.	Nikt nie wie, co tak naprawdę się stało,		
But what we do know at that time that Debbie was not here she had left	ale jesteśmy pewni, że Deborah przy tym nie było. Odeszła.		Bobby Buechler speaking
although she did bring Oliver here and she is…and we know that…	Mimo, że to ona przyprowadziła Olivera w umówione miejsce.		
and she has expressed remorse about that and… and has paid her dues for that act.	Okazała skruchę i zapłaciła już za swój postępek.		

In this sample the subtitle is additive in that it talks about "umówione miejsce" [the arranged place] which brings to the fore the plotting aspect of the event. Based on the Polish version it is plain that Deborah made arrangements with the attackers that she would bring her husband to that exact spot. In the original it is only implicitly mentioned that her bringing Oliver to that place was a part of a plan whose primary aim was to hurt Oliver Wilson.

she has expressed remorse about that and ... and has paid her dues for that act – Okazała skruchę i zapłaciła już za swój postępek. [she showed repentance and has already paid for her (bad) deed]

In this fragment it is the rendition of essentially a single lexeme that introduces a considerable shift. While the source notion of "the act" is very close to neutral – partly because of its broadness – the target variant "postępek" is a less universal word and it is more explicitly evaluative. A query of the National Corpus of Polish shows that the form's semantic prosody (cf. Sinclair 1991, Louw 1993, Partington 2004) is closer to the negative end of the good-bad continuum, with its strongest adjectival collocate being by far "zły" [bad].

Sample 7

most of which went to Oliver's mother – Większość sumy przekazała matce Olivera [she gave a larger part of the sum to Oliver's mother]

Sample 7			
source text	target text	image	comments
After Oliver Wilson was killed Debbie did receive about seventeen thousand dollars in life insurance proceeds,	Po śmierci Olivera Deborah dostała odszkodowanie		Joshua Safran speaking
	w wysokości 17 tys. dolarów.		
most of which went to Oliver's mother and to pay for a very elaborate funeral for Oliver.	Większość sumy przekazała matce Olivera i na jego wykwintny pogrzeb.		

The pecuniary motives of Oliver Wilson's murder are critical for the story because the alleged financial gain was used as the basis for sentencing Debbie. In the source text the agentive component of who gave the money to the bereft mother is not present, therefore implying that the decision whether or not it is given to the mother did not rest with Debbie but had to do more with a standard legal procedure beyond her control. The inference that Debbie volitionally dispensed with the money contributes sincerity to her image and partly contradicts the supposition that she could have wanted Oliver dead for insurance policy profit.

Sample 8

They are always telling about the victim that died in our case – Zawsze mówi się o ofiarach, które przez nas zginęły [the victims that died because of us are always being talked about]

Sample 8			
source text	target text	image	comments
After being sentenced to prison and going to prison,	Po ogłoszeniu wyroku, poszłam do więzienia.		A bird on a barbed wire shot from behind a fence./ Deborah Peagler speaking
five years passed, ten years passed,	Minęło pięć lat, dziesięć lat.		
people started talking about the Battered Women Syndrome,	Ludzie zaczęli mówić o syndromie maltretowanych kobiet.		A photograph of a document with the phrase "Battered Woman Syndrome" highlighted/Deborah Peagler speaking
they even started a domestic violence programme and the prison and group therapy.	Nawet w więzieniu rozpoczął się program o przemocy domowej i terapia grupowa.		
They are always telling about the victim	Zawsze mówi się o ofiarach,		An inmate speaking
that died in our case but we are a victim too	które przez nas zginęły, ale my same przecież jesteśmy ofiarami!		

As has already been mentioned in Sample 5 above, the assignment of roles between victims and their perpetrators is a vital one in the film. In this fragment this division is discussed directly by an inmate during a Battered Women's Support Group meeting. Importantly, the fragment that precedes her speaking concentrates on consciousness raising with respect to the problem of abused women whereby the homicide aspect – pertaining to the male – is similarly present only in an implicit fashion. Therefore, when the woman mentions "the victim that died in our case" the first accessible interpretation can be that it is a woman who is killed by the abusive man rather than the other way round. This ambiguity is partly resolved in the clause that follows – nonetheless originally the element of the woman agency in the homicide is successfully backgrounded as the actor is consistently underdetermined. The Polish version openly talks about "ofiary, które przez nas zginęły" [the victims that died because of[1] us], thus drawing attention to women as perpetrators.

Sample 9

we work for her freedom today – walczę o jej wolność [I fight for her freedom]

The source and target versions foreground different aspects of the process whose objective is to set Deborah free. Taking into account the rest of Nadia's utterance where she alludes to her personal motivation for getting involved in Deborah's case, the verb that she uses at the very end to wrap up the statement is all the more important. Still, despite the painfulness of the topic she tackles, she does not intend to oppose violence with violence – i.e., by fighting. Instead, she promotes a different approach, "work" – which draws on systematicity, methodicalness, and gradual progress rather than violent solutions which are to bring rapid change. Interestingly, she first talks about her individual motivation but then finishes by talking on behalf of the group of people. The Polish translation does not retain this shift.

Sample 9			
source text	target text	image	comments
However, it's been important for me to summon the courage to discuss what I can as part of this film	Jednak bardzo ważne było dla mnie, jako jednego z bohaterów tego filmu,		Nadia Costa working
in order to let people know	odważenie się do pokazaniaś wiatu,		Nadia Costa and Deborah Peagler talking in prison
that abuse doesn't just happen in south-central LA to young black women.	że przemoc nie jest tylko problemem młodych, czarnych kobiet z Los Angeles.		
It happens everywhere,	Takie rzeczy dzieją się wszędzie.		A housing estate filmed from a moving vehicle
it happened to me as a child and also as a young adult all the time	Spotykało mnie to, gdy byłam dzieckiem, gdy dorastałam, cały czas.		
when I was living in affluent communities and it was never stopped.	Mieszkałam w zamożnym środowisku, a ciągłe nadużywanie nie ustawało.		Nadia Costa and Deborah Peagler talking in prison
It's one of the reasons that I became involved in Debbie's case and why we work for her freedom today.	Między innymi, dlatego zajęłam się sprawą Deborah i walczę o jej wolność.		Nadia Costa speaking

Sample 10

The judge characterized this witness's testimony as pretty poor and, quote, extremely ambiguous – Sędzia określił go słowami „bardzo słaby," „dwuznaczny." [the judge described him with the words "very weak," "ambiguous"]

Sample 10			
source text	target text	image	comments
The hearing transcript from Debbie's preliminary hearing in 1983	Transkrypt z roku 1983, z wstępnego przesłuchania Deborah	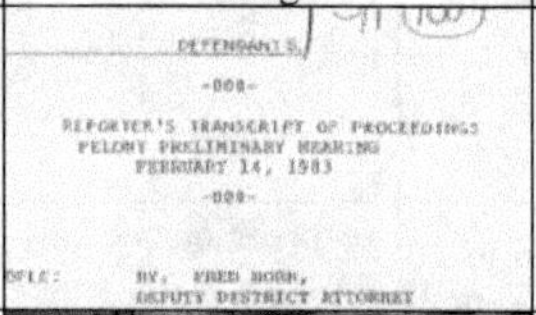	A photo of a transcript of proceedings
shows that the prosecution had only one witness.	ujawnił, że na rozprawie pojawił się tylko jeden świadek.		Joshua Safran gesturing and he speaks
The judge characterized this witness's testimony as pretty poor and, quote, extremely ambiguous.	Sędziaokre ślił go słowami „bardzo słaby", „dwuznaczny".	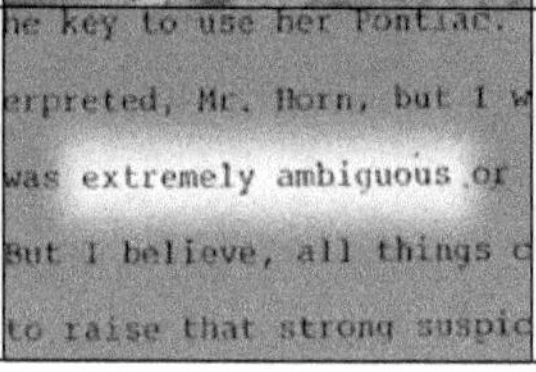	A photo of a transcript with the phrase "extremely ambiguous" highlighted

The Polish viewer can arrive at the intended meaning by metonymically interpreting the "witness" as providing access to the concept closely related to his product (testimony). That the witness himself is being described rather than his testimony makes the message even stronger than originally (cf. Sample 11 below). A viable explanation of this solution is that the pronoun "go" [him] is much more economical than a more analogous construction like "zeznanie tego świadka" [this witness's testimony].

Sample 11

he tried to back out – chciał wycofać zeznania [he wanted to withdraw (his) testimony]

Sample 11			
source text	target text	image	comments
When he heard that they were gonna prosecute Debbie for the death penalty he tried to back out.	Gdy dowiedział się, że grozi jej za to kara śmierci, chciał wycofać zeznania,		Nadia Costa speaking
But the DA wouldn't let him.	lecz prokuratura okręgowa nie dała mu tej szansy.		
In fact he was arrested and he was told that unless he testified against Debbie Peagler	W rzeczywistości Toniego aresztowano i zmuszono do zeznań przeciw Deborah.		A photo of the title page of the transcript of Anthony Reedburg's statement
	Zagrożono mu, że w przeciwnym razie	 CONFIDENTIAL	
they would vigorously prosecute him for an old felony charge that had basically been dormant.	będzie surowo sądzony za dawne, umorzone już przestępstwo.	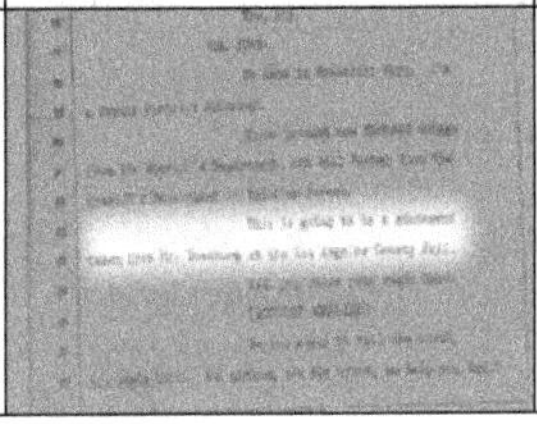	A photo of the transcript of Anthony Reedburg's statement with a highlighted fragment

This case of prominence recombination is the inverse of what can be seen in Sample 10. Here it is the source text that employs the PRODUCER FOR PRODUCT metonymy and the variant introduced by the subtitler dispenses with that mechanism. Originally, the entire person of the witness is being metonymically conceptualized, and in the Polish version it is the man's statement – a product – that operates as the salient element. The source formulation appears to be more powerful, suggesting that it is Reedburg, with all the attributes of a human being, who is involved and who is going to be responsible for Debbie's imprisonment. As a more technical and literal formulation is proposed in the subtitle, a part of the original's appeal and dramatic quality is lost in translation.[2]

he was told – Zagrożono mu [he was threatened]

The target lexeme derived by prefixation from "grozić" [to threaten] activates a narrower profile within the concept originally denoted by "telling." This adds an interpretational tier absent from the source text because the Polish variant can be understood as graver – potentially signalling unprofessionalism on the part of the District Attorney's office, compared to the more neutral notion of "telling" which triggers different framing.

Sample 12

an obligation disclosure that has continued every single day for 25 years – Obowiązek ujawnienia trwał przez 25 lat [a disclosure obligation lasted for 25 years]

Sample 12			
source text	target text	image	comments
And the memo goes on to say that he is an informant.	Notatka służbowa utrzymuje, że on jest informatorem.		Joshua Safran speaking
It turns out Deadman has been a paid informant for law enforcement	Nieboszczyk był płatnym informatorem organu ochrony porządku publicznego	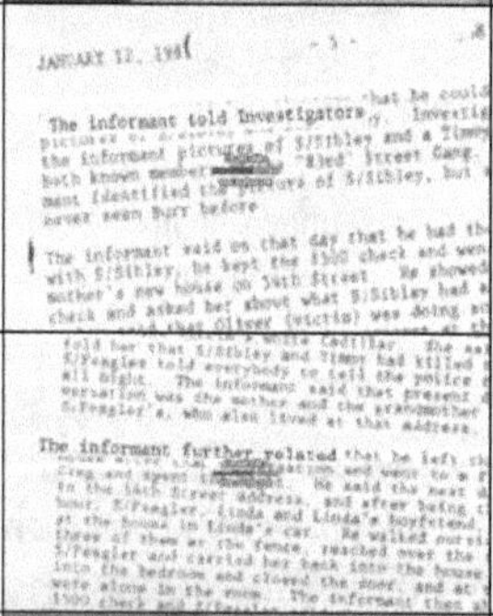	A photograph of a memo with a magnified fragment
in Los Angeles county for decades.	w hrabstwie Los Angeles przez dekady.		
These were facts that the DA was obligated to disclose in 1983,	To są fakty, do których ujawnienia w 1983 zobowiązany był prokurator okręgowy.		Joshua Safran speaking
an obligation disclosure that has continued every single day for 25 years. And the DA's Office has kept it secret.	Obowiązek ujawnienia trwał przez 25 lat, a prokuratura trzymała to w tajemnicy.		

The speaker's profiling of individual days makes us realize better the time span, as if by assuming Debbie's vantage point. The difference can be described using Langacker's (1987) notions of sequential scanning as different from summary scanning or Lakoff's (1987) image schema transformations whereby the conceptualizer would proceed in conceptualization from mass to multiplex.

6. Conclusions

While – in line with the Cognitive orientation – it is here argued that the source and target meanings can never be identical, the translator's task is invariably to maximize the level of analogousness against constraints, taking it as one of the principles that how conceptual content is coded in the form of linguistic expressions is material for the construction and reconstruction of meaning.

As has been demonstrated above, instances of how attention is redistributed over a scene vary in nature, scope and consequentiality. For the purpose of description, they are reducible to multiword expressions or even the translator's singular lexical choices – which may be rather straightforwardly conditioned by systemic cross-linguistic conceptual mismatches, for instance on the axiological level, as well as by other constraints, importantly *stricte* technical ones, too. In some other cases attention re-focusing will result from syntactic shifts like de-passivisation. Clearly, some reconfigurations influence the process of meaning construction more than others but it can be reasoned that even minute modifications matter because they get orchestrated and ultimately contribute to the film's overall interpretation. But in some instances the minuteness of modification can be deceptive if taken for granted. Vitally, it ought not to be assumed that consequentiality of change is reflected in the size of the manipulated component because – as has been indicated in the analysis – even how a single two-letter pronoun is rendered can significantly bear upon the message of the entire cinematic production. In the case of films that openly refer to people and events in the real world with a view to influencing viewers' perceptions and opinions – like documentaries – translation-incurred change merits particularly careful investigation.

On the whole, a major observation is that only a portion of prominence shifts is dictated by reasons that can be traced back with a relatively high degree of certainty. As has been suggested above, these reasons are by and large the technical constraints imposed upon the subtitler and constraints formulated more broadly, necessarily including the parameter of conventionalization and the systemic asymmetries of the languages involved. Still, in a range of cases it is hardly feasible to arrive at explanations of the translator's choices that go beyond conjecturing.

Nonetheless, with the use of Cognitive Linguistics assumptions and constructs the emerging reconfiguration patterns can be identified and quite neatly described. One of this paper's aims has been to argue that using such a usage-based (cf. Barlow and Kemmer 2000) empirically-driven model can help us better understand the mechanisms that underpin meaning. Thus obtained insights might be further utilized to optimize the translation process by being put to use in fields like translator training. Tabakowska (2002: 161) aptly remarks that despite the complexity of the Cognitive Linguistics model, if properly tailored for the classroom setting, "it may be profitably used when providing (more or less probable) interpretations of the original text, trying to understand the systematic potential of the source and target languages, or searching for solutions, which are not necessarily 'better' or 'worse,' but may prove to be just 'different'". It is critical that the translator acknowledge the existence of such difference and mind its potential.

Notes

1 Besides, if used to talk about causal relations, the Polish preposition "przez" generally pertains to what is undesirable, for instance when putting the blame on somebody. In terms of semantic prosody, "because of" is more towards the neutral.

2 What is more, in the source the activity of "hearing" is profiled which is but a phase on the way to the more elaborate result of "finding out."

References

Anderson, J.R. (1983). *The Architecture of Cognition.* Cambridge, MA: Harvard University Press.

Baldry, A. and P. J. Thibault (2006). *Multimodal Transcription and Text Analysis. A Multimedia Toolkit and Coursebook.* London and Oakville: Equinox.

Barlow, M., and S. Kemmer, (eds). (2000). *Usage-based Models of Language.* Stanford, CA: CSLI Publications.

Bell, A. [1984] (1997). "Language style as audience design." In *Sociolinguistics: A Reader and Coursebook,* ed. N. Coupland and A. Jaworski, 242–244. London: Palgrave Macmillan.

Bogucki, Ł. (2004). *A Relevance Framework for Constraints on Cinema Subtitling.* Łódź: Łódź University Press.

Chaume, F. (2002). "Models for research in Audiovisual Translation." *Babel* 48 (1): 1–13. http://dx.doi.org/10.1075/babel.48.1.01cha.

Collins, A.M., and M.R. Quillian. (1969). "Retrieval time from semantic memory." *Journal of Verbal Learning and Verbal Behavior* 8 (2): 240–7. http://dx.doi.org/10.1016/S0022-5371(69)80069-1.

Deane, P.D. (1992). *Grammar in Mind and Brain: Explorations in Cognitive Syntax.* Berlin: Mouton de Gruyter. http://dx.doi.org/10.1515/9783110886535.

Deckert, M. (2013). *Meaning in Subtitling: Toward a Contrastive Cognitive Semantic Model.* Frankfurt am Main: Peter Lang.

Díaz-Cintas, J., and G. Anderman. (eds). (2009). *Audiovisual translation: Language transfer on screen.* Basingstoke: Palgrave Macmillan.

Givón, T. (1990). *Syntax: A Functional-Typological Introduction,* vol. 2. Amsterdam: John Benjamins.

Karamitroglou, F. (1998). "A Proposed Set of Subtitling Standards in Europe." *Translation Journal* 2(2).

Lakoff, G. (1987). *Women, Fire, and Dangerous Things: What Categories Reveal About the Mind.* Chicago: University of Chicago Press. http://dx.doi.org/10.7208/chicago/9780226471013.001.0001.

Lambrecht, K. (1994). *Information Structure and Sentence Form: A Theory of Topic, Focus, and the Mental Representations of Discourse Referents.* Cambridge: Cambridge University Press. http://dx.doi.org/10.1017/CBO9780511620607.

Langacker, R.W. (1987). *Theoretical Prerequisites,* vol. 1. Foundations of cognitive grammar. Stanford, CA: Stanford University Press.

Langacker, R.W. (2008). *Cognitive Grammar: A Basic Introduction.* New York: Oxford University Press. http://dx.doi.org/10.1093/acprof:oso/9780195331967.001.0001.

Lewandowska-Tomaszczyk, B. (1987). *Conceptual Structure, Linguistic Meaning, and Verbal Interaction.* Łódź: Łódź University Press.

Lewandowska-Tomaszczyk, B. (2010). "Re-conceptualization and the emergence of discourse meaning as a theory of translation." In B. Lewandowska-Tomaszczyk and M. Thelen (eds), *Meaning in Translation,* 105–147. Frankfurt am Main: Peter Lang.

Louw, B. (1993). "Irony in the text or insincerity in the writer? – the diagnostic potential of semantic prosodies." In M. Baker, G. Francis, and E. Tognini-Bonelli (eds), *Text and Technology: In Honour of John Sinclair,* 157–176. Amsterdam: John Benjamins. http://dx.doi.org/10.1075/z.64.11lou.

Luyken, G.M., T. Herbst, J. Langham-Brown, H. Reid, and H. Spinhof. (1991). *Overcoming Language Barriers in Television: Dubbing and Subtitling for the European Audience.* Manchester: European Institute for the Media.

Nida, E.A. [1964] (2004). "Principles of correspondence." In L. Venuti (ed.), *The Translation Studies Reader,* 2nd ed, 153–167, New York and London: Routledge.

Nord, Ch. (1991). *Text Analysis in Translation: Theory, Methodology and Didactic Application of a Model for Translation-Oriented Text Analysis.* Amsterdam: Rodopi.

Partington, A. (2004). """Utterly content in each other's company": semantic prosody and semantic preference."" *International Journal of Corpus Linguistics* 9 (1): 131–56. http://dx.doi.org/10.1075/ijcl.9.1.07par.

Reiss, K. (1976). *Texttyp und Übersetzungsmethode: Der operative Text*. Kronberg: Scriptor Verlag.

Reiss, K., and H.J. Vermeer. (1984). *Grundlegung einer allgemeinen Translationstheorie*. Tübingen: Niemeyer. http://dx.doi.org/10.1515/9783111351919.

Schmid, H.-J. (2007). "Entrenchment, Salience, and Basic Levels." In *Oxford Handbook of Cognitive Linguistics*, ed. D. Geeraerts and H. Cuyckens, 117–138. Oxford: Oxford University Press.

Sinclair, J.M. (1991). *Corpus, Concordance, Collocation*. Oxford: Oxford University Press.

Tabakowska, E. (2002). "Aspect and Tense in the narrative: an English original and a Polish translation." In W. Oleksy (ed.), *Festschrift for Professor P. T. Krzeszowski*, 152–162. Frankfurt am Main: Peter Lang.

Talmy, L. (2007). "Attention phenomena." In D. Geeraerts and H. Cuyckens (eds), *Oxford Handbook of Cognitive Linguistics*, 264–293. Oxford: Oxford University Press.

Talmy, L. (in preparation) "The Attention System of Language" – *A Report on Work in Progress*. http://linguistics.buffalo.edu/people/faculty/talmy/talmyweb/Handouts/attention1.pdf. accessed 15 May 2013.

Tomlin, R.S. (1995). "Focal attention, voice, and word order: An experimental, cross-linguistic study." In P. Downing and M. Noonan (eds), *Word Order in Discourse*, 517–554. Amsterdam: John Benjamins. http://dx.doi.org/10.1075/tsl.30.18tom.

Tomlin, R.S. (1997). "Mapping conceptual representations into linguistic representations: The role of attention in grammar." In J. Nuyts and E. Pederson (eds), *Language and Conceptualization*, 162–189. http://dx.doi.org/10.1017/CBO9781139086677.007.

Toury, G. (1995). *Descriptive Translation Studies and Beyond*. Amsterdam, Philadelphia: John Benjamins.

Venuti, L. (1995). *The Translator's Invisibility: A History of Translation*. London, New York: Routledge. http://dx.doi.org/10.4324/9780203360064.

Vermeer, H.J. (1978). "Ein Rahmen für eine allgemeine Translationstheorie." *Lebende Sprachen* 23 (3): 99–102. http://dx.doi.org/10.1515/les.1978.23.3.99.

Other resources

The National Corpus of Polish (http://www.nkjp.uni.lodz.pl/), PELCRA search engine.

Index